TIME OF TRANSITION

TIME OF TRANSITION
The Growth of Families Headed by Women

HEATHER L. ROSS AND ISABEL V. SAWHILL

With the assistance of Anita R. MacIntosh

 THE URBAN INSTITUTE • Washington, D.C.

The Urban Institute is a nonprofit research organization established in 1968 to study problems of the nation's urban communities. Independent and nonpartisan, the Institute responds to
current needs for disinterested analyses and basic information
and attempts to facilitate the application of this knowledge. As
part of this effort, it cooperates with federal agencies, states,
cities, associations of public officials, the academic community,
and other sectors of the general public. The Institute's research
findings and a broad range of interpretive viewpoints are published as an educational service.

The research and studies forming the basis for this report
were supported by grants from the Ford Foundation and the
Department of Health, Education, and Welfare (grant number
31607/D/74-02). The statements and conclusions contained herein do not necessarily reflect the views of the Ford Foundation or
the U.S. Government or the Department of Health, Education,
and Welfare, which make no warranty and assume no responsibility for the accuracy or completeness of the information herein.

The interpretations or conclusions are those of the authors
and should not be attributed to The Urban Institute, its trustees,
or to other organizations that support its research.

LC 75-38209

ISBN 87766-148-0

UI 191-0979-04

Refer to URI 12600 when ordering

List price: $4.95

The Urban Institute
2100 M Street, N.W.
Washington, D.C. 20037

B/76/3M

Contents

Tables

Figures

FOREWORD

This book performs an especially timely service, dealing as it does with the single-parent family, a phenomenon that has grown at a very rapid rate in recent years. As the authors point out, the single-parent family—usually headed by a woman—is transitional in two senses. For a large proportion of the individuals involved, it is a transitional stage between marriages. At the overall societal level, it is a symptom of the transition from what the authors call the "distributive" family of the 19th and early 20th centuries, in which a man working outside of the home provided resources for financially dependent women and children, and a form adapted to the less specialized marital roles we seem to be moving toward, in which both husbands and wives will share more equally in the physical care and financial support of their children. In this present transitional period, the social forms necessary to support these more egalitarian marriages, such as community services and appropriate sex role attitudes, have not yet been worked out while the malfunctions of the older system—gaps in the distributive function—persist. One manifestation of these changes in the economic basis of marriage is a burgeoning of female-headed families, whose numbers increase as the divorce rate rises.

Policy makers, faced with this unprecedented situation, are left with little guidance. Should they design programs to strengthen the family of a now passing distributive economy, or should they design them to support the new, more egalitarian type of family? In the first case, they will lean toward programs that guarantee female heads of families the support which in the old model was supplied by the husband-and-father, either by enforcing the common-law requirement of such support or by supplying it through transfer payments. In the second case, they will lean toward programs that improve women's earnings and wealth-accumulating power. This approach will mean that during the period between the older order and the new, mothers will be in a better position to support or share in the support of their children. Such programs for the improvement of the economic independence of women prepare them for the future more than do transfer payments alone.

The careful and detailed scrutiny of the current situation which the authors have undertaken and the analyses they have made of the data are especially enlightening. They have also put forward their views of two appropriate characteristics of public policies affecting such families which I find compelling. The first is that public policy which may significantly affect the number or well-being of such families should be self-conscious—that is, it should be shaped with as complete an awareness of its impacts as possible. Second, it should be intentionally neutral with respect to family type—that is, it should not be designed either to increase or to decrease the number of individuals in any particular kind of family arrangement. The first stipulation reflects a growing appreciation of the far-reaching, sometimes counter-productive and sometimes counter-intuitive, effects of government intervention on the lives of people but also the decision-maker's concomitant responsibility to try to forecast these effects as completely as possible. In the second stipulation, the point the authors are making is that we do not have a valid factual basis on which the public sector can legitimately favor one family type over another.

The authors, Heather Ross and Isabel Sawhill, are both economists, and while their book emphasizes the economic causes and consequences of changes in family composition, they have tried to integrate relevant insights from the precincts of the sociologist, the psychologist, and the anthropologist. The concepts and the analytical model of family structure which Ross and Sawhill have developed will, I believe, be of continuing usefulness in understanding what is happening and what might happen to the American family. This work is the first major product of a larger program of research whose focus is on the social and economic conditions of women and whose principal objective is to illuminate the kinds of public intervention and nonintervention which are most appropriate in this "time of transition."

William Gorham
President
The Urban Institute

October 1975

ACKNOWLEDGMENTS

It would be impossible to fully express our appreciation to all the many people who have so generously helped in the research undertaking which this book represents. But there are a few key people and institutions whose help and support have been substantial and without whose assistance this monograph could not have been produced.

Critical financial support was provided by the Ford Foundation and by the Department of Health, Education, and Welfare. Various researchers at The Urban Institute have been most generous with their time and ideas. An early draft of chapter 2 was written by Barbara Boland and a draft of chapter 6 by Timmy Napolitano. Rheda Swanson has patiently and expertly typed her way through numerous drafts.

There have been too many outside reviewers to mention them all individually, but we owe a special debt to Jessie Bernard, Lee Rainwater, Reynolds Farley, Barbara Bergmann, Martin Rein, Jonathan Lane, Robert Hampton, Phillips Cutright, and Arthur Norton. There is, of course, no implication that any of these individuals necessarily agree with our findings or conclusions.

TIME OF TRANSITION

Chapter 1

INTRODUCTION

For most people the word *family* brings to mind a picture of husband, wife, and children living together in their own household. Social scientists call these units *nuclear families* while the Census Bureau, as a matter of convention, labels them *male-headed families*.

To a great extent, of course, this popular image accords with the facts since most of the population in the United States lives in these two-parent families. But a sizable and rapidly growing proportion of households are families that consist of a mother and her children living alone. It is with these single-parent families, headed by a woman, that this book is principally concerned. In the following pages, we examine how and why they have been growing and explore the implications of that growth for society and for public policy.

Over the past decade, female-headed families with children have grown almost ten times as fast as two-parent families. This dramatic and rather surprising increase is shown in figure 1. Moreover, as the figure clearly indicates, the trend has been accelerating. As a result, by the mid-1970s one out of every seven children in the United States lived in a family where—whether because of death, divorce, separation, or an out-of-wedlock birth —the father was absent.

REASONS FOR RESEARCH

To some, these changes in family organization are unsettling. Nearly everyone is a member of a nuclear family for at least

1

Figure 1

GROWTH OF FEMALE-HEADED FAMILIES WITH CHILDREN (FHFCH) AND HUSBAND-WIFE FAMILIES WITH CHILDREN (HWFCH) 1950-1974

(1950 = 100)

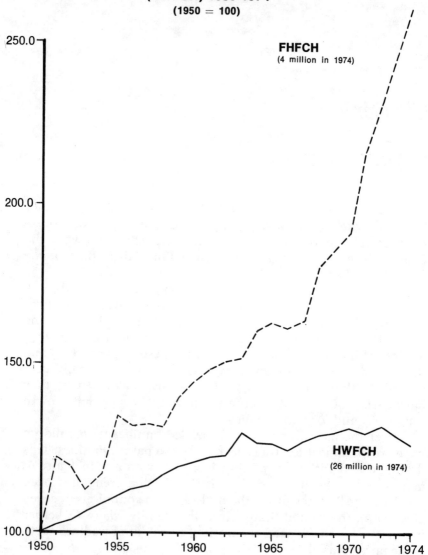

Source: *Current Population Reports,* Series P-20, "Household and Family Characteristics," Washington, D.C.: U.S. Bureau of the Census.

some part of his or her life, and many individuals spend most of their lives in such families. Moreover, the family is a fundamental unit of social and economic organization in our culture, bearing major responsibility for the rearing of children, the achievement of adult satisfaction and social integration, and the distribution of economic resources. Thus, changes that give rise to female-headed families seem to alter a basic institution which touches the lives and emotions of almost everyone.

However, not all change is bad, and much of the constant ebb and flow of change turns out to have little broad or lasting significance. Nor are female-headed families a new phenomenon. Anthropologists and social historians point out that such families have existed throughout human history. So are the trends we have cited a matter for national attention and concern?

One reason they are is the precarious financial status of female-headed families. Whatever their prior income status (and many were middle class), women and children who form their own families run a high risk of poverty. Almost half of them are poor and a similar proportion spend some time on welfare. Indeed, the poverty population is coming increasingly to be dominated by female-headed families. The rapid rate of economic growth during the sixties permitted many husband-wife families to escape from poverty, with the result that a majority of poor families with children are now headed by women. Thus, no one who is concerned about poverty or about distributional equity in our society can ignore the disadvantaged position of this group.

A second reason is the possible effect on children of being reared in a fatherless home. Much of this effect has to do with the loss of income which a father could provide, but other elements include the possible consequences of not having an adult male influence in the home and the strains which can result when a single parent has to shoulder the full burden of child care and decision-making within the family.

A third reason for giving attention to the growth of female-headed families is a lack of clarity about how public policy may have contributed to these changes and whether policy is responding appropriately to the growth that is occurring. Family structure has traditionally been considered outside the realm of acceptable policy manipulation, although the superiority of stable, intact families has generally been assumed. Yet much policy does have a capacity for influencing family structure—as with

divorce laws, family planning or child care services, child support and alimony, welfare benefits, and taxation. Any policy
which treats persons differently based on their marital status,
or which alters the costs or benefits of living in a particular
status, can affect the way people choose to group themselves in
family units. The fact that such effects are largely unintended
does not mean that they are necessarily unimportant.

Whether existing policy has contributed to the growth of
female-headed families or not, there is a need for policy to ac-
knowledge that growth is occurring and to respond to that fact.
The traditional response to the poverty of female-headed families has been income-conditioned transfers, either in cash or in
kind. But the increasing fragility of marital ties—perhaps exac-
erbated by the availability of these transfers—together with
changing attitudes about the economic dependency of women,
have led to the search for alternative solutions. One alternative
is to provide some combination of work incentives, market opportunities, and social services (such as day care) to help low-
income women contribute more earned income to their families.
Another alternative is to improve the flow of nonearned income
to these families by replacing or supplementing public transfers
with private transfers in the form of child support from absent
parents. Given the relatively recent awareness of changing
family structure and the lack of consensus on policy objectives,
very little headway has been made here, despite the fact that
female-headed families present a distinctive new challenge to
social policy.

Thus, the reasons for studying female-headed families are
basically three: (1) the reality of unprecedented and unexplained
growth, (2) the uncertain and possibly harmful social and economic consequences of that growth for individuals and society,
and (3) ignorance about the role public policy has played and
could play with respect to female-headed families.

EXPLANATIONS FOR CHANGE

The total number of female-headed families at any time is a
pool whose size is determined by the volume of flows into and
out of it. To see where growth is coming from and to understand why it is occurring, one must look at the flows—that is,
at the events which create and dissolve female-headed families.
It is here where behavioral change is taking place.

The striking thing when one looks at the various events and processes through which female-headed families appear and disappear is how many of them there are and how much change is going on in each. The breaking up of previous husband-wife families through separation, divorce, or death; the bearing of illegitimate children; the creation of separate households away from prior groupings of relatives or others—all are going on at various paces. At the other end of the sequence, new husband-wife families are forming through remarriage; some earlier marriages are being reestablished through reconciliation; and distinct female-headed family units are disappearing through departure of family members, through death, or through consolidation with other households. In the midst of all this movement, the first task is to see how all the various elements fit together and how each contributes to the whole. The figure for female-headed families in any given year cannot be understood or analyzed except as the net result of a continual movement of a much larger group of people among a much larger array of possible living arrangements.

Once female-headed family growth has been expressed as the net outcome of the various decisions people make or have imposed on them with respect to living arrangements, the next task is to see whether any consistent behavioral pattern can be detected. Is female-headed family growth a happenstance of many small unrelated behavioral changes, or is there some broad explanation for that growth which can be seen operating through each of the many contributing elements of change?

A central hypothesis pursued in this book is that the changing economic and social status of women is a major source of the behavioral evolution leading to female-headed families. This is not to suggest that economic and social independence for women causes families to break up. But income opportunities and social support outside the traditional family arrangements do enable women and children to exist in units of their own during at least transitional periods should they choose or be required to do so. The availability of those income and support opportunities, notably women's own earnings and social welfare benefits in cash and in kind, relieves the constraints which used to bind families together, happily or not, for utilitarian reasons. As the constraints are loosened, people show greater mobility in their living arrangements, searching for those with the greatest personal satisfaction. In a way, this mobility parallels the

great increase in job mobility experienced by the U.S. economy
in the postwar period, as workers who were assured of a minimum economic base sought jobs offering something beyond
simple financial security.

Both the methodology of focusing on behavioral flows from
one family status to another, and the hypothesis that greater
income opportunities for women permit greater marital and
family mobility, lead to a picture of female-headed families
that is dynamic rather than static. Indeed, the evidence to
be presented later strongly suggests that in most instances
female-headed families are transitional units. They are interim
entities of relatively short duration between one traditional
family structure—usually a husband-wife family—and another.
This behavior need not indicate a rejection of life in a nuclear
family, as some have feared; it may, instead, be an affirma-
tion of it and a search for its more satisfying manifestations.
Of course, the general pattern should not obscure the fact that
some families make it back to a husband-wife pattern very slowly, and that other families have no desire to get there at all. The
latter group may be relatively small statistically, but it could be
an important leading indicator of change to come.

Thus our title *Time of Transition* has two distinct meanings. The first refers to the life cycle of individuals, recognizing
that, for most women, heading a family is indeed a time of
transition. They move into that status as a result of the death of
a husband, divorce, or the birth of a child out of wedlock, but
they move out of it again when they marry, remarry, or when
their children grow up and leave home. The second meaning
refers to the evolution of society. It recognizes that the family as
an institution is going through a time of transition, as far-reaching changes in sex roles contribute to undermining the traditional social and economic basis of marriage. Relationships between men and women are moving toward a new more egalitarian mode, and the life-long nuclear family may have to adapt
to this trend or relinquish its predominant position in our social
system.

ORGANIZATION OF THE BOOK

The book is divided into seven chapters. In chapter 2, data are
drawn together which document the growth of female-headed
families in considerable detail. Particular attention is focused

on the demographic events which lead to the creation and dissolution of female-headed families and on how those events fit together to produce the growing pool of such families as measured yearly by the Census Bureau. Attention is also given to the shifting characteristics of this pool as it is transformed by the major inflows and outflows each year.

The task of chapter 3 is to explain why marriages have become less stable than in the past. A model of marital instability is developed and a number of specific hypotheses are evaluated using data from a representative national sample of families. This chapter examines the hypothesis that the changing economic and social status of women (particularly their relative income position) has contributed to higher divorce and separation rates.

Chapters 4 and 5 extend the analysis by highlighting two variables traditionally associated with family instability—race and poverty. Chapter 4 attempts to describe racial differences in family structure and to indicate why these differences have persisted, or even grown, over time. New data are presented which document the extent to which the constrained economic opportunities of blacks contribute to family instability. Chapter 5 explores the common view that welfare programs contribute to female-headed family growth in the poverty population, and concludes that welfare reform could have some effect on the proportion of families headed by women.

In chapter 6, the literature about the effects of father absence on children is reviewed, leaving considerable doubt as to how much is known about any possible pathology associated with female family headship. Chapter 7 sums up the findings of previous chapters, and uses them as a basis for speculating on the broad sweep of family evolution and for identifying important areas for further research. It ends with a discussion of policy actions needed to address the reality of changing family structure and to help newly forming family types—particularly female-headed families—take a less disadvantaged place in the economic and social structure.

Some new data are developed in this book, and some new analytic efforts are undertaken to measure and understand the growth of female-headed families. Much of the work, however, is a synthesis of pieces of evidence which existed in a wide range of places but were never before drawn together because female-headed families had not been taken as a focus of research. This effort indicates both how much and how little is known about the subject. Our hope is that the book will provide both a base and a framework for further inquiry, that it will help us discard some of the myths and prejudices which surround the subject, and that it will assist in the intelligent exploration of what is happening to this most basic of society's institutions—the family.

Chapter 2

FAMILIES HEADED BY WOMEN:
Their Growth & Changing Composition

In the previous chapter we noted that one-parent families headed by women have been growing more rapidly than husband-wife families and that, as a result, more and more children are living in fatherless homes. In this chapter, the essential trends in that growth are documented as we probe behind the aggregate evidence to build a statistical profile of families headed by a mother, and to analyze the diverse demographic events, such as divorce, widowhood, and remarriage, which mark their formation as well as their subsequent dissolution through time.

As noted in chapter 1, our interest in women who head families stems essentially from their status as single parents. In this connection, it should be remembered that there is a sizable group of female-headed families *without* children—as when two sisters live together. These families will be excluded from most of our analysis. Similarly, there are some single-parent families headed by men. However, there are relatively few of these father-headed families (table 3) and they do not face the same economic deprivations as women living alone with their children. As table 1 indicates, the mean income of single-parent, female-headed families is dramatically lower than that of male-headed, single-parent families, which, in turn, is lower than that of husband-wife families. For example, in the 25–44 age group, single-parent families headed by a woman have only half

Table 1

MEAN FAMILY INCOME, 1973

| | | Single-Parent Families | |
Age of Head	Husband-Wife Families	Male-Headed	Female-Headed
Under 25	$ 8,922	$ —	$3,198
25-44	15,114	11,931	5,951
45-64	17,761	12,078	7,205

Source: "Money Income in 1973 of Families and Persons in the U.S.," *Current Population Reports*, Series P-60, no. 97, table 29, Washington, D.C.: U.S. Bureau of the Census.

the income, on the average, of single-parent families headed by a man. Since women, then, head the great majority of one-parent families and face the most severe economic handicaps, we will briefly review the data on all household and family types and then devote the remainder of the book almost exclusively to female-headed families with children.

RECENT TRENDS IN HOUSEHOLD COMPOSITION

In order to understand where female-headed families with children fit into the larger picture of all household and family types, it is useful to have some basic understanding of Census Bureau definitions in this area. Tables 2 and 3 provide the necessary guidance. Table 2 indicates that there were nearly 70 million household heads in 1974. Of these household heads, 79 percent were the heads of primary families, whereas 21 percent were primary individuals. Primary families, in turn, can be divided into those which are headed by a husband and wife (designated male-headed by the Census),[1] those that are headed by a male (no wife present), and those that are headed by a female (no husband present). Finally, in addition to the pri-

1. It is worth noting that the Census-imposed definition of husband-wife families as male-headed is a convention that offers little gain in simplicity for what it costs in observing household differences of possible interest. It is a convention which assumes the social and economic dependency of wives without inquiring into the facts and as such is not only demeaning to many women but is also likely to become an increasingly obsolete description of reality over time. For example, in 1970, 22 percent of wives working full-time year-round contributed over 50 percent of the total income of their respective families. (Bell, 1973, table 1 and p. 20.) The Census Bureau is currently proposing to modify the wording of the question on "household relationship" so as to permit a married woman to be designated as "head" and her spouse as "husband of head."

Table 2

DISTRIBUTION OF TOTAL HOUSEHOLDS BY HOUSEHOLD TYPE, 1974
(Numbers in thousands)

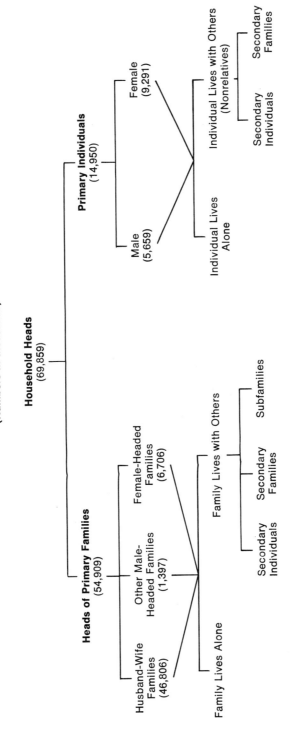

Source: "Households and Family Characteristics: 1974," *Current Population Reports*, P-20, No. 276, Washington, D.C.: U.S. Bureau of the Census.

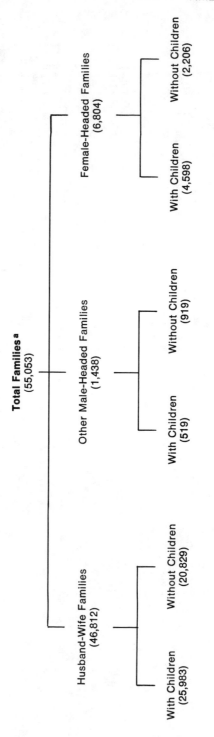

Table 3

**DISTRIBUTION OF PRIMARY FAMILIES BY SEX OF HEAD
AND PRESENCE OF CHILDREN, 1974**

(Numbers in thousands)

Total Families [a]
(55,053)

Husband-Wife Families
(46,812)

With Children
(25,983)

Without Children
(20,829)

Other Male-Headed Families
(1,438)

With Children
(519)

Without Children
(919)

Female-Headed Families
(6,804)

With Children
(4,598)

Without Children
(2,206)

[a] Includes secondary as well as primary families. ,

Source: "Household and Family Characteristics: March 1974," Table 1, Series P-20, No. 276, *Current Population Reports, Population Characteristics*, Washington, D.C.: U.S. Bureau of the Census.

mary families, there are some families who live in other people's households and are designated subfamilies if they are related to the head of that household and secondary families if they are not (see table 4 for definitions).

Table 3 further divides primary families into those where there are children less than 18 years old and those where there are no children in this age category. It shows that there are children present in 56 percent of husband-wife families, in 36 percent of other male-headed families, and in 68 percent of female-headed families.

In the period since World War II some of these household and family types have grown much more rapidly than others. A careful documentation of these differential growth rates, not only by household type but also by age, race, and other factors, is presented in Appendix 1. Here we present the most salient facts which emerge from that detailed analysis.

1) It is clear that husband-wife families, though still constituting a substantial majority of all households are steadily losing ground to other household types. By far the greatest growth in recent decades has been among primary *individuals*, both male and female, but *families* headed by women have grown much more rapidly than those headed by men.

2) The greatest increases in female family headship have occurred among the youngest women. This finding is not changed when the data are adjusted to eliminate the effect of differing rates of population growth in different age groups.

3) Increasingly, the women who head families (with or without children) are divorced or separated rather than widowed. In 1974, about 47 percent were divorced or separated, 37 percent were widowed, and 13 percent were single. (The remaining 3 percent were heads of families because their husbands were temporarily absent.)

4) About two-thirds of all female-headed families contain children under 18. These families with children have been growing over half again as fast as the overall category of female-headed families, which means that the living arrangements of children have been shifting considerably. Thus, 15 percent of all families with children are now female-headed, up from 9 percent in 1960.

5) Since 1960, nonwhite female-headed families with children have grown twice as fast as white female-headed families with children.

Table 4

DEFINITIONS OF HOUSEHOLD AND FAMILY ARRANGEMENTS

Household—all the persons who occupy a housing unit. A household includes the related family members and all unrelated persons, if any, who share the housing unit. A person living alone in a housing unit, or a group of unrelated persons sharing a unit, is also counted as a household. Each household has a designated head.

Family—a group of two or more persons related by blood, marriage or adoption and residing together. A household may contain more than one family. It should be noted here that a household head living alone or with unrelated persons is regarded as a household but not as a family. Thus, some households do *not* contain a family.

Primary Family—one that includes among its members the head of a household.

Secondary Family—a family that does not include the head of the household. Members of secondary families are related to each other and have a designated family head. Examples include guests, lodgers, or resident employees and their relatives living in a household.

Subfamily—a married couple with or without children, or one parent with one or more own single children under 18, living in a household and related to but not including, the head of the household or his wife. Members of a subfamily are also members of a primary family. The most common example of a subfamily is a young married couple sharing the home of the husband's or wife's parents.

Head of Household, Family, or Subfamily—the person designated as the "head." The number of heads is equal to the number of households, families, or subfamilies. The head is usually the person regarded as such by the members of the group except that married women are not classified as heads if their husbands are living with them.

Married Couple—a husband and his wife, with or without children, who are members of the same household. The expression "husband-wife" before the terms "household," "family," or "subfamily" indicates that the household head or family head is a married man whose wife lives with him.

Unrelated Individuals—persons who are not living with any relatives. They may be primary individuals or secondary individuals.

Primary Individuals—a household head living alone or with nonrelatives only.

Secondary Individuals—a nonhousehold head who is not related to any other person in the household.

Note: Both males and females fall into the classifications listed above. Therefore, any woman, age fourteen or over, may head a household unless she is married and living with her husband. She becomes a head by designation of the members of the household. In practice, however, it is not expected that certain types of individuals—for example, unmarried teenage daughters in husband-wife families—will be designated as heads.

6) The trend toward female-headed families with children is not just a poverty phenomenon. It is going on at all income levels, with the nonpoor far outnumbering the poor. But because the number of poor families who are male-headed has declined so significantly over the 1960s, the poverty population has come to be increasingly characterized by female-headed families. The majority of poor families with children are now headed by a woman.

In short, female-headedness is an increasingly common occurrence. Yet little is known about why these families are growing in number or what the significance of recent trends may be. We turn now to a more detailed analysis of the demographic events which have contributed to the phenomenon of mothers and children living alone.

THE DEMOGRAPHY OF FEMALE-HEADED FAMILIES

Having documented that families headed by women are a small but rapidly growing proportion of all families, we now focus on the demographic factors which lie behind these trends. This analysis will show that the flows not only into but also *out of* female-headed status have increased in recent years, and that for a large proportion of these female-headed families their situation may be transitory rather than permanent.

The stock of female-headed families *with children* in any one year depends on:

- the stock in the preceding year.

- the number of husband-wife families with children which became female-headed during the year because of death or a marital separation.

- the number of female-headed families that are created during the year because an unmarried woman has a first illegitimate child and does not give up the child for adoption.

- the number of female-headed families that move out of that status during the year because of marriage, remarriage, death of the mother, or death or aging of the children.

Algebraically, this may be stated as:

$$FC_t = FC_{t-1} + p_1(s + md) MC_{t-1} + p_2bF_{t-1} - (r + fd + a) FC_{t-1} \; [2]$$

2. This can be rewritten in the sparser notation of Appendix 3 as

$$FC_t = P_1 P_{mcfc} MC_{t-1} + P_2 P_{ffc} F_{t-1} + P_{tcfc} FC_{t-1}$$

where:

FC = the stock of female-headed families with children under 18. This includes subfamilies and thus abstracts from the living arrangements of these women.[3]

MC = the stock of husband-wife families with children under 18.

F = the stock of single women, ages 14–44.

p_1 = the proportion of children in disrupted marriages who remain with their mother.

s = the separation rate of husband-wife families with children under 18 (includes divorce, separation, desertion, annulment).

md = the death rate of husbands in husband-wife families with children under 18.

b = the first birth illegitimacy rate among single women 15–44.

p_2 = the proportion of first-born illegitimate children that remain with their mother.

r = the weighted sum of the remarriage rate of widows and divorcees, the reconciliation rate of separated women, and the first marriage rate of single women with children under 18.

fd = the death rate of female heads with children under 18.

a = the rate of disappearance of female-headed families because of the aging or death of the last (or only) child.

The above equation is an attempt to identify all of the events which can cause the number of female-headed families to vary. It also shows very clearly that the number of such families may grow not only because of an increase in the flows into female-headed status but also because of a decrease in flows out of that status. This leads quite naturally to a review of the data available on such basic demographic events as illegitimacy, widowhood, divorce, and remarriage. The approach to these data will become increasingly refined as we move through the chapter. We begin with a very general discussion of the longer-run trends evidenced in published sources. This discussion provides a useful backdrop for the more detailed study of demographic shifts over the decade of the sixties, which is designed to

---

3. See table 4 for a definition of subfamily.

pinpoint recent sources of growth in female-headed families *with children* and which draws on the better data available for this most recent period. We use two approaches in our analysis of change for this decade. The first approach, the analysis of changing stocks (p. 20 ff.), involves using static Census data on the changing proportions of women in different marital states, presence of children, and headship categories to apportion the growth to different demographic factors. The second approach, the analysis of changing flows (p. 24 ff.), takes a more direct look at recent divorce, remarriage, and the other rates of change specified in the foregoing equation, and suggests how a more complete demographic model relating stocks and flows might be developed as part of any continuing research on this subject.[4]

Trends in Illegitimacy.   Since 1940, the first year for which complete statistics on illegitimacy are available, the *proportion* of all births that are illegitimate has steadily risen. By 1973 illegitimate births accounted for 13 percent of all births.[5]

However, the proportion of births that are illegitimate depends on both the legitimate and the illegitimate birth rates. Thus, a decrease in legitimate fertility will increase the proportion of out-of-wedlock births, even if there is no change in illegitimacy. For this reason, demographers generally prefer to study illegitimacy *rates* (the number of illegitimate births per 1,000 unmarried females, aged 15-44) and these data present a more mixed picture. Year-to-year increases in the overall rate were much faster during the 1940s and early 1950s than they have been since 1958.[6] Also, since the mid-sixties, the rate for nonwhites, which has always been substantially higher than the rate for whites, has gradually declined. At the same time, the *proportion* of all nonwhite births that are illegitimate continues to climb because general fertility for nonwhites has been dropping even faster than the illegitimacy rate. For whites, the illegitimacy ratio has risen both because legitimate fertility has declined and illegitimate fertility has increased.[7]

Closer examination of the trends in illegitimacy rates suggests that it is second births (which do not generally result in a new female-headed family) that are exhibiting the strongest

---

4. See Appendix 3 for a more complete description of a model relating stocks and flows.

5. See Appendix 1, table 1-L.

6. National Center for Health Statistics (NCHS), Series 21, no. 15, "Trends in Illegitimacy."

7. See Appendix 1, table 1-M.

tendency toward decline. Also, the rates by age show recent declines among older women while the series for 15-19 year-olds is still rising. Since the latter group accounts for such a large proportion of *single* women aged 15-44 (the illegitimacy population base), their behavior has a significant effect on the overall rate. While the rate of illegitimacy has continued to climb in the 15-19 year-old age group over the past 25 years, the rate of increase has been diminishing.[8]

Another factor which has an important effect on the absolute level of illegitimacy is the size of the population "at risk." Since the late 1950s this population has been expanded by members of the postwar baby boom and, more recently, by the rise in age at first marriage. Even if the overall illegitimacy rate levels off, the number of illegitimate births may continue to rise substantially because of the growth of this population. Projections prepared by the National Center for Health Statistics— using 1965 illegitimacy rates and assuming that the number of unmarried women will increase with no change in their age distribution—show that by 1980 the number of illegitimate births could increase by almost a third from 1965 levels.[9]

Trends in Marriage, Divorce, and Remarriage. Even though unwed mother-child families have exhibited a rapid rise over the last decade, the predominant source of female headedness is still the absence of husbands from former husband-wife families. The overall level of marital disruption due to death and legal divorce has changed little since 1860, but a long-term shift in the relative importance of the two events has taken place with the result that a rising proportion of dissolutions are due to divorce.[10] Indeed, a closer look at divorce rates confirms a definite secular rise. For example, there were 1.2 divorces per 1,000 existing marriages in 1860, 4.0 in 1900, and 9.3 in 1956.[11] Although there has always been a good deal of fluctuation in this rate (with peaks typically occurring during periods of prosperity and after wars), and although the available data leave much to be desired, there is little doubt that American families are more divorce-prone than in the past.

More recent indicators of marital behavior show a signifi-

---

8. Ferris, 1970, pp. 60-61.

9. See Appendix 1, table 1-L. Also see "Trends in Illegitimacy, U.S., 1940-1965," NCHS, Series 21, no. 15, p. 10.

10. See Appendix 1, table 1-H.

11. Goode, 1971, table 4, p. 486. Also see Appendix 1, table 1–I, which gives recent data on divorce rates for women, 14–44.

cant change occurring sometime around the mid-1950s.[12] In the early 1950s all of the crucial statistical series seemed to indicate a relatively high level of satisfaction with family life and the institution of marriage. Median age at marriage was at an all-time low, the annual birth rate was high, and the annual divorce rate was far below its post-World War II peak. In the latter part of the decade this seemingly placid situation gave way to new developments which have continued through the 1960s and into the 1970s. Figure 2, developed by Paul C. Glick and Arthur J. Norton, two demographers who have carefully studied and documented these trends, graphically depicts these new developments. Sometime in the late 1950s divorce and remarriage rates began to rise sharply while first marriage rates continued to fall. The rise in the remarriage rate appears to be primarily a consequence of the increasing number of divorced women among those eligible for a second spouse, since divorced women are more likely to remarry than their widowed counterparts.

Present trends could be viewed as simply another phase in a continually fluctuating pattern of marital behavior, since all of the trend lines in figure 2 show considerable cyclical variation. Yet the long-term upward trend in divorce and remarriage exhibited in the figure is also apparent in retrospective survey data which measure the difference in lifetime experience between successively more recent birth cohorts (age groups). Glick and Norton use this latter type of analysis to look at first marriage, first divorce, and first remarriage experience of women born from 1900 to 1954. While they conclude that it is too early to determine whether the recent downturn in first marriages will result in an increase in lifetime singleness, their analysis does suggest very strongly that there has been a significant rise in divorce in recent decades. Over the last thirty years the proportion of women whose first marriage ended by a given period in life has gone up consistently. The percentage divorced by their early twenties has risen from 2.1 percent for women reaching that age in 1940 to 6.3 percent for those reaching that age in 1970. And the percentage divorced by their early thirties has increased from 6.3 percent in 1940 to 15.8 percent in 1970. Thus, among women in their early twenties or thirties, the proportion divorced more than doubled in little over a generation. The increases have been particularly large among wom-

12. This discussion of the recent increase in divorce is based on the excellent article, "Perspectives on the Recent Upturn in Divorce and Remarriage," by Paul Glick and Arthur J. Norton in *Demography*, vol. 10, no. 3, August 1973.

Figure 2

**FIRST MARRIAGE RATES PER 1,000 SINGLE WOMEN, DIVORCE
RATES PER 1,000 MARRIED WOMEN, AND REMARRIAGE RATES
PER 1,000 WIDOWED OR DIVORCED WOMEN: UNITED STATES,
THREE-YEAR AVERAGES, 1921 TO 1971.**

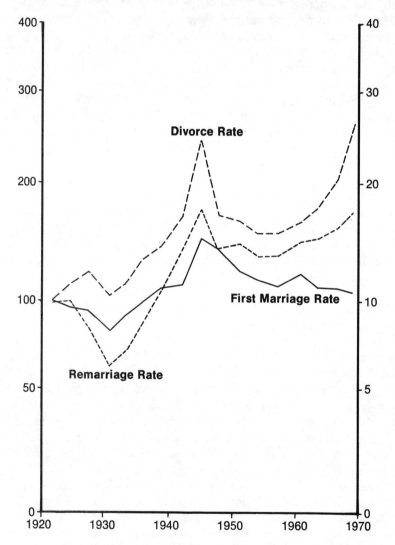

Source: Paul Glick and Arthur J. Norton, "Perspectives on the Recent Upturn
in Divorce and Remarriage," *Demography,* vol. 10, no. 3, August 1973,
p. 303.

en who were 25-34 years old in 1970. These women have already experienced more divorce than their older counterparts experienced in a lifetime and they still have roughly 40 more years of exposure to divorce. Assuming that future increments in divorce for this group will be similar to the divorce experience of older women, Norton and Glick estimate that 25-30 percent of women currently in their late twenties or early thirties will end their first marriage in divorce sometime during their lives.

These authors have also found a long-term rise in the rate of remarriage among widowed and divorced women, which mirrors the long-term rise in divorce. In 1940 less than 1 percent of women in their twenties had remarried, but by 1970 this figure reached 3.5 percent. Similarly, for divorced and widowed women in their early thirties the proportion remarried had increased from 3.8 to 11.1 percent.

The above data indicate that recent years have witnessed increasing amounts of illegitimacy, divorce, and remarriage, but we have not asked how these trends may have contributed to the phenomenon of women and children living alone. Is it illegitimacy or divorce that is more responsible for the growth of this particular population? How important are changes in the living arrangements of these women—that is, their propensity to establish their own households and thus be included in official counts of family heads? And what role have population shifts played in the observed growth? To answer these questions, we turn to an analysis of recent Census statistics on the changing composition of the female population by marital status, presence of children, and household headship.

Analysis of Changing Stocks, 1960-1970. Figure 3 partitions the total growth in female-headed families with children over the decade 1960-1970, into the following demographic components.[18]

(1) Changes in living arrangements (an increasing proportion of never-married or formerly married mothers heading their own households rather than living as a subfamily in someone else's household).

---

13. The method used in coming up with these numbers involves calculating how many *additional* female-headed families with children there would have been in 1960 if the relevant 1970 proportion for each factor had prevailed and everything else had remained the same. For example, the proportion of white never-married women with children increased from .3 percent in 1960 to .9 percent in 1970. Plugging the higher proportion for 1970 into the components formula (see Appendix 4), we estimate that there would have been 63,000 additional white female heads even if nothing else had changed since 1960. This number represents 9 percent of the total increase of 700,000 white female heads.

Figure 3

COMPONENTS OF GROWTH
IN FEMALE-HEADED FAMILIES WITH CHILDREN
1960-1970

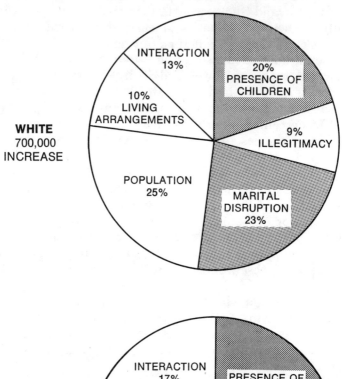

WHITE
700,000
INCREASE

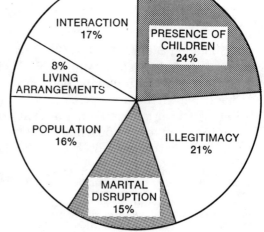

NONWHITE
392,000
INCREASE

Source: See Appendix 4, Table 4-A.

(2) Increased marital disruption (an increasing proportion of ever-married women who are separated, divorced, or widowed).

(3) Increased presence of children (an increasing likelihood that dependent children will be present when a marriage is disrupted and will live with their mother).

(4) Higher "illegitimacy" (an increasing proportion of never-married women who have children less than 18 years old).

(5) Population growth (increasing numbers of adult women).

(6) A residual interaction term which represents the effect of two or more of the above factors operating in conjunction with one another.

The figure shows that population growth was responsible for 25 percent and 16 percent of the total observed increase in female headship among whites and nonwhites respectively.[14] More adult women would mean more women heading families with children even if the proportion of women heading such families had not changed.

The share of the growth attributable to marital disruption was 23 percent for whites and 15 percent for nonwhites. This reflects primarily an increase in divorce and separation, since the probability of becoming a widow has changed little over the last decade. Furthermore, the probability that a woman who experiences marital disruption will have one or more children living with her has also increased considerably and is labeled "presence of children" in the chart. This indicates more divorced or separated women and fewer widows among the maritally disrupted population, the younger ages of divorced women, and declining childlessness among the population as a whole. The increased presence of children accounts for 20 percent of the growth among whites and 24 percent among nonwhites.

The probability that an unmarried woman will have a child living with her has also grown. The figures show, however, that "illegitimacy" is a much more important factor for nonwhites than for whites, accounting for only 9 percent of the growth among the latter but for 21 percent of the growth among the former.

---

14. This does not necessarily mean that there was greater population growth in the white population. Instead, it should be interpreted to mean that, relative to nonwhites, a larger *share* of the total growth in white female-headed families was associated with more adult women being at risk rather than with other types of change.

Finally, there is an increasing probability that an un-married or formerly married mother will set up her own house-hold rather than live with relatives. These changes in "living arrangements" reflect increasing economic ability to establish independent households and are consistent with a trend away from extended-family living patterns throughout society. But this type of change has made only a modest contribution to total growth, accounting for 10 percent of the growth for whites and 8 percent for nonwhites.[15]

Summarizing the results, most of the growth in female-headed families has been related to increased marital disrup-tion and to the higher proportion of marital dissolutions which involve children. Illegitimacy has contributed to a larger share of total growth among nonwhites than among whites, but even in the black population it appears to be the higher proportion of marital separations involving children which has dominated recent trends.

Analysis of Changing Flows, 1960-1970. The foregoing analysis provides no direct evidence on what has happened to rates of divorce, illegitimacy, and other demographic flows over the decade. It is as if we had used changes in the moisture content of the soil to make inferences about the amount of rainfall, or changes in the composition of durable goods to make inferences about the kind of investment activity which has taken place. Clearly, we would be in a better position to understand recent developments if we could relate changes in the stock of female heads directly to changes in such demographic flows as divorce and remarriage.

In principle, there is no reason why this cannot be done,

---

15. This conclusion runs counter to that reported by Phillips Cutright and John Scanzoni who argue that a change in "the propensity to live in separate households" was the single most important factor in explaining increased fe-male headedness between 1940 and 1970. But these researchers appear to have given insufficient attention to the possible effects of (1) more marital disruption among younger women, (2) generally higher fertility, (3) an increase in the age at which children leave home, or (4) a decline in other types of living arrange-ments for children. All of these factors would tend to increase family headship among formerly married women, 15–44, who have ever borne a child because in each case they would be more likely to have a dependent child to care for. In any case, our own analysis shows that between 1960 and 1970 only 10 percent of the growth for whites and 8 percent for nonwhites was due to the increased propensity of women to establish their own households rather than live as a subfamily. While changes in housing patterns may indeed have been a more important factor over the longer period covered by the Cutright and Scanzoni analysis (i.e., 1940 to 1970), it clearly has not been an important factor over the last decade. Unfortunately, lack of appropriate data prevents us from extending our own analysis (which differs somewhat from the Cutright-Scanzoni approach) to the 1940-1960 period.

and in Appendix 3 we describe a model which could be used to evaluate the specific contribution of various demographic events to the growth of female-headed families. Unfortunately, all of the data required for this more ambitious analysis are not readily available, although they probably could be developed in future research on this topic.

In the meantime, we have attempted to piece together *some* of the necessary information, which is presented in table 5. (The reader is referred to the equation and definitions on pp. 15–16 for help in interpreting the symbols used in the table.) These data tend to confirm our earlier conclusions. They indicate that the growth in female-headed families over the decade of the sixties was related both to higher rates of marital instability and to higher rates of illegitimacy. The largest absolute increases, however, are associated with marital instability because of the much larger number of husband-wife families relative to single females of child-bearing age. It is interesting to note that almost all of the increase in female-headed families flowing out of husband-wife families appears to be associated with a rise in divorce rates, since the stock of husband-wife families with children has grown very little. The increase in illegitimacy, however, is associated with both a rise in rates and an increase in the population at risk. The number of single females 14–44 increased by about 50 percent over the decade.

The remarriage rate among divorced mothers—the most important flow out of female-headed status—also increased substantially over the decade. By 1970, almost one out of every five divorcees remarried in a given year. Or viewing the same data in a slightly different way, we can conclude that the mean duration between divorce and remarriage is about 5 or 6 years. Remarriage rates are highest in the first year after a divorce and decline gradually thereafter. The probability of remarrying is also quite strongly and inversely related to a woman's age and the number of children she has.[16]

High rates of remarriage have not been sufficient to offset the increase in divorce rates—hence the growth in female-headed families we have been witnessing.[17] Our calculations also suggest that the gross flows into female headship are about

---

16. See *Current Population Report* (CPR), P-20, no. 223, "Social and Economic Variations in Marriage, Divorce, and Remarriage, 1967" and Sweet, 1973.

17. It can be shown that, under certain assumptions, the proportion of families headed by women equals "flows in" divided by the sum of the "flows in" and "flows out." Thus, if marital instability increases faster than remarriage rates, we would expect this proportion to increase. See Appendix 3.

Table 5

STOCKS AND FLOWS OF FEMALE-HEADED FAMILIES WITH CHILDREN

	STOCKS (in thousands)			FLOWS IN						FLOWS OUT					
	FC	MC	F	p_1	s	d	md	p_2	b	r^w	r^d	r^{d+s}	r^f	fd	a
Total															
1960	2,012	24,610	10,185	*	*	8.9	5.0	.61	10.6	30.8	149.8	130	*	4.2	*
1970	3,230	25,855	15,345	*	*	14.4	5.0	.69	16.2	30.8	188.6	159	*	3.2	*
White															
1960	1,450	22,302	8,806	*	*	8.7	4.9	.34	5.9	30.8	151.3	131	*	3.1	*
1970	2,199	22,616	12,972	*	*	14.4	5.0	.38	9.7	30.8	190.5	160	*	2.1	*
Nonwhite															
1960	562	1,704	1,379	*	*	10.9	10.8	.93	40.0	30.8	137.8	121	*	6.5	*
1970	1,031	2,332	2,379	*	*	17.6	10.8	.95	49.1	30.8	173.5	147	*	5.1	*

Notes: *not available.

Stocks in thousands. All flows are rates per thousand except p_1 and p_2 which are proportions.

d is the divorce rate used as a proxy for the total separation rate.

r^w and r^d represent remarriage rates for widows and divorcees respectively.

r^{d+s} represents the remarriage rate when the stock of separated women who eventually divorce is added to the denominator in calculating the remarriage rate of divorcees. It is based on the assumption that such women spend an average of one year between separation and divorce.

r^f represents the first marriage rate of unwed mothers.

Source: See Appendix 2 for source and derivations.

four or five times as large as the net increase in a given year, showing that there have been many more families involved in recent growth than the net change in the static data would indicate.[18]

Differences in the data for whites and nonwhites suggest that the pattern of recent growth varies significantly by race.[19] For nonwhites all of the flows into female-headed status occur at a much higher rate than for whites. Even the probability of widowhood is much higher for nonwhites. Also, the most important flow out of female-headed status, the remarriage of divorcees, is lower for nonwhites. This implies that one of the reasons a higher proportion of nonwhite families is female-headed is not only the higher levels of marital disruption but also the higher probability of remaining in disrupted status.[20] However, this appears to be true only for divorcees; widows, whether black or white, do not remarry to a very great extent.

One dramatic difference by race observable in table 5 is in the level of illegitimacy. For nonwhites the basic rate is higher, the proportion not adopted is higher, and the size of the population at risk is much larger relative to the number of husband-wife families. By 1970 the number of single females, 14–44 (with no children) in the nonwhite population was equal to the number of husband-wife families. For whites, the comparable ratio of single females to husband-wife families is 1 to 2.

Not much appears to be changing in the demography of widows. Male death rates and the remarriage rates of widows have remained fairly constant over the last decade. Husband-wife families continue to dissolve at a much slower rate because of death, as opposed to divorce, and a widowed family head is much less likely to remarry than one who is divorced.

---

18. Using the data for 1970 in table 5, we estimate a total annual flow into female headedness of 855,000 and a total flow out of 684,000 for a net increase of 171,000. This compares with an actual average net increase of 127,000 for the period 1960-1972 and 223,000 for the period 1968-1972 from table 1-F.

19. The most important caveat for the reader to keep in mind in assessing the validity of this analysis is that aggregate trends in divorce and remarriage have been assumed to apply to both racial groups. The relative differences by race, however, are based on more detailed calculations for widowed and divorced women with children which were available for the early years of the 1960s. Thus, the figures should be fairly accurate for an assessment of relative differences.

20. In figure 3, marital disruption was shown to account for 15 percent of total female-headed family growth for nonwhites and 23 percent for whites. This does not mean that there was *more* marital disruption among whites, only that whatever marital disruption took place accounted for a larger *share* of total growth relative to other factors among whites. See *Current Population Report,* P-2, no. 276, "Household and Family Characteristics: March 1974," table 4.

It should be remembered, however, that the aging of children is an important route out of female headedness for this last group. In 1974, almost 56 percent of widows who headed families with children under 18 were over 45, suggesting that many of the children in these families were close to the age of 18.[21] By way of illustration, if we assume that the youngest child is 14, on average, when the father dies, then the typical widow spends four years with at least one child under 18 and the rate at which such families "dissolve" due to the "aging" of children is 250 (per 1,000). Thus, in spite of their much lower remarriage rates, it is not at all clear that widows spend more time as single-parent heads of families than their divorced counterparts.

The absence of data on total separation rates, and the necessity of relying on divorce rates instead, tends to underestimate the flows into, and overestimate the flows out of, female-headed status. Women who separate but have not divorced are not picked up in divorce rates or in the base population for which most remarriage rates are estimated. From one standpoint, their exclusion from the base of the remarriage rate makes sense since such women are legally ineligible to remarry. But conceptually, separations should be included in the numerator of the divorce rate and the denominator of the remarriage rate in order to give a more accurate picture of the total flows we are interested in. However, there is no good data with which to make such estimates. The inaccuracy which this lack of data creates is particularly serious for black women because, relative to whites, a much larger proportion of them are separated rather than divorced.[22]

---

21. The average woman has her last child around age 30. See Wattenberg, p. 42, and Norton, p. 164.

22. If P = the proportion of all ever-married (nonwidowed) adult women who are separated or divorced

s = the total separation rate

r = the remarriage rate of separated and divorced women

Then (from Appendix 3) $P = \dfrac{s}{s + r}$ or $\qquad$ (1)

$$r = s \left(\frac{1 - P}{P} \right) \qquad (2)$$

For 1970, we calculate the following values for $(1 - P)/P$ (from Appendix 4)

	$(1 - P)/P$
white women	11.82
nonwhite women	4.92

Another important piece of information that is missing from table 5 is the rate at which unmarried mothers marry. Most of them eventually do marry and we suspect that their marriage rate is higher than that of divorcees but lower than that of other single women.[23]

Finally, it is impossible to tell from standard Census materials how many mothers make informal arrangements for their children to live in other households, affecting the living arrangement parameter (p_1) in table 5. However, a study by Farley and Hermalin indicates that approximately 3 percent of all children under six are not living with their mothers,[24] and the Census does count a sizable number of related, non-own children (e.g., nieces, nephews, grandchildren) who live with relatives other than their own parents.[25]

(footnote 22 cont'd)

Now assume (based on evidence from the University of Michigan's Panel Study of Income Dynamics presented in chapters 3 and 4) that total separation rates are:

white women	18
nonwhite women	27

Then, from equation 2, the remarriage rate is:

white women	$18 \times 11.82 = 213$
nonwhite women	$27 \times 4.92 = 133$

We can now compare these estimates to those presented in table 5.

	divorce rate from table 5	estimated separation rate
white women	14	18
nonwhite women	18	27

	remarriage rate of divorced women	remarriage rate of divorced and separated women
white women	191	213
nonwhite women	174	133

Although one would expect the remarriage rate of white divorced and separated women to be somewhat lower than that of divorced women alone, the data on which these calculations are based come from different sources and are not entirely comparable. Nevertheless, the general conclusions which they illustrate are of interest.

23. Phillips Cutright has shown that among a sample of mothers under age 59 whose first child was born out of wedlock, 93 percent of white and 81 percent of nonwhite mothers had married. (Cutright and Scanzoni, table 10.)

24. Farley and Hermalin, 1971.

25. In 1970, 5 percent of all children under 18 living in families were "related" rather than "own" children. It is also interesting to note that a dramatic increase occurred between 1960 and 1970 in the number of "own" and "related" children living in male-headed families, spouse absent—80 percent. (1970 Census of Population, PC(2)-4B, "Persons by Family Characteristics".) This subject is discussed further in chapter 6.

CONCLUSIONS

This chapter has indicated that much is changing in the demography of female-headed families. They are the fastest growing household type, significantly outdistancing husband-wife and male-headed households in their rate of increase. Their growth stems from trends in demographic events and living arrangements which have changed the characteristics of the female-headed household population as well as its size. It is in these events and trends that an explanation of the growth of female-headed households, and ultimately a judgment on the implications of that growth, must be sought.

Recent years have seen an upsurge of flows both into and out of female-headed status. Most women become heads of their own families because of divorce or separation, but most also remarry within a relatively short time. Thus, for large numbers of women, female-head-of-household status appears to be a transitional situation between membership in other types of households. Since these other household types, notably husband-wife families, have traditionally characterized marital and living arrangements in this country, and appear to be as popular as ever (as measured by the proportion of the population engaging in such arrangements), it is tempting to see female-headedness as in large part a high turnover phenomenon in a marriage market that in a number of ways is analogous to the labor market.

This approach offers a number of interesting parallels. Jobs and families have traditionally been the pre-eminent elements of adult life. Both institutions are undergoing change as the growing mobility of the population makes increasing demands on them, demands which may go beyond simple economic security. Yet despite greatly changing norms, a good steady job and a good steady marriage appear to be preferred by most people.

However, the fact that the great majority of people in both markets are employed at any point in time does not lessen the significance of those who are not. Among the labor market unemployed are those who chronically cannot find a job. These people would like to be a more integral part of the market but cannot find a place for themselves. Similarly, among the large number of women moving through female-headed-household status, there are no doubt *some* who would like to find marriage situations for themselves but are unable to do so over long periods of time. These "chronically unemployed" need to be identified and their situation evaluated in any analysis of female-headed households.

Then again, at any point in time, some people are out of the labor market because they reject the life style of regular market work. They may be relatively few in number, but they could be important leading indicators of future patterns of making a living. Analogously, there are surely women, although perhaps relatively few, who have chosen not to enter into traditional husband-wife arrangements and do not consider themselves a part of that market or life style. They too may be leading indicators.

There are more adult women traditionally in the marriage market who are not at work as wives, than there are adult men traditionally in the labor market who are not at work in jobs. This may mean (1) that the labor market works more efficiently (or at least more rapidly) to handle frictional unemployment, (2) that there is more chronic unemployment in the marriage market, or (3) that the marriage market has a lower participation rate. Perhaps all three are true. Determining the mix of these, and the change in the mix over time, is important in explaining and evaluating the growth of female-headed households.

In conclusion, this chapter raises many questions for further analysis. Specifically, what has led to higher rates of illegitimacy and marital instability over time? What is the role of changing norms, changing economic conditions, and shifts in government policy in creating more female-headed families, and how can we explain rates of female headship which are much higher for some subgroups than for others? Finally, what are the implications of these changes for individual and social welfare? In the chapters which follow we turn our attention to these questions.

BIBLIOGRAPHY

Bell, Carolyn Shaw. "Women's Earnings and Family Income." *Eastern Economic Journal* 1:3 (July 1974).

Carter, Hugh, and Glick, Paul C. *Marriage and Divorce: A Social and Economic Study.* Cambridge, Mass.: Harvard University Press, 1970.

Cutright, Phillips, and Scanzoni, John. "Income Supplements and the American Family." Paper no. 12 of the Sub-Committee on Fiscal Policy, Joint Economic Committee of the Congress, Nov. 4, 1973.

Davis, Kingsley. "The American Family in Relation to Demographic Change." Commission on Population Growth and the American Future, Research Reports, vol. 1, *Demographic and Social Aspects of Population Growth*, edited by Charles F. Westoff and Robert Parke, Jr., 1972.

Farley, Reynolds, and Hermalin, Albert I. "Family Stability: A Comparison of Trends Between Blacks and Whites." *American Sociological Review* 36:1 (Feb. 1971), pp. 1-17.

Ferris, Abbott L. *Indicators of Change in The American Family*. New York: Russell Sage Foundation, 1970.

————. *Indicators of Trends in the Status of American Women*. New York: Russell Sage Foundation, 1971.

Glick, Paul C., and Norton, Arthur J. "Perspectives on the Recent Upturn in Divorce and Remarriage." *Demography* 10:3 (Aug. 1973), pp. 301-14.

Goode, William J. "Family Disorganization." In *Contemporary Social Problems*, edited by Robert N. Merton and Robert Nisbet. New York: Harcourt Brace Jovanovich, 1971.

Helco, Hugh; Rainwater, Lee; Rein, Martin; and Weiss, Robert. "Single-Parent Families: Issues and Policies." Working paper prepared for The Office of Child Development, DHEW, Oct. 1973.

Hill, Robert B. *The Strengths of Black Families*. New York: Emerson Hall, 1971.

Kobrin, Frances E. "Household Headship and Its Changes in the U.S., 1940-1960, 1970." *Journal of the American Statistical Association* 68:344 (Dec. 1973).

National Center for Health Statistics (NCHS). HSM 73-1121, vol. 21, no. 13, "Annual Summary for U.S. 1972" (June 27, 1973).

————. Series 21, no. 18, "Children of Divorced Couples: U.S., Selected Years" (Feb. 1970).

————. Series 21, no. 15, "Trends in Illegitimacy, U.S. 1940-1965" (Feb. 1968).

Norton, Arthur J. "The Family Life Cycle Updated: Components and Uses." In *Selected Studies in Marriage and the Family*, edited by Robert F. Winch and Graham P. Spanier. New York: Holt, Rinehart and Winston, 1974.

Sweet, James. "Differentials in Remarriage Probabilities." Working Paper no. 73-29. Madison, Wis.: University of Wisconsin (Sept. 1973).

Wattenberg, Ben J. *This USA: An Unexpected Family Portrait of 194,067,296 Americans Drawn from the Census*. New York: Doubleday, 1965.

United States Bureau of the Census. "Household and Family Characteristics." *Current Population Report (CPR)*, Population Characteristics, Series P-20, nos. 173, 191, 200, 218, 233, 246, 258, and 276.

————. "Marital Status and Family Status." *CPR*, Population Characteristics, Series P-20, nos. 187, 198, and 212.

————. "Marital Status and Living Arrangements." *CPR*, Population Characteristics, Series P-20, nos. 225, 242, 255, and 271.

————. "Social and Economic Variations in Marriage, Divorce and Remarriage: 1967." *CPR*, Population Characteristics, Series P-20, no. 223.

————. "Marriage, Divorce, and Remarriage by Year of Birth: June 1971." *CPR*, Population Characteristics, Series P-20, no. 239.

————. "The Social and Economic Status of the Black Population in the U.S., 1971." *CPR* Special Studies, Series P-23, no. 42.

————. "Population Estimates and Projections." *CPR*, Series P-25, no. 483 (April 1972).

————. "The Extent of Poverty in the U.S. 1959 to 1966." *CPR,* Consumer Income Series P-60, no. 54.

————. "Poverty in the U.S. 1959 to 1968." *CPR,* Consumer Income Series P-60, no. 68.

————. "Characteristics of the Low-Income Population 1970." *CPR,* Consumer Income Series P-60, no. 81.

————. "Characteristics of the Low-Income Population 1971." *CPR,* Consumer Income Series P-60, no. 86.

————. "Characteristics of the Low-Income Population 1972." *CPR,* Consumer Income Series P-60, no. 91.

————. "Characteristics of the Low-Income Population 1973." *CPR,* Consumer Income Series P-60, no. 98.

————. "Income of Families and Persons in the U.S." *CPR,* Consumer Income Series P-60, nos. 43, 47, 51, 53, 59, 66, 75, 80, and 85.

————. United States Census of Population 1960. Subject Reports, "Families," PC(2)-4A and "Marital Status," PC(2)-4E.

————. 1970 Census of the Population. Subject Reports, "Family Composition," PC(2)-4A, "Marital Status," PC(2)-4C, and "Persons by Family Characteristics," PC(2)-4B.

U.S. Commission on Population Growth in the American Future. *Demographic and Social Aspects of Population Growth.* Vol. I of Commission Research Reports. Edited by Charles F. Westoff and Robert Parke, Jr. Washington, D.C.: GPO, 1972.

Chapter 3

MARITAL INSTABILITY

We have seen that a rising divorce rate is the single most important factor in explaining the observed growth in female-headed families. But this discovery leads to a whole new set of questions. What is responsible for the longer-term increase in the divorce rate and for its most recent upward swing? Are families "breaking down" under the pressure of inadequate private or public resources or are they "breaking up" as individuals seek new identities or new personal relationships in a relatively affluent era? Is a life-long marriage to one person less satisfying than in the past or is it just that there are new expectations and new options interacting with the old realities of married living? What role has government policy played in shifting expectations or widening options, if any? And can one generalize about these matters or do the explanations vary sharply by income or social class? This chapter searches for some possible answers.[1]

The purpose of the chapter is not to explain *individual* behavior by probing the deeper psychological factors which may determine why some people divorce or separate while others don't. Rather, the focus is on those social and economic deter-

___
1. In principle, there is a need to explain all of the different types of demographic behavior discussed in chapter 2: not only marital instability but also illegitimacy, remarriage, and changing living arrangements. We are currently doing some research in several of these areas but since most attention thus far has been given to analyzing the determinants of marital instability, it is this work which is reported here.

minants of behavior which may tip the aggregates in one direction or another, and which may help to explain changes over
time or intergroup differences.

The chapter begins with a brief digression on methodological perspectives and then proceeds to a discussion of those personal, economic, and cultural variables which appear to affect
a couple's decision to separate.

METHODOLOGICAL PERSPECTIVES

Given their desire to abstract and simplify the world, social scientists have not been averse to approaching even such a complex subject as marriage or divorce with the standard tools of
their respective disciplines. However, with a few exceptions,
the social science literature is richer in empirical detail than in
conceptualization of the issues.[2] In short, we are dealing with
an area where the facts are still very much in search of a theory
and where a given set of facts may be equally consistent with
several hypotheses.

As economists with an interdisciplinary commitment, we
have made an effort to bridge the gap between the different social science perspectives, recognizing that in spite of these efforts, we may have leaned too heavily on economic variables or
misinterpreted the contributions of sociologists. As Duesenberry
has quipped, economics is all about how people make choices
while sociology is all about why they don't have any choices to
make.[3]

Yet, cross-fertilization does occur. An increasing number of
economists have become interested in what most people would
consider "noneconomic" issues and have applied the rigor of
mathematical models of utility maximization to household decisions about marriage and divorce.[4] A few have even become
attuned to the softer variables and less rationalistic assumptions
of some of their colleagues in sociology. In this last category,
one might cite Kenneth Boulding's work on "grants economics"
in which he emphasizes those one-way transfers that are moti-

2. Exceptions include efforts by Gary Becker, George Levinger, John Scanzoni, and F. Ivan Nye, but none of these has reached the stage of being widely
used and accepted. In reporting here the results of previous empirical research,
which is quite voluminous, we have relied heavily on the literature reviews by
Hicks and Platt (1971), Levinger (1965), and Goode (1971). Readers interested in
original sources will need to go to these articles for further citations.

3. Duesenberry, 1960, p. 233.

4. Becker, 1973 and 1974.

vated by "love" or "fear" and form part of the "integrative" or "threat" sectors of the social system.[5] Sociologists and psychologists, in turn, have been influenced by the economic paradigm. Social exchange theorists, following in the tradition of George Homans, emphasize that most interpersonal relationships involve mutual benefits, even though the quid pro quo may not be immediate or measurable in dollar terms.[6] In our own view, it is probably useful to think of a range of transactions, with the market exchange of goods for money at one end of the spectrum and pure altruism (one-way transfers based on love or caring) at the other, but with many transactions involving at least an expectation of reciprocity falling somewhere in between.

Where does marriage fit into this scheme of things? Although there have been societies where wives were bought and sold and treated as property, or where alliances were formed for purely political reasons, in most modern cultures the institution of marriage has fallen toward the altruistic, or "integrative," end of the spectrum.[7] But, there is also an implicit exchange between husband and wife, symbolized by the roles which each is expected to perform, and the superior physical and economic power of men may occasionally cause women's behavior to be motivated by fear (or security needs) as well as by love. Ideally, in building research models it would be desirable to capture each of these aspects of the marital relationship. In practice, we are far from having a grand scheme for guiding the interpretation of facts along such lines. What follows is an eclectic summary of some existing ideas, freshly synthesized and influenced by our own judgments of what is salient.

Specifically, the approach taken is to argue that people choose a particular marriage over its alternatives for a combination of personal, cultural, and economic reasons. That is, marriage provides benefits in the form of love, companionship, emotional security, and sexual satisfaction. In addition, it is clearly the most generally approved way of living in our culture. And finally, it generates economic utility which is derived from the way in which resources are combined, transferred, or exchanged

---

5. Boulding, 1973.

6. See Simpson, 1972, for an excellent review of this literature.

7. Jessie Bernard (1974) argues that women have been socialized to perform in the integrative system and that relationships in the home sector ("women's sphere") are still dominated by ascribed status rather than by achievement.

within marriage. The central hypothesis is that individuals[8] implicitly weigh these social, economic, and personal benefits (or costs) of marriage and that they choose to divorce only when the future, expected net benefits of a marriage compare unfavorably to its perceived alternatives.[9]

The remainder of the chapter is organized as follows. First, there is a general discussion of (1) marriage as a psychological (interpersonal) experience, (2) marriage as an economic institution, and (3) marriage as a social institution. Next, we formulate a model of marital instability which is then tested against new data from the University of Michigan's Panel Study of Income Dynamics. Finally, there is a concluding section which speculates about the significance of these findings for explaining past and future trends in divorce and separation and the quality of married life.

MARRIAGE AS A PSYCHOLOGICAL EXPERIENCE

Although there are obvious difficulties in measuring "marital satisfaction," a great deal of research has been reported on this topic. This research suggests that there are some very "happy" marriages, some very "unhappy" marriages, and a much larger

---

8. One problem with our model of marital instability is that it gives too little attention to the fact that every separation involves *two* people whose experiences and perception of benefits and costs may differ. We need to develop an exchange type model which deals with this problem explicitly. In the meantime, one can perhaps think of husband and wife as bringing the net benefits of marriage to a common level by bargaining or exchange. (One unhappy spouse may make life quite intolerable for the other.) To the extent that such "exchange" is incomplete, it is the spouse deriving the least benefits from marriage whose status will have the greatest effect on stability. Bernard believes that, more often than not, this is likely to be the wife (Bernard, 1972, chapter 3). In general, it has been argued that because marriage and family life are more central to their lives, women tend to make a greater investment in marriage than men, tend to expect a higher return, and tend to be more disappointed if these expectations are not achieved; and, further, that whether or not they act upon their disappointment will depend upon the social and economic benefits associated with remaining married relative to the benefits available outside of the existing arrangement. The fact that about 75 percent of divorces are initiated by women and that this proportion has been increasing lends some support to this argument, although who initiates the divorce, in many cases, has only legal significance. (Bernard, 1972, chapter 3; Goode, 1962; Levinger, 1974; Goode, 1971, p. 509.)

9. It is assumed that people implicitly weigh costs and benefits over some future period, e.g. their own expected lifetime. However, both because of uncertainty and because of a preference for near-term versus longer-term benefits, current net benefits will loom large in the decision.

number that fall somewhere in between.[10] Sociologists and psychologists who have studied this distribution have given names to the different types of marriages they have observed along this spectrum and have even affixed some crude numbers to the relative frequencies of each. For example, Cuber and Harroff speak of "total," "vital," "passive-congenial," "devitalized," and "conflict-habituated" marriages and suggest that after 15 to 20 years of marriage about half are either conflict-habituated or devitalized while the other half fall in the other three categories.[11] Lederer and Jackson use a similar system of labels to discriminate the happiest ("the heavenly twins") from the unhappiest marriages ("the gruesome twosome").[12] More important than these descriptions, and the distribution which they imply, is the finding that a significant proportion of marriages provide little in the way of positive satisfactions to the participants—or are what William Goode has called "empty shell" marriages which are held together for social and economic reasons rather than by any intrinsic benefits flowing from the relationship itself.[13] Numerous studies have demonstrated the importance of these social and economic constraints in marital stability.[14] In short, stable marriages are not necessarily happy marriages, since stability may be related as much to a lack of attractive alternatives to marriage as it is to positive gratifications within marriage.

Nevertheless, other things being equal, a higher level of marital satisfaction is clearly related to greater stability. But what produces happy marriages? It is not within the purview of our research to delve into the psychological literature on the subject, and, in fact, no one has ever had much success in identifying the psychological correlates of marital adjustment. However, it does appear that individuals with similar values experience greater marital satisfaction. Thus, there is evidence that marital satisfaction is lower and divorce rates are higher for those who marry dissimilar mates—such as, individuals outside

---

10. Norman Bradburn reports that psychological satisfaction is represented by a balance between positive and negative feeling (or "affect"). These two components are not necessarily correlated with one another and thus should not be thought of as a continuum. However, the balance between them (Affect Balance Scale) may be thought of as a continuum (see Bradburn, 1969, Ch. 9). Bradburn and others have also shown that reported happiness in marriage is skewed toward the "very happy" end of the continuum. For example, see Bernard, 1942.

11. Cuber and Harroff, 1965.

12. Lederer and Jackson, 1969.

13. Goode, 1971.

14. Hicks and Platt, 1971. Also, see the recent study by Levinger (1974) on factors associated with the outcome of divorce applications.

of their age, education, and religious groups. Similarly, those who marry young, or because of a premarital pregnancy, may reduce the time spent searching for appropriate (like-minded) mates, and may also marry at a time when their values and expectations are still undergoing rapid change, thus increasing the risk that these values will later diverge.[15]

Age at marriage is especially critical. In table 6, we report two sets of findings on this issue, both of which suggest a marked decline in the proportion of marriages ending in divorce or separation as age at first marriage increases. In both cases, this relationship holds, even after adjustments are made for a number of social and economic factors which tend to be correlated with age at marriage. (For example, those who marry young typically have less education and more limited occupational opportunities.) In general, those who marry while they are still in their teens are three or four times as likely to divorce as those who marry in their mid-twenties.

Another interesting finding is that reported satisfaction tends to decline with the duration of a marriage—probably because a high level of emotional involvement is difficult to sustain over a long period and a relationship eventually becomes somewhat stale. In spite of this, divorce rates decline sharply as marriages age.[16] There are a number of possible explanations for this apparent paradox. First, long-term marriages represent "the survival of the fittest" out of an initial cohort. Second, older couples have made a number of specific investments in their marriages, the most important of which is children. Third, the individuals involved have few alternatives to their present relationship—remarriage rates decline precipitously with increasing age, especially among women; and fourth, the period over which any future benefits can be enjoyed becomes shorter, so the expected benefits compare less favorably with the costs of dissolution.

We note, further, that some sociologists have found greater marital satisfaction reported among higher income couples and have hypothesized that a wife's marital satisfaction increases with her husband's occupational success.[17] Because these issues are so intertwined with expectations about marriage as an economic institution, we defer further discussion of them to the next section.

---

15. Levinger, 1965; Hicks and Platt, 1971; Bumpass and Sweet, 1972.
16. Hicks and Platt, 1971, p. 70.
17. Hicks and Platt, 1971, p. 68; Scanzoni, 1972, chapter 1.

Table 6

THE RELATIONSHIP BETWEEN MARITAL INSTABILITY AND AGE AT FIRST MARRIAGE

Wife's Age at Marriage	Number of Cases	Proportion of White Ever-Married Women under 45 in 1970 whose first marriage ended in separation or divorce [a] (N = 5366)
14-17 years	1111	.26
18-19	1791	.16
20-21	1278	.11
22-24	814	.08
25-29	320	.08
30+	52	.03

Husband's Age at Marriage	Number of Cases	Proportion of White Husband-Wife Families in 1968 whose first marriage ended in separation or divorce between 1968 and 1972 [b] (N = 1306)
14-17 years	43	.12
18-21	569	.09
22-24	385	.06
25+	309	.04

a. After controlling for duration; wife's education; status of first pregnancy and birth; wife's religion, family status, and residence while growing up; first husband's marital history. Based on data from the 1970 National Fertility Study. Source: Bumpass and Sweet (1972), table 1, p.756.

b. After controlling for duration of marriage, wife's annual earnings, employment problems of the head, homeownership, employment status of wife, husband's income relative to potential welfare benefits, the ratio of actual to expected husband's earnings, presence of children, marriage-birth interval, church attendance, urban residence, and region and race. Based on data from the Michigan Panel Study of Income Dynamics.

MARRIAGE AS AN ECONOMIC INSTITUTION

In a modern industrialized nation, the family has two basic economic functions. The first is to provide a mechanism by which resources are transferred from those who work in the market (most often men) to those who don't (most often women and children). We will argue that these transfers affect both family stability and the distribution of power within marriage. When a woman acquires direct access to economic resources as a worker, rather than indirect access as a wife, it improves her bargaining position within marriage and reduces the cost of marital dissolution.

The second economic function of the family is to establish the socioeconomic status of its individual members within the social structure. Thus the viability of a marriage may depend, in part, on the level of income and consumption the family achieves relative to other families in the same culture.

In short, both the distribution of resources *within* the family (especially the relative contribution of husband and wife) and the distribution of resources *among* families have implications for marital stability.

The Distribution of Resources within the Family. Gary Becker has argued that there are economic gains associated with marriage.[18] If we assume that women's market wages are lower than men's and that women are at least as productive within the home as men, then this gain is achieved, in part, by substituting the wife's less expensive time for the husband's in household production, and the husband's more highly-paid time for the wife's in market production. The gains from marriage will be directly related to (1) the amount of household production to be done (more household production permits more specialization of the wife's time), (2) the relative wages of men and women (which determine the gains from this specialization), and (3) the extent to which there are economies of scale in a married household's consumption or production (e.g., whether two can live more cheaply together than apart).

The numerical example presented in table 7 should help illustrate the point. It is based on the assumptions that men can earn twice as much as women, that household work is valued at the female wage rate,[19] and that the total output of a married household is shared equally by husband and wife. In the example used, it can be seen that, in pure economic terms, married women gain $2500 while married men lose $1500 relative to their single counterparts. Using the assumption that household work should be valued at male wage rates, women gain $4000 over their single counterparts while men lose nothing. Note that in

---

18. Becker, 1973.

19. It has been argued that this underestimates the value of a wife's contribution because she would choose to work if the wage she could earn were as great as or were greater than the value of her time at home. Thus, the alternative assumption that her time should be valued at male wage rates is also incorporated into table 7. This sets an upper bound because men would stay home if the value of home production were greater than the wages they earn.

Table 7

THE ECONOMIC GAINS FROM MARRIAGE

Single Households

	Value of Household Production	Money Income	Value of Total Output Accruing to Each Person
Male	$1,000 (2,000)	$8,000	$ 9,000 (10,000)
Female	$1,000 (2,000)	$4,000	$ 5,000 (6,000)
Total			$14,000 (16,000)

Married Households

	Value of Household Production	Money Income	Value of Total Output Accruing to Each Person
Male	0	$10,000	$ 7,500 (10,000)
Female	$5,000 (10,000)	0	$ 7,500 (10,000)
Total			$15,000 (20,000)

Explanatory Notes:

a. Single households devote 2,000 hours to paid work and 500 hours to unpaid work (housekeeping activities, etc.).

b. Married households allocate all unpaid work to lower-paid spouse and have enough such work to fully employ one person. They divide total output equally between the two spouses.

c. Men earn $4 per hour; women earn $2 per hour.

d. Household work is valued at female wage rates. Figures in parentheses show the results when household work is valued at male wage rates.

e. Given the higher opportunity cost of their time, male single households probably allocate less time to household production than female single households but this will not change the general conclusions.

both cases the strictly economic gain from marriage (an improved standard of living) accrues entirely to the wife because we assume equal sharing of total output. Of course, men would not marry if they did not reap some compensating (noneconomic) benefits—a point to which we return below. Also, note that the value of total married output is greater than the sum

of the value of output in the two single households.[20] Specialization has created some clear-cut economic efficiencies. These
economic gains will be even greater to the extent that there are
economies of scale in household consumption or production.
They will be smaller to the extent that there is insufficient work
at home to fully employ the wife. They will also vary directly
with relative differences in the wages of men and women or
differences in their home productivity. (The fact that these differences in both wages and home productivity tend to widen
with years spent in a marriage may be another reason for the
positive correlation between marital stability and duration.)[21]

The data in table 8 give some indication of the "cost of marriage" to men. The average prime-age male family head (aged
35-54) spends $7,238 to support his family. This represents the
difference between his income and the market goods and services he personally consumes. In the younger age groups most of
these intrafamily transfers are from fathers to children with
young mothers tending to produce (in both earned income and
household services) about what they consume. Older wives, on
the other hand, consume more than they produce partly because
their labor force participation is lower than that of younger
wives and partly because the value of their housework contribution decreases as children grow up and leave home. One
could argue that these data tend to underestimate the contribution of nonworking wives since their time is valued at the market wage rate in domestic-type occupations. On the other hand,
whatever the value of household production, the fact that it is
unpaid leaves the housewife in a financially dependent position.

Since women gain more financially from marriage than
men, we would expect that more women than men would be
willing to enter, or remain in, marriage, *other things being equal.*
Moreover, the marriage and remarriage prospects of women
depend on the supply of eligible men which is not very high rel-

---

20. These results are similar to those postulated by the theory of compara-
tive advantage which emphasizes the gains from trade when two different countries (or people) have different initial resource endowments. The distribution of
gains between the two countries or individuals will depend on their relative
bargaining power and there is no necessity that all gains accrue to the wife as
we have assumed in table 7. However, given the difficulty of maintaining un-
equal consumption standards within the family, this seems the most probable
outcome.

21. For evidence that the earnings difference between married men and
women widens with age, see Sawhill, 1973. We would also expect the wife's
specialization in the home and the husband's in the market to increase the
relative productivity of women in the home over time.

Table 8

INTRAFAMILY TRANSFERS, 1970

Male Heads	Mean ($)	Aggregate (billion $)
less than 35	3549	49.37
35-54	7238	150.12
55-64	4398	35.76
65 and over	2611	18.85
Wives		
less than 45	33	.82
45 and over	—1898	—36.12

Note: Transfer = Income minus consumption where income includes imputed rent and housework contribution and excludes taxes and work-related expenses, and where consumption of income is allocated in proportion to food needs. Housework is valued at the market wage rate in similar occupations.

Source: Baerwaldt and Morgan, 1971, table 11.

ative to the demand once women reach middle age.[22]

The result of this inequality in both earning power and numbers is an inequality in marital power between husband and wife.[23] The husband may use his position to redistribute family income in his favor, to establish greater authority within the family, or to obtain other nonmonetary perquisites.[24] Women,

---

22. In 1970, the ratio of unmarried (widowed, divorced, single) women to unmarried men was as follows:

Age	Ratio
14-19	.7
20-24	.7
25-34	.9
35-44	1.2
45-54	1.7
55-64	2.5

These data are from the 1970 Census, "Marital Status," PC (2)-4C, table 1.

23. This type of inequality has been termed the "Principle of Least Interest" which states that the individual with the least to lose in a relationship has the most bargaining power. Waller, 1951.

24. Evidence for this kind of bargaining or exchange within marriage comes from the literature on family power (Blood and Wolfe, 1960; Heer, 1963; Scanzoni, 1970, chapter 6). In their classic study in Detroit, Blood and Wolfe found that the distribution of power within marriage was dependent upon the distribution of resources between husband and wife. Research has also shown that high-income men have more authority than those with lower incomes and that women who work (or who do not have children) have more decision-making power within the family than those who don't. Thus, there appears to be some adjustment of status relationships within the family to compensate for differences in economic circumstances, although given the strength of social norms, such adjustments tend to be incomplete.

in turn, generally defer to and accept these male prerogatives as the "price" of being wives, although Jessie Bernard has produced convincing evidence that the "price" they pay often takes its toll on their own mental health.[25]

Two factors may soften or condition the exchange process within marriage. The first is love, or what Becker calls "full caring," within the family.[26] With full caring, the husband receives as much satisfaction from his wife's (or children's) consumption of economic resources as from his own and there is no necessary quid pro quo expected from these transfers. The second factor is community pressure, which insures that both men and women accept the prevailing intrafamily transfers as the norm. Most husbands do not resent their responsibilities as breadwinners nor wives their homemaking role or financially dependent status. Expectations are set by the socialization process which gives men greater rights and status both within and outside of marriage, in return for which they provide some degree of economic security to women and children. Except for a small number of men and women who have consciously chosen a different arrangement, there is no necessity for each couple to negotiate its own marriage contract. The exchange process has been institutionalized; the terms of trade are set in the market and are generally known and accepted.

Turning now to the implications of the intrafamily distribution of resources for marital stability, we suggest two hypotheses:

- *The role specialization hypothesis.* The greater the specialization of husband-wife economic roles, the greater the benefits from exchange and the more stable a marriage.
- *The ideological consistency hypothesis.* The greater the consistency between actual role performance in a marriage and the ideological beliefs of each spouse about what the roles should be, the more acceptable the terms of exchange and the more stable a marriage.

The role specialization hypothesis. We have already noted that the economic benefits of marriage depend on the gains derived from specialization. Thus, we would expect more instability where these gains are small, either because there is little demand for the wife's time at home (e.g., few or no children) or because her wage rate is competitive with that of her husband. Put somewhat differently, the kind of specialization of economic roles and the kinds of implicit exchange which occur

---
25. Bernard, 1972, pp. 30-35.
26. Becker, 1974.

in traditional marriages, especially where there are children involved, create a degree of interdependence that makes dissolution of the relationship costly. Specialization in the home makes women particularly vulnerable since they then have few alternatives to being supported by men. Although society tries to insure that men will share in the costs of divorce through alimony and child support arrangements, the system seems to work poorly in practice.[27] On the other hand, where women have other means of support in the form of welfare or their own earnings, they may be less constrained to remain in a personally unsatisfying relationship.

Existing data are at least consistent with the above hypothesis. Childless marriages are less stable than those with children even though recent research suggests that the presence of children interferes with satisfactions derived from the husband-wife relationship.[28] This apparent paradox can be resolved if we hypothesize that children provide an economic (and sometimes a social) reason for preserving a marriage. In addition, there is evidence of greater instability in families with working wives.[29]

The ideological consistency hypothesis. Our second hypothesis suggests that, whatever the degree of role specialization in marriage, instability will be greater when there is incongruity between role performance and ideology. In other words, given that there is an exchange between husband and wife, each spouse must believe that the terms of the exchange are fair if there is to be an equilibrium in the relationship.

The essential features of this hypothesis are illustrated in table 9 where we postulate a matrix of eight different marital types based on two possible role behaviors that are combined with four possible ideological positions. The two possible role behaviors are "traditional" (wife works in the home) and "non-

27. One of the few existing pieces of evidence on this question (for a metropolitan county in Wisconsin in 1955) shows that within one year of divorce, 42 percent of fathers had made no court-ordered child support payments and that after 10 years, the proportion rose to 79 percent. A nationwide study made by the American Bar Association in 1965 found that alimony was awarded in a very small percentage of all divorce cases. See Citizens' Advisory Council on the Status of Women, "The Equal Rights Amendment and Alimony and Child Support Laws," Washington, D.C., 1972. Also see the data cited in chap. 7, pp. 175–76.
28. Hicks and Platt, 1971, p. 65; Plateris, 1970, p. 3; Levinger, 1965. In our analysis reported below, we did not find higher instability in marriages where there were no children *under 18*. These marriages are not necessarily childless, but we expected to find more divorce where there were no children living at home.
29. Levinger, 1974.

traditional" (wife works in the market). The four possible ideological positions are: (1) both spouses are traditional (i.e., they believe that husbands should be breadwinners and that a wife's place is in the home), (2) both spouses are nontraditional (i.e., they both believe in sex role equality), (3) the husband is traditional and the wife nontraditional, and (4) the husband is nontraditional and the wife traditional.

The role specialization hypothesis leads us to expect more instability when the wife is working than when she is not (more instability in the cells numbered 2, 4, 6, and 8 than in those numbered 1, 3, 5, and 7). The ideological consistency hypothesis then makes some further distinctions based on the interaction between attitudes and behavior. The most conventional, and probably most stable, marriages are represented by cell 1. In these marriages, there is the traditional division of labor between husband and wife, an arrangement which each spouse believes to be appropriate and accepts as mutually beneficial.

Table 9

**ROLE IDEOLOGY AND PERFORMANCE:
EIGHT MARITAL TYPES**

| | | Role Performance | |
		Traditional	Nontraditional
Role Ideology	Both Spouses Traditional	1	2
	Both Spouses Nontraditional	3	4
	Husband Traditional Wife Nontraditional	5	6
	Husband Nontraditional Wife Traditional	7	8

Cell 2 marriages (wife working, both spouses traditional) might include cases where men have been relatively unsuccessful in their breadwinner role and where wives are working out of economic necessity. Both spouses believe that supporting a family is a male responsibility and the incongruity between actual and desired roles undermines the husband's self-esteem, frustrates the wife, and creates marital dissatisfaction for both. Participant-observer studies suggest that this is a common situ-

ation in lower-class families and is one cause of their instability.[30] There is also evidence that marital dissatisfaction is
greater where wives work out of necessity rather than by choice,
suggesting more instability in cell 2 than in cell 4.[31] Cell 3 marriages are probably uncommon since they would normally
achieve cell 4 status; however, there may be some egalitarian
couples whose behavior is constrained by a traditional environment or a lack of job opportunities for the wife.

Cell 4 marriages include those two-career families, currently most prevalent among young, well-educated professionals,
where a mutual commitment to greater equality reduces the
tensions created by the wife's assumption of a nontraditional
role.

In cells 5 through 8 there is disagreement between husband
and wife about family roles, and this husband-wife dissonance
is likely to undermine the marriage relationship.[32] For example,
it has been shown that where husbands do not support a wife's
decision to work (cell 6), marital problems occur more frequently.[33] Where this dissonance is combined with less role
specialization, as in cells 6 and 8, separation is an especially
likely outcome.

The economic role of women has been shifting rapidly. The
proportion of married women in the labor force increased from
25 percent in 1950 to 43 percent in 1973. Since the economic
contribution of wives has probably changed more rapidly than
beliefs about traditional sex roles,[34] we suggest that an increasing proportion of all marriages fall into categories 2, 6, and
8. The result is higher instability caused both by declining specialization and increased ideological dissonance.[35] If and when
attitudes change to accord with the facts, more marriages will
fall into category 4. These marriages may be more stable than
2, 6, or 8 but may be less stable than the traditional relationships of the past (cell 1 marriages).

The Distribution of Resources between Families. Previous re-

---

30. Liebow, 1967; Rainwater, 1970.
31. Orden and Bradburn, 1969; Hicks and Platt, 1971, p. 64.
32. Goode (1971) cites higher divorce rates where husband and wife disagree
about their role obligations.
33. Nye, 1961.
34. See Sawhill, 1974, or Oppenheimer, 1970, for a review of some evidence
on this question.
35. In his provocative book, *Sexual Bargaining*, Scanzoni argues that long-
term changes in family structure have been mainly related to women's demands
for greater rights combined with male reluctance to concede them.

search has established a generally positive relationship between the socioeconomic status of the family and marital stability,[36] and the most recent work in this area suggests that income, rather than education or occupation, is the determining factor.[37] There is also some agreement that what is important in this context is a family's relative position, or "station," in the income scale, rather than any absolute measure of well-being.[38] This latter would explain why rising standards of living over time have not, in themselves, led to greater family stability, although a more equal distribution of income could have this effect.

What is not known is why this empirical relationship between marital stability and the family's economic position exists. One theory ("the husband-wife role affect model") emphasizes the impact of the husband's success or failure as a breadwinner on mutual esteem and affection between husband and wife.[39] Another hypothesis ("the constraint model") is that the greater accumulation of assets in higher-income families makes dissolution more costly.[40] A third possibility is that there are personal factors common to success both in marriage and on the job. Finally, more economic resources may simply alleviate some of the factors contributing to interpersonal tensions (e.g. crowding, disagreeable living conditions, and competition for a limited amount of money).

To date, research has not been able to discriminate effectively between these various hypotheses. Most existing studies have been based on cross-sectional evidence that provides information on the current income of divorced males rather than on the total income of the family before divorce, which makes it difficult to say whether low income causes divorce or divorce causes low income.[41] Also, few of these studies [42] have controlled for other factors and most have not discriminated between various types of income (income from husband's earnings, income from wife's earnings, income from property or income

36. Levinger, 1965; Goode, 1971; Carter and Glick, 1970; Cutright, 1971.
37. Cutright, 1971.
38. Ibid, p. 303.
39. Both "the role affect model" and "the constraint model" are Cutright's terms for distinguishing between what he sees as the two major competing hypotheses in this area. He also makes some interesting suggestions for how researchers might disentangle them empirically. See Cutright, 1971.
40. This is similar to Becker's (1973) contention that the economic gains from marriage vary directly with the level of *nonearned* income.
41. Peabody, 1975.
42. See Goode, 1971; Levinger, 1965; Bumpass and Sweet, 1972. The effects of these variables generally persist even after controlling for various demographic and economic variables. This is less true of some other attitudinal proxies such as education.

from a public transfer program). Findings that emerge from our own empirical analysis, which is reported below, suggest that these distinctions are important.

MARRIAGE AS A SOCIAL INSTITUTION

Whatever personal satisfactions or economic benefits may or may not be gained from marriage, many individuals have strong feelings about maintaining their families intact or respond to community pressures which applaud stability and stigmatize those who are divorced. The strength of these values or pressures is difficult to measure but appears to vary with religious affiliation and commitment, current residence, and where one grew up. Instability is higher among Protestants than among Catholics, as one would suspect, but the lowest separation rates are found among Jewish women and the highest among Episcopalians. Even more important than religious affiliation is degree of religious commitment. People who attend church regularly maintain more stable marital ties than those who don't.[43]

Growing up in the South or on a farm is also associated with greater stability, while couples residing in the West or in large cities are more divorce prone. These facts suggest that community norms vary systematically with residential environment, and we hypothesize that social as well as economic constraints are important in determining who divorces and who doesn't.[44]

Moreover, there is little doubt that attitudes toward marriage and divorce have been changing for a long time. As William Goode points out:

It seems likely that public opinion in the United States during the nineteenth century considered bearable a degree of disharmony that modern couples would not tolerate. People took for granted that spouses who no longer loved one another and who found life together distasteful should at least live together in public amity for the sake of their children and their standing in the community.[45]

Thus, over time, changes in attitudes have probably led to higher divorce rates, and these, in turn, may have fueled a further change in attitudes as divorce has become a more common and increasingly acceptable event.

---

43. Ibid. On religious differences, see particularly Bumpass and Sweet, 1972.

44. It has sometimes been suggested that there are racial or ethnic differences in attitudes or norms which partially explain higher rates of instability for some groups. Since this is a complex question, and one to which a considerable body of research has been devoted, we defer consideration of it until chapter 4.

45. Goode, 1971, p. 480.

A MODEL OF MARITAL INSTABILITY[46]

We are now ready to formulate a model of marital instability drawing on the general hypotheses outlined earlier in this chapter. The kinds of variables which can be incorporated into the model are limited by the available data, but working within this constraint, an attempt has been made to measure a number of the determinants of marital instability and to disentangle several of the hypotheses concerning the relationship between income and instability.

The data come from the University of Michigan's Panel Study of Income Dynamics which includes a national sample of about 5,000 families who were followed longitudinally (interviewed each year) from 1968 to 1972. Of these, there are 1894 who were intact husband-wife families and whose head was less than 54 years old in 1968. It is this group which forms our analysis sample. Some descriptive statistics for the group are shown in table 10.[47]

The basic model can be summarized as follows:

$$S = B_0 + B_1D + B_2I + B_3Y + B_4C + E$$

where S = the probability that an intact family in 1968 will separate during the next four years.

    D = variables measuring the initial timing (age of head at time of marriage) and the current duration of the marriage.

    I = variables measuring the resources available to the wife (the *"independence effect"*).

    Y = variables measuring resources available to the family (the *"income effect"*).

    C = variables measuring the cultural environment or possible variations in social attitudes.

    E = measurement error, the variation in marital satisfaction across marriages, and other unspecified influences.

The specific set of variables used in the final testing of this model are listed in table 11 and the final estimated regression equation is reproduced in table 12. Our hypotheses about these variables will now be briefly reviewed and the results of the analysis summarized.[48]

---

46. For a more detailed discussion of the model, data and results, see Sawhill et al., 1975.

47. Ibid.

48. A more complete description of these results (the data, sample, variables, different model specifications tried, etc.) is included in Sawhill et al., 1975.

Table 10

SUMMARY STATISTICS FROM THE MICHIGAN PANEL STUDY OF INCOME DYNAMICS

Husband-Wife Families with Head <54

	Total	White	Nonwhite
Number	1,894	1,306	588
Duration of marriage (years)	14.3	14.3	14.4
Mean age of head at first marriage (years)	22.7	22.7	22.6
Mean number of children <18 (includes those with no children)	2.1	2.0	2.6
Proportion with no children <18	.21	.21	.23
Proportion of families who attend church once a week or more	.40	.41	.28
Proportion nonwhite	.11	0.0	1.0
Proportion living in the South	.30	.27	.50
Proportion living in the North Central	.30	.32	.18
Proportion living in the West	.16	.16	.16
Proportion living in the Northeast	.24	.25	.16
Proportion of families living in central city of one of 12 largest metropolitan areas	.09	.07	.29
Proportion of husbands who experienced serious unemployment problems in last 3 years	.06	.06	.08
Proportion of families with income a lot higher than usual in 1967	.37	.37	.38
Proportion of families with income a lot lower than usual in 1967	.14	.14	.13
Average annual AFDC income potentially available to mother and children in the state where the family resided in 1968	$1,801	$1,804	$1,770
Husband's mean annual earnings (includes those with no earnings)	$8,110	$8,406	$5,689
Wife's mean annual earnings (includes those with no earnings)	$1,346	$1,336	$1,426

Table 11

DEFINITIONS OF VARIABLES USED IN
SEPARATION REGRESSION

(All variables measure family status in 1968 unless otherwise noted.)

Dependent Variable (S)

DEP1 = dummy representing those families with head under 54 years of age in 1968 that separated because of marital problems at some time between 1968 and 1972.

Duration and Timing (D)

DROM = duration of marriage (years since head's first marriage).[a]
AGHD = age of head at first marriage.

Independence Effect (I)

WERN = wife's 1967 annual earnings (in thousands of dollars).
WELF = monthly average AFDC income per recipient in state where family resides, 1968, times 12, times number of children plus mother (in thousands of dollars).
KIDB = dummy for families who have no children less than 18.

Income Effect (Y)

Family Income
HERN + WERN = husband's 1967 annual earnings plus wife's 1967 annual earnings, used as a proxy for total family income (in thousands of dollars).[b]

PY1 =   family income a lot higher than usual in 1967.

PY2 =   family income a lot lower than usual in 1967.

a.   Includes some men in a second or later marriage for whom this overestimates duration in present marriage.

b.   Our hypothesis is that

$$S = B_o + B_x X + B_i (WERN) + B_y (HERN + WERN) + E.$$

where X is a vector of control variables.
Simplifying, we have

$$S = B_o + B_x X + (B_i + B_y) WERN + B_y HERN + E.$$

The income effect is measured by the coefficient B_y and the independence effect by subtracting B_y from the estimated coefficient for WERN in the above equation. Note that if B_y has the expected negative sign, then $B_i > (B_i + B_y)$. In other words, the pure independence effect is larger than the estimated coefficient for WERN because the latter measures an independence effect partially or totally offset by an income effect.

Table 11

Income Effect (Y)—*Continued*

Assets
ASSETA = asset index taking a value of 1-6 was created by assigning one point for each of the following:
1) two months' income saved
2) more than $200 in property income
3). owns home
4) no mortgage
5) owns two or more cars
6) no debt on car

Husband's Role Performance
EP5 = husband experienced serious unemployment in last three years (1965-1968).

ART1-4 = set of dummies indicating variations in the ratio of actual to expected annual earnings of husband. Expected earnings were derived by regressing actual earnings of each family head against their relevant characteristics (race, age, education, father's education, occupation, and local wage rates). The dummy variables were then defined as follows:

$ART1 = ART \geq 1.5$
$ART2 = 1.1 \leq ART < 1.5$
$ART3 = .5 < ART < .9$
$ART4 = ART \leq .5$
Omitted category $= .9 \leq ART < 1.1$

Cultural Environment (C)
COMH = dummy representing families living in central city of one of 12 largest metropolitan areas.
SOUTH = dummy representing families living in the South.
NC = dummy representing families living in the North Central region.
WEST = dummy representing families living in the West.
RACE = dummy representing nonwhite families.
CHRB = dummy representing families attending church once a week or more.
SOUTHNW = dummy representing nonwhite families living in the South.
NCNW = dummy representing nonwhite families living in the North Central region.
WESTNW = dummy representing nonwhite families living in the West.

Table 12

REGRESSION RESULTS:
SEPARATION DATA FROM THE MICHIGAN PANEL STUDY OF INCOME DYNAMICS

Dependent Variable: Probability that an Intact Family with Head under Age 54 Separates, 1968-1972 (D)

Variables	Coefficients	T Ratios
Intercept	.18***	4.1
WERN	.01***	3.4
WELF	.004	.7
KIDB	−.005	.3
HERN	−.00007	.04
PY1	−.016	1.2
PY2	.053***	2.9
ASSETA	−.011**	2.2
EP5	.073***	2.8
ART1	.044**	2.0
ART2	.002	.1
ART3	.031*	1.7
ART4	.038	1.6
COMH	.058***	2.6
SOUTH	.025	1.2
NC	.019	1.1
WEST	.057***	2.7
SOUTHNW	−.097*	1.8
NCNW	−.111*	1.7
WESTNW	−.201***	3.0
CHRB	−.041***	3.3
RACEA	.096**	2.1
DROM	−.003***	4.1
AGHD	−.004***	2.6

R^2 (corrected) .061   Significance levels denoted by: *** $p < .01$
N = 1894   ** $p < .05$
F = 6.4***   * $p < .10$
$\overline{D}$ = Mean separation rate over four years = .076

Duration and Timing (D). Although marital satisfaction tends to decline with increasing duration, as suggested previously, there are reasons for expecting less instability as a marriage ages. Each spouse makes certain investments in knowing and understanding the other and in creating a family entity; the supply of alternative partners decreases; the time in which alternative benefits could be enjoyed shortens; and, over time, the population of intact couples is purged of the least successful marriages in an initial cohort. Whatever the reasons, our analysis shows a marked decline in separation rates at higher marital durations. On the average, an additional 10 years of marriage reduces the separation rate by three percentage points.

With respect to the timing-of-marriage variable, other things being equal we expect those who marry very young to experience greater instability, probably because these are the marriages in which there is the least value congruence initially and the greatest value divergence over time.[49] The results for this variable indicate a strong effect. For example, a five-year delay in age at marriage reduces the separation rate by two percentage points, on the average.[50]

The Independence Effect (I). Here we are testing the role specialization hypothesis we presented earlier. Where wives are less specialized as homemakers or are less financially dependent upon their husbands, the economic benefits of marriage (or the costs of separation) are expected to be correspondingly lower.

To test this hypothesis, we look at the effects of (1) the wife's annual earnings, (2) the potential welfare benefits available to the wife and children in the state where they resided in 1968, and (3) the presence of children under 18. We find a substantial increase in separation rates as the wife's annual earnings increase. Other things remaining the same (including husband's earnings), a one thousand dollar increase in the wife's earnings is associated with a one percentage point increase in separation rates. On the other hand, we do not find that the availability of higher welfare benefits or the presence of children has any significant effect on stability.

These results merit further discussion. First, although we believe that the positive relationship between the wife's earnings and separation strongly suggests an independence effect, there are other possible interpretations. It may be, for example, that wives seek employment in anticipation of a divorce, although the fact that we are comparing separation rates over the 1968-1972 period with 1967 earnings makes it somewhat unlikely

---

49. Early marriage is often associated with premarital pregnancy, but the inclusion of a variable measuring the marriage-birth interval for our sample of couples was usually not significant and did not change the above conclusions in any important way.

50. Further results for this variable are reported in table 6.

that this is what we are finding. Alternatively, it may be that husbands think their working wives are performing their home-maker and maternal roles less adequately, creating marital strains, or that the time pressures in two-earner families under-mine the marital relationship. To investigate these issues further, it would be desirable to measure the effect of expected as well as actual earnings of the wife on marital stability, since the former would provide a sharper test of the independence effect. We also need to examine how the wife's earnings (or work behavior) and the sex role attitudes of husband and wife inter-act in influencing marital behavior, so that we can test the ideological consistency hypothesis outlined earlier in the chap-ter. Unfortunately, neither of the above can be accomplished with the available data.

Although we can find no evidence of a welfare effect in these data, detecting such effects is an extremely difficult task. First, welfare benefits are a contextual variable rather than a family attribute, and researchers are forced to rely on the existing variation in benefit levels across states to test hypotheses in this area. Yet, in a mobile society, the significance of this variation may be blurred, since the general availability of welfare assist-ance may be as relevant in affecting behavior as welfare benefit levels for specific locations. Moreover, the recent rather dramatic growth in federally-mandated food stamp benefits, available to all low-income families, has reduced both interstate variation in total (cash plus in-kind) benefits and the incentive for husband-wife families to separate in order to qualify for cash assistance.

Second, in searching for a possible welfare effect, it is im-portant to identify that subset of families—largely the poor or near-poor—who are most likely to be affected by whatever variation in welfare benefits does exist. If the availability of welfare does have an effect on family stability, it is within this low-income group that we would expect to find it. For this reason, we ran separate regressions for lower and higher income couples in our sample, but even this strategy failed to reveal any significant association between separation rates and the generosity of the welfare system.

Finally, the level of welfare benefits potentially available to a wife depends not only on the state where she resides (or ends up) but also on the number of dependent children in the family. Thus, our measure of potential welfare benefits includes an adjustment for family size and is highly correlated with the number of children in the family. Based on some evidence not reported here, we found that marital instability was positively correlated with number of children in the lower income families in our sample. It is impossible to say whether this is because larger families can qualify for more welfare assistance or because children put an added financial or emotional strain on a marriage, but we suspect the latter is the more plausible interpretation.[51]

The Income Effect (Y). As noted above, past research has shown a strong positive correlation between socioeconomic status and marital stability. The model presented here attempts to answer a number of questions about this relationship. First, does the correlation found in cross-sectional evidence hold up in a longitudinal analysis where what is measured is the economic status of the *family before* the separation occurs rather than the income of the *husband after* the separation occurs? Second, does this correlation hold in a multivariate context in which variables such as duration and age at marriage (which are correlated with socioeconomic status) are held constant? Third, what aspect of socioeconomic status is most important in understanding marital stability? Is it successful role performance on the part of the husband relative to social expectations? Is it the constraint imposed by an accumulation of assets? Or is it a "pure" income effect whereby the strains associated with having insufficient resources destabilize the family? The set of variables that we have chosen to measure socioeconomic status attempts to discriminate between these possibilities (see table 11).

If a history of unemployment is a good indicator of a husband's inability to provide for his family, then our data strongly confirm that this is what matters more than anything else. Separation rates are at least twice as high among families where the husband experienced serious unemployment over the three years preceding the start of the survey. We also formed a ratio which compared the husband's actual earnings to what he might be expected to earn on the basis of his race, age, education, occupation, family background, and local labor market conditions and found that the ratio had somewhat more explanatory power than the absolute level of his earnings. This again suggests that is is the husband's performance as a breadwinner

---

51. In other words, there is a high degree of correlation between the number of children in the family and the potential welfare benefits. Either variable is significant in a regression that includes race-region interaction effects and is restricted to low-income couples.

relative to expectations in his own social group that is relevant.[52] Somewhat surprisingly, however, being highly successful was just as destabilizing as being highly unsuccessful.

There is very little evidence of any "pure income effect" in these data. The absolute level of husband's earnings has no effect on separation. (And even if it did, the fact that wife's earnings operate to *reduce* stability suggests that this is a "role performance" rather than a "pure income effect" since an extra dollar of earnings increases income equally no matter who contributes it.) On the other hand, large fluctuations in family income, especially in the downward direction, are associated with higher separation rates, and this result, combined with the finding that a history of unemployment is important, suggests that the *stability* of income may be more important than the *level* in explaining marital outcomes.

Finally, the greater the family's assets, the less likely it is that a separation will occur. Perhaps these assets increase the cost of dissolving a marriage—especially if they are relatively illiquid or indivisible. Or perhaps couples who accumulate wealth are more risk averse, or more conventional in their attitudes toward marriage. Or perhaps assets act as a buffer which offsets temporary declines in income.

To summarize, there is some indication here that men who are relatively successful (but not too successful) have more stable marriages, and that fluctuations in income or employment, or a lack of assets, lead to higher separation rates. On the other hand, the level of family income is not predictive of greater marital stability. This last finding is somewhat surprising in view of past research on this subject, but it is a result which has held up throughout our work with this data base, regardless of the particular formulation of the model being tested. Some of our disaggregated analysis, however, has suggested that higher male earnings are associated with lower separation rates among the poorest families, but this correlation does not hold up as one moves into the middle-income group.

Cultural Environment and Social Attitudes (C).   Although we can not measure social attitudes directly with the available data, there are a number of variables which may partially capture attitudinal differences—region, city size and urban location (central city vs. suburbs), church attendance, and possibly race.

---

52. There is a positive correlation between HERN and ART1 and a negative correlation between HERN and ART4 of about +.4 and −.4 respectively.

(Since we will have much more to say about race and family structure in the next chapter, here we simply introduce it as one independent variable without discussing past or present findings on its association with marital stability in any detail.)

In the initial testing of the model, we found the effects of region on separation rates were very different for whites and nonwhites. This led to the present formulation of the model which explicitly incorporates the interrelationships between race and region as a set of independent variables. The results indicate that separation rates are highest for nonwhites living in the northeast, followed by whites living in the west. Although nonwhite rates are about nine percentage points higher than white rates in the northeast, they are about eleven percentage points lower in the west where nonwhites experience the lowest separation rates of all eight subgroups examined. There are no significant racial differences in either the south or the north central region although separation rates are somewhat higher generally in the south than in either the northeast or north central part of the country.[53]

Living in the central city of a large urban area has a significant negative impact on marital stability. Again, there were some racial differences in the strength of the effect, the destabilizing impact of city living being somewhat stronger among white couples.

Finally, couples who attend church regularly are much less likely to separate than those who don't.

There is no way of knowing whether these correlations are the result of the selective migration (or association) of groups who are differentially at risk of marital separation to begin with, whether there is something in the environment itself which produces changes in the attitudes or behavior of the couples involved, or whether these variables are simply proxies for some omitted but unknown influences.

CONCLUSIONS

As we have seen, recent years have brought a marked rise in divorce rates and this is the major cause of the growth in

---

53. The results for the eight race-region subgroups are summarized below. The regression coefficients which are listed represent percentage point deviations from the separation rates experienced by whites in the northeast. Only those deviations which are statistically significant are reported.

West, nonwhite	− .05
Northeast, white; North Central, white and nonwhite	0.0
South, white and nonwhite	+ .025
West, white	+ .057
Northeast, nonwhite	+ .09

families headed by women. Since it is unlikely that the ability of men and women to "live happily ever after" has changed much, we have sought an explanation for this trend in structural or institutional changes. We can now suggest what those changes may have been.

The first change to be identified is the postwar trend toward early marriage. There was a sharp drop in age at first marriage after 1940 and the average age remained low until the mid-sixties, at which point it began to rise again.[54] The initial decrease probably contributed to a rise in divorce rates, and the more recent turnaround may have a stabilizing impact in the future. Certainly, this is what we would expect on the basis of the well-documented association between marital instability and youthful marriage.

The second change we have identified is economic. Women have been moving into the work force and acquiring some independent means of support for a long time, but there was an acceleration in their labor force participation during the postwar period coincident with the sharp upturn in divorce rates. Combined with evidence that separation rates are correlated with the amount of family income contributed by the wife, this suggests that new economic opportunities for women are one explanation for rising divorce rates.

The third trend which has undoubtedly contributed to marital instability is cultural. It is difficult to document a shift in attitudes toward divorce or to say whether such a shift is a cause or a consequence of a change in behavior. We have shown, however, that such things as church attendance, the region, and the type of community in which a family lives are associated with differences in marital stability, and we take this as indirect evidence that attitudes and social constraints do matter.

It is interesting to speculate about what will happen if women's economic opportunities continue to expand relative to men's and if cultural norms about the sanctity of marriage continue to erode. How will the future of marriage unfold?

First, if traditional attitudes about husband and wife roles lag behind changes in the economic status of women, there may be a period during which men and women will be less happy with marriage than in the past due to an increasing dissonance between role performance and ideology. Secondly, if attitudes change to accord with the facts and restore "an ideological equilibrium to the marriage market," marriages will become

54. See Appendix 1, table 1-J.

much more egalitarian than in the past. Thirdly, people will increasingly marry and remain married because of the personal satisfaction involved rather than for economic reasons. There will be fewer transfers of income within marriage and a less rigid division of labor between husband and wife, although within each household there will continue to be economies of scale which may make marital-type living arrangements more desirable than their alternatives. We can thus speculate that divorce rates will rise quite rapidly at first as women's economic opportunities expand, but we would expect some eventual restabilization accompanied by a redefinition of rights and responsibilities within marriage. However, structural constraints, economic interdependence, and thus the utilitarian basis for marriage, will have been steadily eroded, and in the absence of any change in the general quality of interpersonal relationships, we can probably expect a permanently higher level of marital dissolution. This trend will be significantly strengthened to the extent that more liberal attitudes toward divorce become more pervasive. Those marriages which do endure will be, on the average, more satisfying than the marriages which endure today but there will be fewer of them, and those people whose marriages do not endure may end up better off in their unmarried (or, more likely, remarried) state than their present day counterparts who remain married because of more pressing social and economic constraints.

For the more disadvantaged, often minority, segments of the population husband-wife sharing of financial responsibility within the family is nothing new. It is the result of sheer economic necessity. Here, the issue is whether new feminist attitudes will emerge to rationalize this sharing or whether society will find ways to make it possible for these families to adopt the more traditional life styles to which many of them still aspire in spite of shifting social norms. A more detailed discussion of the interactions between race, poverty, and family structure appears in the next chapter.

Another question which we have only touched on in this chapter concerns the role of government policy in influencing marital outcomes. Existing policies were fashioned in an earlier era when both the reality and the ideology of family life were quite different from what they have become today. We have seen that the current welfare system does not appear to contribute to marital instability but we will review further evidence on this question in chapter 5.

Finally, perhaps the most important unanswered question here is what will happen to children in a world in which traditional marriages are less prevalent and in which marital instability is even higher than it is today. We return to this subject in chapters 6 and 7.

BIBLIOGRAPHY

Baerwaldt, Nancy A., and Morgan, James N. "Trends in Inter-Family Transfers." A working paper from OEO Study of Family Income Dynamics for the Office of Economic Opportunity. Dec. 1971.

Becker, Gary S. "A Theory of Marriage: Part I." *Journal of Political Economy* 81:4 (July-Aug. 1973).

————. "A Theory of Marriage: Part II." *Journal of Political Economy* 82:2 (March-April 1974).

Bernard, Jessie. *American Family Behavior.* New York: Harper, 1942.

————. *Remarriage.* New York: Dryden, 1956.

————. "Marital Stability and Patterns of Status Variables." *Journal of Marriage and the Family* (Nov. 1966).

————. *The Future of Marriage.* New York: World, 1972.

————. "Women and New Social Structures." In *The American Woman: Who Will She Be?* Edited by Mary Louise McBee and Kathryn A. Blake. Beverly Hills: Glencoe, 1974.

Blood, Robert O., and Wolfe, Donald M. *Husbands and Wives: The Dynamics of Married Living.* Glencoe: Free Press, 1960.

Boulding, Kenneth E. *The Economy of Love and Fear.* Belmont, California: Wadsworth, 1973.

Bradburn, Norman. *The Structure of Psychological Well-Being.* Chicago: Aldine, 1969.

Broderick, Carlfred B., ed., *A Decade of Family Research and Action, 1960-1969.* Minneapolis: National Council of Family Relations, 1971.

Bumpass, Larry L., and Sweet, James A. "Differentials in Marital Instability: 1970." *American Sociological Review* 37 (Dec. 1972), pp. 754-66.

Carter, Hugh, and Glick, Paul C. *Marriage and Divorce: A Social and Economic Study.* Cambridge, Mass.: Harvard University Press, 1970.

Coombs, Lolagene C., and Zumeta, Zena. "Correlates of Marital Dissolution in a Prospective Fertility Study: A Research Note." *Social Problems* 18 (Winter 1970), pp. 92-101.

Cuber, John F., and Harroff, Peggy B. *The Significant Americans.* New York: Appleton-Century-Crofts, 1965.

Cutright, Phillips. "Income and Family Events: Marital Stability." *Journal of Marriage and the Family* (May 1971).

Duesenberry, James. Comment on "An Economic Analysis of Fertility" by Gary S. Becker. In *Demographic and Economic Change in Developed Countries.* Universities—National Bureau Conference Series 11. Princeton, N.J.: Princeton University Press, 1960.

Furstenberg, Frank F. Jr. "Work Experience and Family Life." Paper prepared for Secretary's Committee on Work in America, Department of Health, Education and Welfare, 1973.

Goode, William J. *After Divorce*. New York: Free Press, 1956. (Later published in paperback under the title *Women in Divorce*).
_____. "Marital Satisfaction and Instability: A Cross-Cultural Class Analysis of Divorce Rates." *International Social Science Journal* 14 (1962), pp. 507-26.
_____. *World Revolution and Family Patterns*. New York: Free Press, 1963.
_____. "Family Disorganization." In *Contemporary Social Problems*, Third Edition. Edited by R. K. Merton and R. Nisbet. New York: Harcourt Brace Jovanovich, 1971.
Heer, David M. "The Measurement and Bases of Family Power: An Overview." *Marriage and Family Living* 25:2 (Nov. 1963).
Hicks, Mary W., and Platt, Marilyn. "Marital Happiness and Stability: A Review of the Research in the Sixties." In *A Decade of Family Research and Action*, edited by Carlfred B. Broderick. Minneapolis: National Council on Family Relations, 1971.
Homans, George C. *Social Behavior: Its Elementary Forms*. New York: Harcourt, Brace and World, 1961.
Johnson, Shirley. "The Impact of Women's Liberation on Marriage, Divorce and Family Life Cycle." In *Sex, Discrimination, and the Division of Labor*. Edited by Cynthia B. Lloyd. Columbia University Press, forthcoming.
Lederer, William J., and Jackson, Don D. *The Mirages of Marriage*. New York: W. W. Norton, 1969.
Levinger, George. "Marital Cohesiveness and Dissolution: An Integrate Review." *Journal of Marriage and the Family* 27 (1965), pp. 19-28.
_____. "Marital Cohesiveness at the Brink: The Fate of Applications for Divorce." Mimeoed Draft. Jan. 1974.
Morgan, James N.; Dickinson, Katherine; Dickinson, Jonathan; Benus, Jacob; and Duncan, Greg. *Five Thousand American Families—Patterns of Economic Progress*, vols. 1 and 2. Ann Arbor, Mich.: Survey Research Center of the University of Michigan, 1974.
Nye, F. Ivan. "Maternal Employment and Marital Interaction: Some Contingent Conditions." *Social Forces* 40 (Dec. 1961), pp. 113-119.
Nye, F. Ivan, and Berardo, Felix M. *The Family: Its Structure and Interaction*. New York: Macmillan, 1973.
Oppenheimer, Valerie K. *The Female Labor Force in the U.S.* Berkeley: University of California, 1970.
Orden, Susan R., and Bradburn, Norman M. "Working Wives and Marriage Happiness." *American Journal of Sociology* 74:4 (Jan. 1969).
Peabody, Gerald E. "Income and Marital Stability: A Review of Empirical Findings." Paper 979-02. Washington, D.C.: The Urban Institute, April 9, 1975.
Plateris, Alexander A. "Children of Divorced Couples." Vital and Health Statistics, Series 21, no. 18, National Center for Health Statistics. Washington: U.S. Government Printing Office, 1970.
Rainwater, Lee. *Behind Ghetto Walls*. Chicago: Aldine, 1970.
_____. "Crucible of Identity: The Negro Lower-Class Family." *Daedalus* (Winter 1966), pp. 172-216.
Sawhill, Isabel V. "The Economics of Discrimination Against Women: Some New Findings." *Journal of Human Resources* (Summer 1973).
_____. "Perspectives on Women and Work in America." In *Work and the Quality of Life*. Edited by James O'Toole. Cambridge: MIT Press, 1974.
Sawhill, Isabel; Peabody, G.; Jones, C.; and Caldwell, S. "Income Transfers and Family Structure," Urban Institute Working Paper 979-03, July 1975.

Scanzoni, John. "A Reinquiry into Marital Disorganization." *Journal of Marriage and the Family* 27 (1965), pp. 483-491.

_____. *Opportunity and the Family.* New York: Free Press, 1970.

_____. *Sexual Bargaining.* Englewood Cliffs, N.J.: Prentice-Hall, 1972.

Simpson, Richard L. "Theories of Social Exchange." New York and Morristown, N.J.: General Learning Press, 1972.

Udry, J. Richard. *The Social Context of Marriage.* Philadelphia: Lippincott, 1966a.

_____. "Marital Instability by Race, Sex, Education and Occupation, Using 1960 Census Data." *American Journal of Sociology* (Sept. 1966b), pp. 203-209.

_____. "Marital Instability by Race and Income based on 1960 Census Data." *American Journal of Sociology* (May 1967).

Waller, Willard. *The Family, A dynamic Interpretation.* Revised by Reuben Hill. New York: Dryden, 1951.

Chapter 4

RACE AND FAMILY STRUCTURE

The great majority of black families, like their white counterparts, are headed by two parents. However, in the black community the proportion of all families with a female head is not only higher than among whites but also, as indicated in chapter 2, has been increasing at a faster rate. By 1973, one-third of all nonwhite families, and nearly two-thirds of nonwhite families that were poor and had children, were headed by women. The parallel figures for whites are considerably lower, as indicated in table 13.

A great deal of attention has already been devoted to interpreting these facts. A decade has passed since the Department of Labor issued its publication entitled "The Negro Family: The Case for National Action." In this document, Daniel Patrick Moynihan argued that there was a unique black culture, rooted in slavery, segregation, and deprivation, to be sure, but now indelibly printed on the social fabric and responsible for many of the problems endemic to life in the ghetto. In his words:

At the heart of the deterioration of the fabric of Negro society is the deterioration of the Negro family. . . .

There is no one Negro community. There is no one Negro problem. There is no one solution. Nevertheless, at the center of the tangle of pathology is the weakness of the family structure. Once or twice removed, it will be found to be the principal source of most of the aberrant, inadequate or antisocial behavior that did not establish, but now serves to perpetuate the cycle of poverty and deprivation.[1]

---

1. Moynihan, 1965, pp. 5 and 30.

Table 13

SELECTED MEASURES OF FAMILY STABILITY, BY RACE
(Percentages)

	White	Nonwhite
Proportion of all Families with a Female Head		
1960	9	22
1973	10	33
Proportion of Low-Income Families with a Female Head		
1960	20	33
1973	33	63
Proportion of Low-Income Families with Children under 18 with a Female Head		
1960	25	35
1973	48	71
Proportion of Children under 18 Living with both Parents		
1960	92	75
1973	87	52
Proportion of Children under 18 Living with both Parents in Low-Income Families		
1960	N.A.	N.A.
1973	61	34
Proportion of Births which Were Illegitimate		
1960	2	22
1973	6	42

Sources: "Poverty in the U.S. 1959-1968," *Current Population Reports* (CPR).
Consumer Income Series P-60, no. 68, Washington, D.C.: U.S.
Bureau of the Census.

"Household and Family Characteristics," Series P-20, no. 246, CPR,
Population Characteristics, Washington, D.C.: U.S. Bureau of the
Census.

"Marital Status and Living Arrangements: March, 1972," Series P-20,
no. 242, CPR, Population Characteristics, Washington, D.C.: U.S.
Bureau of the Census.

"Characteristics of the Low Income Population," Series P-60, nos.
86, 88 and 91, CPR, Consumer Income, Washington, D.C.: U.S.
Bureau of the Census.

"Vital Statistics of the U.S., vol. I—Natality," 1968 and 1969, Rockville, Maryland: National Center for Health Statistics.

Much controversy and interest was generated by the "Moynihan Report," and its author's views have not gone unchallenged.[2] In fact, they have spawned a considerable volume of new research, which has improved our understanding of these issues even though there is still more to learn. Past research has been directed toward two basic questions. The first concerns the degree to which racial differences in family structure and functioning are a direct result of differences in the economic and social circumstances confronting each group. Thus, a number of studies have suggested that blacks hold to the same set of values and norms as the dominant culture but that past and present discrimination, along with its economic consequences, has forced them to adopt a different set of behavior patterns. Direct observations of lower-class black families by Lee Rainwater, Elliot Liebow and others have been especially useful in documenting the way in which poverty and unemployment breed family instability, impair self-esteem, and produce a cultural milieu which in turn may help to generate another cycle of poverty.[3]

The second question which has concerned researchers relates to the way in which these cultural adaptations in family life affect the achievement and well-being of its members. Moynihan argued that children raised in female-headed families would be more prone to juvenile delinquency, would have greater difficulties in school, and would generally be disadvantaged relative to children raised in intact families.[4] Other scholars have strongly resisted the notion that female-headed families, black or white, are dysfunctional.[5] In chapter 6 we critically review the mixed and rather unsatisfactory evidence on this question. Here, it is sufficient to point out that one undisputed consequence for children growing up in a female-headed family is a greater risk of growing up poor.

The purpose of the present chapter is to review the most recent evidence on two questions. The first is why have black families traditionally been more likely than white families to be headed by a woman? The second is why has female-headedness continued to increase more rapidly in the black community than in the white? In each case, the discussion begins with a

2. Rainwater and Yancey, 1967.

3. Liebow, 1967; Rainwater, 1966.

4. Moynihan, 1965, chap. 4.

5. Staples, 1971; Billingsley, 1973; Hill, 1972.

demographic analysis of racial differences and then moves on to discuss the basic social and economic conditions which impinge upon these demographic processes. Drawing on the model of marital instability introduced in the last chapter, we present new evidence that economic opportunities, especially stable job prospects for men, are critical elements in explaining racial differences in family structure.

RACIAL DIFFERENCES IN FEMALE HEADEDNESS

Demographic Components. In chapter 2, we examined the immediate determinants of female headedness through a series of accounting relationships which showed that the proportion of families headed by a woman depends on total inflows to that status (divorce, separation, death, illegitimacy) as well as on total outflows (remarriage, death, aging of children). A review of the numbers in that chapter quickly reveals that for all of the transition probabilities on which there are any data by race the observed racial differences contribute to the higher incidence of female-headed families with children in the black community (see table 5). For 1970, we estimate that the nonwhite divorce rate was slightly higher than the white rate while the total separation rate was about one and a half times higher than the white rate.[6] Moreover, nonwhite women were twice as likely to be widowed and thirteen times as likely to enter female headedness by having and keeping an illegitimate first child. This latter probability reflects not only higher illegitimacy rates but also a much greater tendency among black women to raise their out-of-wedlock children rather than put them up for adoption. Finally, both a longer lag between separation and divorce and lower remarriage rates among divorced women also contribute to more female headedness among nonwhites.[7]

Next, we turn to Census data to partition out the relative contribution of some of these demographic factors to racial differences in family structure by means of a components analysis similar to that used in chapter 2. To perform this analysis, we first calculate the proportion of women in various family or household statuses. These proportions are reproduced in table 14 and, as we would expect from the data just reviewed, the table shows a much higher proportion of both single and sepa-

6. This last estimate is based on two separate pieces of evidence: (1) mean separation rates from the Panel Study (table 12) and (2) adjusted Census data (table 16).

7. Glick and Norton, 1971.

Table 14

PROPORTION OF ADULT WOMEN IN VARIOUS STATUSES, BY RACE, 1970
(Percentages)

	White	Nonwhite
Proportion of Never-Married Women, 14+, with children under 18	1	12
Proportion of Ever-Married Women, 14+, in disrupted marital status (divorced, separated, or widowed)		
Widowed, divorced, or separated but without children <18	5	4
Widowed with children <18	5	8
Divorced with children <18	8	8
Separated with children <18	4	18
Proportion of unmarried women[a] with children <18 heading their own household	86	84
Proportion of all women, 14+, who were never-married	22	29

a. Includes single, divorced, separated, and widowed women.
Source: Appendix 4.

rated women with children in the nonwhite population although identical proportions of each racial group are divorced with children. The tremendously high rates of separation relative to divorce evidenced in the data for nonwhites are particularly striking. Another interesting finding is that a high proportion of all unmarried women with children head their own households rather than live with relatives and that this choice of living arrangements does not vary much by race. The small difference that does exist is probably related to the fact that white women can more readily afford to establish a separate household. In fact, other research has shown that there are no racial differences in the tendency to establish an independent household once such factors as income, age, marital status, location, and presence of children have been taken into account.[8]

The results of the components analysis of racial differences in female headship for 1970 appear in table 15. The number of female heads in that year has been translated into a rate per 1,000 adult women in order to standardize for the difference in

8. Carliner, 1972, p. 13; Sweet, 1971.

Table 15

COMPONENTS ANALYSIS OF RACIAL DIFFERENCES IN FEMALE HEADSHIP, 1970

Female-Headed Families with Children less than 18, 1970[a]	Number	Rate Per 1,000 Women, 14+
White	1,891	27.4
Nonwhite	840	103.4
Difference		76.0

Components of Difference[b]		Percent
Total Difference	76.0	100
Living Arrangements		−1[d]
Marital Disruption and Presence of Children Combined		78
Independent Effect of Disruption		23
Independent Effect of Children Being Present		32
Interaction Between Disruption and Presence of Children		23
Population Composition[c]		−2[d]
Illegitimacy		18
Residual Interaction		7

a. Includes female-headed subfamilies but excludes married women, spouse absent.

b. Calculated by substituting nonwhite proportions for white proportions in the following formula:

$$FHFC = \frac{EFHFC}{DC} \cdot \frac{DC}{D} \cdot \frac{D}{E} \cdot E + \frac{NFHFC}{NC} \cdot \frac{NC}{E} \cdot N$$

where E and N are number of ever-married or never-married women per 1,000 women, 14+. See Appendix 4 for basic data and definitions.

c. Proportion of women, 14+, who were never-married.

d. These negative components indicate that if nonwhites headed households with the same relative frequency as whites or if relatively as many of them were married, racial differences would be larger than currently observed.

Source: Appendix 4.

population size between the two subgroups. The nonwhite-white difference is then partitioned into a number of demographic components. Roughly four-fifths of this difference is due to greater marital disruption among black families with children, while most of the remaining one-fifth is related to higher illegitimacy in the black community.

The marital disruption component can be further disag-

gregated into that portion which represents more widowhood
or separation among nonwhites (independent effect of disruption), that portion which represents their greater likelihood of
having children within the home at the time of disruption (independent effect of children), and a third portion which represents
the interaction between these two factors. Thus, the analysis
indicates that, relative to whites, nonwhite women are more
likely to be widowed or separated (but especially the latter)
and are also more likely to have dependent children within the
household at the time their marriage ends.

Table 16

**FACTORS ACCOUNTING FOR BLACK-WHITE DIFFERENCES
IN THE PROPORTION OF WOMEN REPORTING THEMSELVES
SEPARATED OR DIVORCED**

	White	Black
Total women first married in 1965-1967 still living in 1970	3,645,000	454,000
Percent	100	100
Currently separated or divorced	7	19
Divorced but subsequently remarried	4	2
Total divorced or separated since first marriage (line 1 + line 2)	11	21
Adjusted for possible misreporting (black separations reduced by one-fourth)	11	16

Source: U.S. Bureau of the Census, 1970 Census of Population, vol. II-4D,
Age and First Marriages, table 4; and Glick and Mills, 1974, p. 17.

Since there are no good data on separation and remarriage
rates by race, we rely on Census counts of the proportion of
women in different marital states, and it is these counts which
comprise the basic data for the components analysis. It is important to note, however, that racial differences in the proportion of women whom the Census reports as separated or
divorced in a given year reflect not only differences in marital
instability but also differences in remarriage rates, as well as
some possible error in the reporting of marital status. Some
data which illustrate this point are presented in table 16. Looking at the group of women who first married in the years 1965-
1967, we find that by 1970, more blacks than whites were
currently separated or divorced. This was partly because blacks

experienced more marital instability, but it was also due to the fact that more whites than blacks divorced *and* subsequently remarried. Finally, Glick and Mills have suggested that as many as one-fifth to one-fourth of black women heading households could be the wives of the black men who fail—with much greater frequency than white men—to show up in Census counts of the population.[9] Making a rough adjustment for the mis- reporting of marital status that these undercounts suggest, we end up with a separation rate that is about one and a half times higher for blacks than for whites in contrast to the proportion "currently separated," which is 2.7 times higher for blacks.

To summarize the analysis thus far, less than one-fifth of the racial difference in female headship rates is related to the higher proportion of *single* women with children among non- whites. Most of the remaining difference is due to the higher proportion who are *separated or divorced* with children. The higher proportion separated or divorced, in turn, reflects not only greater marital dissolution but also lower remarriage rates and probably greater misreporting of marital status among non- whites.

Differences in Marital Instability. A number of writers have argued that blacks have the same values and attitudes towards marriage and the family as middle-class or working-class whites but that the environment in which they operate precludes their behaving in a similar fashion. Black men often do not have the jobs or the income which would enable them to be stable pro- viders. In other words, it appears to be economics rather than culture which is responsible for the greater instability found among black families.

To test this hypothesis, researchers have used Census data to examine the extent to which differences in income, education, occupation, and employment account for the higher incidence of marital instability among nonwhite men. Studies of these variables have explained some but not all of the observed racial differences.[10] Farley, for example, found that one-third of the black-white differential in headship of husband-wife families by men, aged 25-54 in 1960, could be explained by differences in education, employment, and income. Our own analysis of 1970

---

9. Glick and Mills, 1974. This estimate is based on the assumption that uncounted black males are heads of husband-wife families in the same pro- portion as those who are counted in each age group.

10. Udry, 1966 and 1967; Bernard, 1966b; Farley, 1972; Cutright, 1971a.

Census data also indicates that roughly one-third of the racial differential in the marital stability of males, aged 45-54,[11] was related to differences in current earnings, occupation, and education. The results of this analysis are presented in table 17.

Table 17

PROPORTION OF NEGRO AND WHITE MALES, 45-54, MARRIED ONCE, WIFE PRESENT, STANDARDIZED FOR EARNINGS, EDUCATION, AND OCCUPATION 1970

Negro Actual	.55	
White Actual	.75	
Differential	.20	

Standardized for[a]	Negro Proportion Using White Weights	White Proportion Using Negro Weights
Earnings	.59	.69
Earnings and education	.59	.69
Earnings, education and occupation[b]	.61	.68

Analysis of Differential[c]	Percentage Points	Percent Distribution
Total	20.0	100
Explained by earnings, education & occupation	6.5	33
Unexplained	13.5	67

a. The formulas were $\sum_i P_{iW} F_{iN}$ (Negro weights) and

$$\frac{}{\sum_i F_{iN}}$$

$$\frac{\sum_i P_{iN} F_{iW}}{\sum_i F_{iW}}$$ (white weights) where P is the proportion married once, wife present in an earnings-education-occupation cell (i) and F is the frequency or number of men in a cell.

b. Standardization using Negro weights was based on 272 cells and that using white weights was based on 175 cells. In both cases the potential number of cells is 300 but the cell sizes are too small to calculate proportions in some instances.

c. Average of results using white and Negro weights.

Source: 1970 Census of Population, Subject Report "Marital Status," PC(2)-4C, table 9, Washington, D.C.: Bureau of the Census.

---

11. This is the only age group for which the data needed to do this analysis have been published.

Although these findings suggest that differentials in economic status are only partially responsible for the greater marital instability among blacks, they should not be accepted uncritically. Census data measuring current income tell us nothing about expected lifetime earnings prospects, about asset levels, or about the stability of income or employment. In addition, current income may depend on, as well as determine, marital status—a fact which holds most strongly in the case of women but which has some importance for men as well.[12] For all of the above reasons, the analysis of the Michigan Panel data reported in the last chapter is more illuminating than studies relying on Census data, and after first looking at some other variables, we will review the findings from that analysis below.

Other socioeconomic factors alleged to be of some importance in explaining racial differences in family stability are the *relatively* high educational achievement, occupational prospects, and earnings of black women compared to black men, and the presumed matriarchal family life that this produces.[13] As Rainwater states, black women "are disillusioned with marriage as providing any more secure economic base than they can achieve on their own. . . . Marriage is regarded as a fragile arrangement held together primarily by affectional ties rather than instrumental concerns."[14] Certainly there is evidence that the earnings of black women are more nearly equal to black men's than those of white women (table 18), and that black wives contribute a larger share of total family income than white wives.[15]

With respect to sex roles within the family, numerous analyses of attitudinal data have been conducted to determine whether or not black families are matriarchal in character.[16]

---

12. Duncan, Featherman, and Duncan report that men in a disrupted marital status have somewhat lower occupational achievement scores than those in intact families even after controlling for the respondent's social background, education, and first job. Duncan et al., 1972, p. 235.

13. Moynihan, 1965, chap. 4.

14. Rainwater, 1966, pp. 188 and 197.

15. Using 1960 Census data, Cutright found that nonwhite wives provided 17 percent of total family income, versus 12 percent for all wives in families where the head was 25 to 64. The greater contribution of nonwhite wives was apparent at every income level except the very lowest. (Among families where the head was under 25, the contribution of nonwhite wives was lower than that of white wives.) Cutright, 1971b, table 3. In the panel data used for our own analysis, we found that the average hourly earnings of nonwhite wives more nearly approximated their husband's average hourly earnings than in the case of whites.

16. Rainwater, 1970; Blood and Wolfe, 1969; Staples, 1971; Hyman and Reed, 1969; Mack, 1971; Billingsley, 1969.

"Matriarchy" is usually defined as a form of family life in which the wife or mother exercises a greater amount of authority and has more responsibility than the husband or father relative to cultural norms. The accumulated research on this question is somewhat inconclusive, partly because "matriarchy" is difficult to measure and is fraught with normative connotations. However, the evidence suggests that *economic insecurity* and its actual and expected effects on family life are the principal explanations for whatever matriarchal tendencies may exist. In short, as we argued in the last chapter, male authority within the family is closely linked to the income which men are able to provide.

Table 18

THE RELATIVE INCOME OF WHITE AND NEGRO WOMEN, 1972

(Year-round, Full-Time Workers)

	White Females	White Males	Ratio	Negro Females	Negro Males	Ratio
Northeast	$6,440	$11,283	.57	$6,063	$7,730	.78
North Central	6,190	11,151	.56	5,949	9,084	.65
South	5,631	9,690	.58	4,405	6,043	.73
West	6,873	11,834	.58	6,889	9,056	.76

Source: "Money Income in 1972 of Families and Persons in the U.S.," CPR, Consumer Income, Series P-60, no. 87, Washington, D.C.: Bureau of the Census, June 1973, table 7.

Finally, separation rates are particularly high in the central cities of our large urban areas (see chapter 3, p. 61). Interestingly enough, Farley has found that marital instability is significantly greater for blacks born and living in Northern urban areas than for those who migrated from the South.[17] Thus, it appears to be urban living itself rather than the "cultural shock" of migration that leads to family dissolution. It may be that social controls are weaker in an urban setting, that there is a "contagion effect" whereby marital instability spreads through the population as an increasing number of younger people are exposed to female-headed families, or that more crowded living conditions are inhospitable to family stability.

Since low-income black families are more concentrated in the central cities of urban areas than are low-income white

17. Farley, 1971, chap. 2.

families, these differences in residential location may partially explain the higher incidence of female headedness among the former. To test this hypothesis, we have standardized the data for the differing distributions of blacks and whites in various-sized cities, central city location, and farm or nonfarm status outside of metropolitan areas. The results are summarized in table 19 and indicate that these differences in location account for about 15 percent of the observed differences in female headship.

Table 19

PROPORTION OF NEGRO AND WHITE LOW-INCOME FAMILIES WITH A FEMALE HEAD, STANDARDIZED FOR CITY SIZE, CENTRAL CITY LOCATION, AND FARM-NONFARM STATUS OUTSIDE OF METROPOLITAN AREAS, 1971

Negro Actual	.57
White Actual	.30
Differential	.27

Proportion of low-income families with a female head, standardized for residential distribution[a]

Using Negro weights	.33
Using White weights	.52

	Percentage Points	Percent Distribution
Total Differential[b]	27	100
Explained by residential distribution	4	15
Unexplained	23	85

a. The formulas were $\sum_{i} P_{iW} F_{iN}$ (Negro weights) and

$$\frac{\sum_{i} P_{iW} F_{iN}}{\sum_{i} F_{iN}}$$

$$\frac{\sum_{i} P_{iN} F_{iW}}{\sum_{i} F_{iW}}$$
(white weights) where P is the proportion of low-income families with a female head by residence status cell (i) and F is the frequency or number of families in a cell.

b. Average of results using Negro and white weights.

Source: "Characteristics of the Low-Income Population, 1970," CPR, Consumer Income, Series P-60, no. 81, Washington, D.C.: Bureau of the Census.

To shed further light on all of the above factors, we turn now to a review of the analysis of marital instability reported in chapter 3. This analysis has the advantage of being based on longitudinal data which provide a rich source of information about the economic and social status of intact husband-wife families *prior* to divorce or separation and which permit a multivariate analysis of a number of factors which appear to contribute to family dissolution.

The 588 nonwhite couples in the sample experienced an annual separation rate of 2.7 percent and the 1,306 white couples a rate of 1.8 percent. However, the nonwhite couples were found to have almost all of the characteristics associated with marital instability in much higher proportions than the white couples (table 10). They were more likely to have low-earning husbands and fewer assets, to live in the central cities of large urban areas, to have working wives, and to have incomes more evenly split between husband and wife. Most importantly, they reported much more unemployment in recent years and this was the single most important variable accounting for the higher instability among nonwhite families. After controlling for these and other differences between the two groups, there were no statistically significant differences in separation rates by race, although there was a strong interaction between race and region, as reported in chapter 3.[18] Among the youngest couples in the sample, the expected separation rate tended to be *lower* for nonwhites than for whites.

What these findings imply is that reliance on cross-sectional data, such as census counts of the proportion of males married once, may not provide accurate indicators of *current* marital behavior,[19] and that using longitudinal data leads to quite different conclusions about race and family stability. We have also been able to control for some of the employment-related and other variables which have not been well measured in

---

18. Initially we ran separate regressions for each racial group, but a Chow test showed that only the race-region (and possibly race-city size) interactions were important. Using the regression coefficients from table 12, we then calculated the expected separation rates of each racial group on the assumption that they have the mean characteristics of the entire sample. This procedure produces an expected four-year separation rate which is only .4 percentage points higher for nonwhites. Another regression for the group of couples where the head was under 46 in 1968 produced separation rates which were higher for whites after all adjustments, although in this case there is some misspecification of the model because we failed to incorporate a race-region interaction.

19. For a similar conclusion and more evidence on this question, see Cutright, 1971a.

previous studies. Further research may reveal problems peculiar
to the data set used here, but in the meantime we suggest that
some re-evaluation of past conclusions about these issues is in
order.

Differences in Illegitimacy. We have seen that illegitimacy is of
much less importance than marital instability in explaining the
high incidence of female headedness among nonwhites. Still it
is not inconsequential and some further explanation of racial
differences may be of interest.

Higher illegitimacy among blacks could reflect (1) higher
rates of premarital intercourse, (2) less effective use of contraception, leading to a higher pregnancy rate among the sexually active, (3) less legitimation of the pregnancy through
marriage, (4) fewer abortions, leading to a higher proportion of
births among those pregnant, and (5) less adoption, leading to
a higher proportion of single mothers living with their children.
There is evidence that all of these factors play a role (table 20).[20]
Based on data from a national probability sample, black teenagers are twice as likely as whites to engage in premarital coitus
and they become sexually active at an earlier age.[21] Among those
sexually active, twice as many blacks as whites become pregnant
and this seems to be primarily related to the use of less effective
contraception. The lower legitimation rate among black teenagers is more difficult to explain, but may simply reflect the
limited ability of marriage rates to adjust upwards to accommo-
date high levels of unwanted births, since marriage rates among
black teenagers are generally comparable to rates for whites of
the same age.[22] The higher proportion of live births among
pregnant black teenagers reported in table 20 is almost entirely
due to their relatively lower utilization of abortion, although
recent changes in the availability of legal abortion may have
altered this conclusion.[23] Finally, white unwed mothers are much

20. The discussion of these factors draws heavily on the findings of Zelnik
and Kantner based on a national probability sample of the female population,
aged 15 to 19. Racial stratification produced 1,479 blacks and 3,132 whites and
other races. A good discussion of these issues also appears in Cutright, 1973a.
    21. However, the frequency of intercourse and the number of partners is
somewhat lower than in the case of whites.
    22. Cutright, who has shown a strong negative correlation between the out-
of-wedlock-conceived birth rate and the legitimation rate cross-culturally, seems
to argue that this is the case and that there is no evidence for accepting a more
ethnological theory emphasizing differential social stigma. See Cutright, 1972,
pp. 406-7.
    23. Black unmarried women have far *more* abortions than white unmarried
women but because their pregnancy rate is so much higher, they have fewer
abortions per pregnant woman. See Cutright, 1973a; Tietze, 1973; Sklar and
Berkov, 1973.

more likely to give up their babies for adoption, and this difference largely explains the lower proportion of these white mothers who become female heads.

Table 20

FACTORS ACCOUNTING FOR RACIAL DIFFERENCES IN THE INCIDENCE OF NEVER-MARRIED, FEMALE-HEADED FAMILIES AMONG WOMEN 15 TO 19[a]

	White	Black
Number (000) of Women, 14-19, 1971[a]	9,925	1,514
Percentage who had premarital intercourse	27	54
Percentage of sexually active premaritally pregnant	23	46
Percentage of premaritally pregnant who remained unmarried[b]	49	91
Percentage of unmarried who had live birth[b]	42	72
Percentage of illegitimate babies living in mother's household	72	92
Expected number out of 1,000 who		
are sexually active	270	540
become premaritally pregnant	62.1	248.4
do not marry before birth	30.4	226.0
have an illegitimate live birth	12.8	162.7
become unwed female heads	9.2	149.7

a. No. of women, *14-19,* from *Current Population Survey,* P-20, no. 225, table 1. Proportions from Zelnick and Kantner refer to women *15-19.*

b. Those premaritally pregnant and unmarried (NM) include some currently pregnant teenagers whose eventual marital status and birth outcome are unknown.

Source: Zelnik and Kantner, 1974.

In table 20, we have used data on the above proportions to calculate an expected rate of never-married, female-headed families per 1,000 women, 15-19. The black-white ratio is roughly 15-to-1, somewhat higher than the 12-to-1 ratio reported in table 14 for all adult women over 14. More importantly, this table makes it clear that all of the listed factors are important in understanding the sources of illegitimacy and that in combination they interact to produce large differences in female headship by race among very young single women.

Illegitimacy declines with increasing education, income,

and other measures of status. Cutright estimates that about 45 percent of the white-nonwhite illegitimacy rate difference during 1964-66 is related to the greater incidence of poverty in the nonwhite population.[24] Nevertheless, at almost every socioeconomic level, researchers have found a different set of sexual attitudes and higher rates of premarital intercourse and pregnancy among blacks.[25]

But perhaps too much attention has been focused on illegitimacy within the black community. It is not the legitimacy of a birth per se but the overall level of fertility which is contributing most to the problem of dependency. Most black women who have their first child illegitimately eventually marry,[26] and the timing of fertility (before or after marriage) may not be as important as the amount in increasing both the risk of female headship and the economic burden for those women who end up heading their own families.[27] Low-income black families, whether male- or female-headed, are much larger than similarly situated white families as shown in table 21 (although the reverse is true at higher levels of income).[28] The existence of large numbers of children makes it financially difficult to sustain a marriage,[29] and, as we have seen, it is marital instability rather than illegitimacy which is the major source of female headship in both racial groups.

Table 21

MEAN SIZE OF LOW-INCOME FAMILIES, BY RACE, 1972

	White	Negro
Male-Headed Families	3.7	4.8
Female-Headed Families	3.3	4.3

Source: "Characteristics of the Low-Income Population: 1972," CPR, Consumer Income Series P-60, no. 91, table 21, Washington, D.C.: U.S. Bureau of the Census.

24. Cutright, 1973a, p. 114.
25. Farley, 1971, chap. 7; Gebhard et al., 1958; Cutright, 1973a, p. 101; Zelnik and Kantner, 1972; Reiss, 1967, chap. 3
26. Cutright and Scanzoni, 1973a, table 10.
27. See Cutright, 1973b for evidence that the timing of fertility is not an important factor in future family status. Also see the discussion of this factor in chap. 3.
28. 1970 Census, "Family Composition," PC(2)-4A, table 15.
29. See chap. 3. There is additional support for this view in Farley's analysis of 1960 Census data. He found that relative to black women in husband-wife families, black female heads had married younger, had less education, and had experienced much higher fertility even after controlling for education and age at marriage. Farley, 1971, chap. 6.

RECENT TRENDS IN FEMALE HEADEDNESS IN THE BLACK COMMUNITY

The decade of the sixties brought a rapid increase in female-headed families with children among all income and racial groups but the increase has been considerably greater for black women than for their white counterparts.[30] What can account for this more rapid growth within the black community?

In chapter 2, we analyzed the demographic factors in recent family changes and identified increased illegitimacy as one source of the growth observed among nonwhites. Although the illegitimacy rate has declined for nonwhites generally since the mid-60s, it has continued its upward trend among teenagers who are the most likely to bear a *first* illegitimate child. About three-fourths of all illegitimate first births occur to women under 19, and in this age group, illegitimacy rates have increased more rapidly for nonwhites than for whites.[31] Add to this the fact that the number of black teenagers (15 to 19) has increased much more dramatically than the number of white teenagers over the past decade,[32] and we find that the *absolute* increase in illegitimate births among teenagers has been greater among blacks although the *percentage* increase has been greater for whites starting from their much lower base.

One possible explanation for the increased illegitimacy we have witnessed is improvements in health (reduced sterility and miscarriage, together with greater fecundity among young girls).[33] In Malthusian terms, it appears that "positive" (health-related) checks on fertility have declined faster than "preventive" (contraceptive) checks have become available and effective, at least among the relatively young and disadvantaged segments of the population. For this group, which is disproportionately black, improved standards of living, and the health

---

30. The 1960-1970 increase calculated from Census data on female-headed families (excluding spouse absent for reasons other than separation) was 59 percent for whites and 88 percent for nonwhites (Appendix 4). Using CPS data for 1960-1972 (Appendix 1, table 1-F), we calculate increases of 45 and 79 percent respectively. The latter data include related as well as own children and women whose husbands were absent for reasons other than separation.

31. See chap. 2, table 5. Also, National Center for Health Statistics, "Trends in Illegitimacy," Series 21, no. 15, table 7, and "Teenagers: Marriages, Divorces, Parenthood, and Mortality," Series 21, no. 23, table 3.

32. The increases were 40 percent for white and 67 percent for nonwhite respectively. 1970 Census, PC(1)-B1, "U.S. Summary," table 52.

33. Cutright estimates that health-related factors explain 88 percent of the increase in nonwhite illegitimacy rates but only 19 percent of the white increase between 1940 and 1968. The corresponding estimates for teenagers are 102 percent and 26 percent respectively. Cutright, 1973a, p. 111.

benefits they bring, have given rise to a high level of unwanted[34]
births at a young age, and thus a greater risk of female headship. Since fertility rates—both legitimate and illegitimate—
have declined among mature women, it may only be a matter of
time before these trends affect the teenage population as well.[35]
Given that one-quarter of white and one-half of black young
women are sexually active and that these proportions appear to
be on the rise,[36] the most immediate solution to excessive fertility appears to be greater access to contraception and abortion.
Moreover, there is evidence that these young women, especially
the black group, are quite naive or misinformed about basic
biological facts relating to conception.[37] Sex education at the
junior high school level might help to lower the risk of unwanted pregnancy by improving the effectiveness of contraceptive effort.

Although higher illegitimacy has contributed significantly
to recent trends, it has combined with high and continually increasing levels of marital dissolution to produce more female-
headed families with children. There are no good data from vital
statistics records on recent trends in divorce and separation
rates broken out by race, but Census counts of the proportion
of ever-married women in these statuses suggest a somewhat
greater increase in marital instability among nonwhites over the
past decade (table 22). Alternatively, it could be that other
factors such as lower remarriage rates among blacks or greater
misreporting of marital status (perhaps to take advantage of
more generous welfare benefits) are responsible for the higher
proportions separated or divorced in 1970 relative to 1960.[38]

Finally, there is the possibility that all of the above estimates hide divergent trends in marital instability by income or
social class. Moynihan has suggested that it is precisely this di-

---

34. Based on a review of the evidence, Cutright (1973a, p. 91) reports that
90 percent of illegitimate children are not wanted by their mothers. Zelnik and
Kantner (1974, table 4) found the following percent distribution of pregnancy
intentions among unmarried pregnant girls, aged 15–19, in 1971:

	Total	Black	White
All	100%	100%	100%
Intended	20	24	16
Not Intended	73	73	73
No Response	7	3	12

Finally, Ryder and Westoff (1972, p. 480) have found that nonwhite women have
many more unwanted births than white women although there is little difference between the two groups with respect to desired births.

35. See Appendix 1, table 1-M, for trends in fertility by race.

36. Udry, 1971.

37. Zelnik and Kantner, 1972.

38. See the equation on pp. 15 and 16 for an identification of these factors.

vergence, or what he calls the "up-down" model of black community development, which should be the focus of our attention.[39] He finds support for this view in Andrew Brimmer's documentation of the "deepening schism between the able and the less able, between the well-prepared and those with few skills" within the black community.[40] Presumably, the "ups" are the well-educated young men and women who have nearly achieved income parity with whites and have established stable middle-class families as a result. The "downs" are the "street-corner" men who have fathered but have not been able to support—except perhaps temporarily or sporadically—increasing numbers of children who then end up in female-headed families.

Table 22

TRENDS IN MARITAL DISSOLUTION BY RACE AND PRESENCE OF CHILDREN, 1960-1970

	Percentage of All Ever-Married Women		Percentage Point Change 1960-1970	Percent Increase in Number of Women, 1960-70
	1960	1970		
Divorced				
White	3.4	4.8	+1.4	59
Nonwhite	4.6	7.1	+2.5	66
Separated				
White	1.6	1.9	+0.3	34
Nonwhite	10.7	12.5	+1.8	26
Widowed				
White	14.6	15.7	+1.1	23
Nonwhite	17.8	18.6	+0.8	13
Divorced with Children				
White	1.2	1.8	+0.6	72
Nonwhite	1.6	3.1	+1.5	108
Separated with Children				
White	0.7	0.9	+0.2	50
Nonwhite	5.0	7.0	+2.0	51
Widowed with Children				
White	1.1	1.1	0.0	14
Nonwhite	2.5	2.9	+0.4	26

Source: Appendix 4.

---

39. Moynihan, 1972, p. 13.
40. Brimmer, 1970.

This hypothesis is difficult to test but there are bits and pieces of evidence that tend to support it. We have suggested that marital stability is directly related to the husband's relative socioeconomic standing, and to the size of the earnings difference between men and women. For one group of black Americans these economic factors seem to have increased stability while for another group the reverse is true. We find that among well-educated young men, the nonwhite to white income ratio increased quite dramatically during the sixties, while the earnings differential between men and women widened somewhat. Conversely, at lower levels of education, the gains in economic status which black men have made relative to their white counterparts are almost imperceptible, but the earnings differential between black men and black women has narrowed appreciably as the latter have moved out of menial service jobs into semi-skilled blue collar and white collar work.[41] To the extent that welfare also provides an increasingly generous and stable source of income for these women, they have still less to gain from marriage.[42]

Richard Freeman has noted that the above trends have been accompanied by another important development—a decline in the labor force participation of prime-age black men. He does not investigate the underlying causes for this change but speculates that it may well be related to changes in family structure since married men typically have higher participation rates than those who don't head families.[43] At present, we have no way of knowing whether this development is a cause or consequence of increased female headship—or if, indeed, the two are related. Nevertheless, it should be remembered that although the unemployment rates of black men declined during the latter part of the sixties, there were also increasing numbers of young men who dropped out of the job market entirely, and there is still a great deal of hidden unemployment and underemployment in the ghetto which is not picked up in official counts of the unemployed.

Finally, we noted earlier that marital instability and female headship appear to be correlated with growing up and living in a city. Since 1950, an increasing proportion of blacks have moved into the central cities of our larger metropolitan areas

41. Freeman, 1973.
42. See chap. 5 for further discussion of this question.
43. Freeman, 1973, p. 128.

while whites have been rapidly moving to the suburbs.[44] This means that more and more black children are being raised in an environment which, for reasons we do not fully understand, is conducive to less stability in family life. Whether this represents a contagion effect, a different set of economic opportunities and expectations, or the general anomie of urban life is hard to say.

To summarize, the trend toward greater female headship within the black community may be related to (1) improvements in health and a change in sexual attitudes, both of which have probably had a disproportionate impact on the fertility of young black women, especially teenagers; (2) the inability of young black men with little education to improve their economic position, combined with a significant increase in the alternative sources of income available to black women; and (3) the increased urbanization of the black population.

CONCLUSIONS

What, in conclusion, have we learned about race and family structure? We have seen that higher separation rates, lower remarriage rates, and more out-of-wedlock births all contribute to racial differences in female headship. And we strongly suspect that misreporting of marital status also contributes to these differences. But, of all of these factors, it is the difference in separation rates which contributes most to the greater prevalence of female-headed families within the black population. But why are black separation rates about half again as high as those of whites?

To date, other researchers have not been able to demonstrate convincingly that *all* of the differences in marital instability are related to differences in current socioeconomic status. However, in our analysis of separation we found no differences by race in recent rates of family dissolution, after we controlled for economic variables, especially the less stable job market faced by black men. This is not surprising since much of the previous literature has emphasized the employment prospects of males as a critical determinant of family stability, but it is the first time that this variable has been unambiguously identified as a major factor affecting separation rates in a carefully controlled analysis of the marital behavior of individual families.

The high rate of illegitimate fertility among black women,

---

44. The proportion of all Negroes who lived in central cities moved up from 43 percent in 1950 to 58 percent in 1974 while the white proportion went from 34 percent in 1950 to 23 percent in 1974 (Netzer, 1970, p. 14, and *CPR*, P-23, no. 54).

especially among teenagers, also contributes to racial differences in female headedness, although we have shown that it is not nearly as important as marital instability in explaining these differences. Higher illegitimacy among blacks is due to a higher incidence of premarital intercourse, less utilization of effective contraceptives and abortion, less chance that the pregnancy will be legitimated through marriage, and a lower probability that the child born out of wedlock will be adopted. More analysis of each of these factors would be useful.

Much more research also needs to be devoted to racial differences in remarriage rates and in the reporting of marital status. Are these differences related to the greater dependence of black women on the welfare system (given their larger families and less adequate earnings)—a dependence which creates an incentive for them not to remarry or report their marital status accurately? Do low remarriage rates simply reflect the low incomes and other disadvantages faced by these women which, together with their dependent children, make them less desirable as marriage partners? Or, even in the absence of such disadvantages, does a shortage of black males (or an inappropriate distribution of these men by age, social class, or location) constrain the marriage and remarriage opportunities of black women?

Turning to the reasons behind the continued rapid growth in female-headed families in the black community, our conclusions must be even more tentative; but the limited analysis we have done on this question leads us to speculate that the recent higher rate of growth among blacks is related to the continuing urbanization of the black population; to increased sexual activity and improved health, combined with a low level of effective contraception, among teenagers; to the bleak employment prospects for black men with little education; and to the greater availability of income outside of marriage for the poorest group of black women.

BIBLIOGRAPHY

Bernard, Jessie. *Marriage and Family Among Negroes.* Englewood Cliffs, N.J.: Prentice-Hall, 1966a.

————. "Marital Stability and Patterns of Status Variables." *Journal of Marriage and the Family* (Nov. 1966b) p. 437.

Billingsley, Andrew. *Black Families in White America.* Englewood Cliffs, N.J.: Prentice-Hall, 1969.

————. "Black Family Structure: Myths and Realities." In Paper no. 12 of the Sub-Committttee on Fiscal Policy, Joint Economic Committee of the Congress (Nov. 4, 1973).

Blood, Robert O., Jr., and Wolfe, Donald M. "Negro-White Differences in Blue-Collar Marriages in a Northern Metropolis." *Social Forces,* vol. 48 (Sept. 1969) pp. 59-64.

Brimmer, Andrew F. "Economic Progress of Negroes in the U.S.: The Deepening Schism," Remarks at Founders' Day Convocation, Tuskegee Institute, Tuskegee, Alabama, March 22, 1970.

Broom, Leonard, and Glenn, Norval D. "Negro-White Differences in Reported Attitudes and Behavior," *Sociology and Social Research,* 50:199 (Jan. 1966).

Bumpass, Larry L., and Sweet, James A. "Differentials in Marital Instability: 1970." *American Sociological Review,* vol. 37 (Dec. 1972) pp. 754-66.

Carliner, Geoffrey. "Determinants of Household Headship." Institute for Research on Poverty, University of Wisconsin, 1972.

Carper, Laura. "The Negro Family and the Moynihan Report." *Dissent* (March-April 1966) pp. 266-67. Reprinted in Rainwater and Yancey.

Clark, Kenneth. *Dark Ghetto.* New York: Harper and Row, 1965.

Coale, Ansley J., and Rives, Norfleet W., Jr. "A Statistical Reconstruction of the Black Population of the United States 1880-1970: Estimates of True Numbers by Age and Sex, Birth Rates, and Total Fertility." *Population Index,* vol. 39, no. 1 (Jan. 1973).

Cutright, Phillips. "Illegitimacy in the United States: 1920-1968." In *Demographic and Social Aspects of Population Growth,* vol. 1 of The Commission on Population Growth and The American Future Research Reports, ed. Charles F. Westoff and Robert Parke, Jr. Washington, D.C.: Government Printing Office, 1972.

_____. "Income and Family Events: Marital Stability." *Journal of Marriage and the Family* (May 1971a).

_____. "Income and Family Events: Family Income, Family Size, and Consumption." *Journal of Marriage and the Family,* vol. 33, no. 1 (Feb. 1971b) pp. 161-73.

_____. "Illegitimacy and Income Supplements." Paper no. 12 of the Sub-Committee on Fiscal Policy, Joint Economic Committee of the Congress (Nov. 4, 1973a).

_____. "Timing the First Birth: Does it Matter?" *Journal of Marriage and the Family,* vol. 34, no. 4 (Nov. 1973b).

Cutright, Phillips, and Scanzoni, John. "Income Supplements and the American Family," Paper no. 12 of the Sub-Committee on Fiscal Policy, Joint Economic Committee of the Congress (Nov. 4, 1973).

Duncan, Otis Dudley; Featherman, David L.; and Duncan, Beverly. *Socioeconomic Background and Achievement.* New York: Seminar Press, 1972.

Etzkowitz, Henry, and Schaflander, Gerald M. *Ghetto Crisis: Riots or Reconciliation?* Boston: Little, Brown, 1969.

The Family, Poverty, and Welfare Programs: Factors Influencing Family Instability. Paper no. 12 (Part I), a Volume of Studies in Public Welfare, prepared for the use of the Subcommittee on Fiscal Policy of the Joint Economic Committee of the Congress (Nov. 4, 1973).

Farley, Reynolds. *Growth of the Black Population: A Study of Demographic Trends.* Chicago: Markham, 1970.

_____. "Black Families in the U.S.: Demographic Trends and Consequences." Coop Research Project #10-P-56022/5-03. Ann Arbor: University of Michigan, 1971.

_____. "Family Types and Family Headship: A Comparison of Trends

Among Blacks and Whites." *The Journal of Human Resources,* vol. 6, no. 3 (1972) pp. 275-90.

Fogel, Robert W., and Engerman, Stanley L. *Time on the Cross,* vols. 1 and 2. Boston: Little, Brown, 1974.

Frazier, E. Franklin. *The Negro Family in the United States.* Chicago: University of Chicago Press, Reprinted 1966.

Freeman, Richard B. "Changes in the Labor Market for Black Americans, 1948-72." In *Brookings Papers on Economic Activity,* vol. 1 (1973).

Furstenberg, Frank. "Work Experience and Family Life." In James O'Toole, ed. *Work and the Quality of Life.* Cambridge: M.I.T. Press, 1974.

Gans, Herbert J. "The Negro Family: Reflections on the Moynihan Report." *Commonweal* (Oct. 15, 1965). Reprinted in Rainwater and Yancey.

Gebhard, Paul, et al. *Pregnancy, Birth and Abortion.* New York: Harper, 1958.

Glick, Paul C. "Marriage and Marital Stability Among Blacks." In *Demographic Aspects of the Black Community,* ed. Clyde V. Kiser, *The Milbank Memorial Fund Quarterly,* vol. 48, Part 2 (April 1970).

Glick, Paul C., and Mills, Karen M. "Black Families: Marriage Patterns and Living Arrangements." Papers prepared for the W. E. B. DuBois Conference on American Blacks, Atlanta, Ga., Oct. 1974.

Glick, Paul C., and Norton, Arthur J. "Frequency, Duration, and Probability of Marriage and Divorce." *Journal of Marriage and The Family* (May 1971).

Hannerz, Ulf. *Soulside: Inquiries into Ghetto Culture and Community.* New York: Columbia University Press, 1969.

Hays, William, and Mendel, Charles H. "Extended Kinship Relations in Black and White Families." *The Journal of Marriage and the Family* (Feb. 1973) pp. 51-57.

Herzog, Elizabeth. "Is there a 'Breakdown' of the Negro Family?" *Social Work* (Jan. 1966). Reprinted in Rainwater and Yancey.

Hill, Robert. *The Strength of Black Families.* N.Y.: Emerson and Hall, 1972.

Hyman, Herbert, and Reed, John S. "Black Matriarchy Reconsidered: Evidence from Secondary Analysis of Sample Surveys." *Public Opinion Quarterly* (Fall 1969) pp. 346-54.

Jackson, Jacquelyne J. "Where Are the Black Men?" *Ebony* (March 1972) pp. 99-106.

Kardiner, Abram, and Ovesey, Lionel. *The Mark of Oppression.* New York: Meridian Books, 1962.

Kiser, Clyde. "Demographic Aspects of the Black Community." *Milbank Memorial Fund Quarterly* (April 1970).

Krause, Harry D. "Child Welfare, Parental Responsibility and the State." In Paper no. 12 of the Sub-Committee on Fiscal Policy, Joint Economic Committee of the Congress, Nov. 4, 1973.

Ladner, Joyce Ann. *Tomorrow's Tomorrow: The Black Woman.* Garden City: New York: Doubleday, 1971.

Lefcowitz, M. Jack. "Differences Between Negro and White Women in Marital Stability and Family Structure." Discussion paper, no. 13-68. Madison, Wisconsin: Institute for Research on Poverty, 1968.

Lewis, Hylan. *Blackways of Kent.* Chapel Hill: University of North Carolina Press, 1955.

————. "Agenda Paper no. V: The Family: Resources for Change—Planning Session for the White House Conference 'To Fulfill These Rights,' Nov. 16-18, 1965." Reprinted in Rainwater and Yancey.

Liebow, Elliot. *Talley's Corner*. Boston: Little, Brown, 1967.

Lincoln, C. Eric. "A Look Beyond the Matriarchy." *Ebony* (Aug. 1966) pp. 111-16.

Mack, Delores E. "Where the Black-Matriarchy Theorists Went Wrong." *Psychology Today*, vol. 4 (Jan. 1971) pp. 86-88.

Moynihan, Daniel P. "A Family Policy for the Nation." *America*, vol. 113 (Sept. 1965) pp. 280-83.

_____. "Employment, Income and the Ordeal of the Negro Family." *Daedalus* (Nov. 4, 1965) p. 94.

_____. "The Negro Family: The Case for National Action." Washington, D.C.: Office of Policy Planning and Research, U.S. Department of Labor, 1965.

_____. "The Schism in Black America." *The Public Interest*, no. 27 (Spring 1972) pp. 3-24.

National Center for Health Statistics. "Trends in Illegitimacy, United States, 1940-1965," Series 21, no. 15 (Feb. 1968).

_____. "Teenagers, Marriages, Divorces, Parenthood, and Mortality," Series 21, no. 23 (Aug. 1973).

"The Negro American." *Daedalus*, vols. 1 and 2 (Fall 1965) and Winter 1966).

Netzer, Dick. *Economics and Urban Problems, Diagnoses and Prescriptions*. New York: Basic Books, 1970.

O'Toole, James J. Testimony before the Senate Committee on Labor and Public Welfare, Subcommittee on Children and Youth, Sept. 24, 1973.

Parker, Seymour, and Kleiner, Robert J. "Characteristics of Negro Mothers in Single-Headed Households." *Journal of Marriage and the Family*, vol. 28 (Nov. 1966) pp. 507-13.

Pope, Hallowell. "Unwed Mothers and Their Sex Partners." *Journal of Marriage and the Family*, vol. 29 (Aug. 1967) pp. 187-93.

Rainwater, Lee. "Crucible of Identity: The Negro Lower Class Family." *Daedalus* (Winter 1966) pp. 172-216.

Rainwater, Lee, and Yancey, William L. *The Moynihan Report and the Politics of Controversy*. Cambridge: MIT Press, 1967.

_____. *Behind Ghetto Walls*. Chicago: Aldine, 1970.

Reiss, Ira. *The Social Context of Premarital Sexual Permissiveness*. New York: Holt, Rinehart and Winston, 1967.

Report of the National Advisory Commission on Civil Disorders. U.S. Riot Commission. New York: E. P. Dutton, 1968.

Rodman, Hyman. *Lower-Class Families*. New York: Oxford University Press, 1971.

Rovere, Richard. "Letter from Washington." *New Yorker* (Sept. 11, 1965).

Ryan, William. "Savage Discovery—The Moynihan Report." *The Nation* (Nov. 22, 1965). Reprinted in Rainwater and Yancey.

Scanzoni, John H. *The Black Family in Modern Society*. Boston: Allyn and Bacon, 1971.

Schulz, David. *Coming Up Black: Patterns of Ghetto Socialization*. New Jersey: Prentice-Hall, 1969.

Sklar, June, and Berkov, Beth. "The Effects of Legal Abortion on Legitimate and Illegitimate Birth Rates: The California Experience." *Studies in Family Planning*, vol. 4, no. 11 (Nov. 1973).

Stack, Carol B., and Semmel, Herbert. "The Concept of Family in the Poor Black Community." In Paper no. 12 of the Sub-Committee on Fiscal Policy, Joint Economic Committee of the Congress (Nov. 4, 1973).

Staples, Robert. "Towards a Sociology of the Black Family: A Theoretical and Methodological Assessment." *Journal of Marriage and the Family*, vol. 33, no. 1 (Feb. 1971) pp. 119-38.

————. ed. *The Black Family: Essays and Studies.* Belmont, California: Wadsworth, 1971.

————. "The Influence of Race on Reaction to a Hypothetical Pre-Marital Pregnancy." *Journal of Social and Behavioral Science* (Spring 1972) pp. 32-35.

————. "Sex Life of Middle Class Negroes." *Sexology* (1966) pp. 86-88.

————. "Public Policy and the Changing Status of Black Families." *The Family Coordinator,* vol. 22 (July 1973) pp. 345-51.

Sweet, James A. "The Living Arrangements of Separated, Widowed, and Divorced Mothers." Working Paper 71-4, Center for Demography and Ecology, The University of Wisconsin (May 1971).

Tietze, Christopher. "Two Years' Experience With a Liberal Abortion Law: Its Impact on Fertility Trends in New York City." *Family Planning Perspectives,* vol. 5, no. 1 (Winter 1973) pp. 36-41.

Udry, J. Richard. "Marital Instability by Race and Income Based on 1960 Census Data." *American Journal of Sociology* (Sept. 1966) pp. 203-9 and (May 1967) pp. 673-74.

————. "Estimating the Need for Contraceptive Services in the Younger Age Groups." FPEP Report #1-71, an informal news items from the Family Planning Evaluation Project, Department of Maternal and Child Health, School of Public Health, University of North Carolina, Chapel Hill, N.C., April 1, 1971.

U.S. Commission on Population Growth and the American Future. *Demographic and Social Aspects of Population Growth.* Ed. Charles F. Westoff and Robert Parke, Jr., Vol. 1 of Commission research reports. Washington, D.C.: Government Printing Office, 1972.

Valentine, Charles. *Culture and Poverty.* Chicago: University of Chicago Press, 1968.

Willacy, H. M. "Men in Poverty Neighborhoods: A Status Report." *Monthly Labor Review,* vol. 92, no. 2 (Feb. 1969) pp. 23-27.

Willacy, H. M., and Hilaski, H. J. "Working Women in Urban Poverty Neighborhoods." *Monthly Labor Review,* vol. 93, no. 6 (June 1970) pp. 35-38.

Willie, Charles V., and Weinandy, Janet. "The Structure and Composition of 'Problem' and 'Stable' Families in a Low-Income Population." *Marriage and Family Living* (Nov. 1963).

————. Ed. *The Family Life of Black People.* Columbus, Ohio: Charles E. Merrill, 1970.

Yancey, W. L. "Going Down Home: Family Structure and the Urban Trap." *Social Science Quarterly,* vol. 52, no. 4 (March 1972) pp. 893-906.

Zelnik, Melvin, and Kantner, John F. "Sexual Experience of Young Unmarried Women in the United States." *Family Planning Perspectives,* vol. 4, no. 4 (Oct. 1972).

————. "Contraception and Pregnancy: Experience of Young Unmarried Women in the United States." *Family Planning Perspectives,* vol. 5, no. 1 (Winter 1973).

————. "The Resolution of Teenage First Pregnancies." *Family Planning Perspectives,* 6:2 (Spring 1974).

United States Bureau of the Census. "The Social and Economic Status of the Black Population in the United States 1974." *Current Population Report* (CPR), Series P-23, no. 54.

Chapter 5

WELFARE AND
FEMALE-HEADED FAMILIES

Although the number of female-headed families with children has been growing in all income groups in the population, 45 percent of these families are still poor and the great majority of them are on welfare. Thus the long-standing concern that welfare might be in part responsible for female-headed family growth is still with us. In fact, with unprecedented increases in both female-headed families with children and welfare caseloads in the late 1960s and early 1970s, it has taken on a new significance.

The traditional argument has been that welfare breaks up families by denying assistance to them as long as there is an able-bodied male parent in the home. Thus, men who are able to earn only meager, unstable incomes leave or are pushed out of their families so that wives and children may qualify for welfare aid.

In this chapter, we want to find out whether welfare programs have in fact contributed to female-headed family growth, and—if they have—whether that contribution has come through breaking up existing intact families or through some other mechanism. In chapter 3, we hypothesized that welfare payments might contribute to family instability by encouraging separation and divorce, but found no empirical evidence for it in the microdata analyzed there. In this chapter, we will look more closely at the institution of welfare, the findings of other researchers, and the potential impact that welfare has on family structure when one considers a range of behavioral channels broader than just separation and divorce. We will begin our discussion with a look at the historical development of the welfare system and at its current rules which limit eligibility to certain family types.

THE ORIGINS OF WELFARE

Public Assistance, the major federal-state program of cash assistance to needy families and individuals, originated in the Social Security Act of 1935. The goal of the Public Assistance titles of the act was to alleviate economic insecurity by providing publicly supported sources of income to economically deprived groups. However, given the overwhelming magnitude of need in the depression-recovery era during which it was enacted, and the limited public resources available at that time, the act began by singling out particular groups of people to be aided first. The three initial groups were the aged, the blind, and children in fatherless homes, the third group being helped through Aid to Dependent Children (ADC), later renamed Aid to Families with Dependent Children (AFDC).[1]

The ADC program was essentially an early version of revenue sharing. It provided federal support for pre-existing programs, generally called Mothers' Aid, which many states had adopted prior to the 1930s. ADC did not require much change in those programs and, by adopting their approach on a national scale, carried a major inequity over into federal policy. Children in families headed by able-bodied fathers who had little or no income were not eligible for assistance even though they might be just as needy as fatherless children. This inequity was translated further into a non-neutrality. Needy children would be better off without fathers, which might encourage impoverished families to become female-headed in order to qualify for aid. Framers of the act appear to have concerned themselves only minimally with these effects, however, because they viewed their

1. A fourth group, the disabled, was added in 1956. On January 1, 1974, the adult categories—the aged, blind, and disabled—were consolidated into a new, totally federal Supplemental Security Income program operated by the Social Security Administration.

work as only a first step in a broad strategy of income security.[2]

This is an important point to make, since it has generally been ignored or misrepresented in discussions of welfare. According to conventional wisdom, ADC was intended for widows, and in time it was expected to wither away, along with the Public Assistance program as a whole. This reasoning has been used to explain why virtually no constructive attention was given to the program after its inception.

The withering away argument assumed that the expansion of the contributory programs of the act—originally the Old Age and Survivors Insurance provisions[3] would eventually cover the elderly, the incapacitated, and children without a parent or parents through the contributions of breadwinners in their earning years. Thus, as the contributory programs expanded and matured, the benefits paid to needy persons under the noncontributory Public Assistance titles would gradually end.

Several things went wrong with this scenario. Expansion of OASI coverage to earners not included in the original act proceeded slowly, and even today 10 percent of paid employment is still not covered.[4] Widowhood, which accounted for the great majority of female-headed families in the 1930s, dwindled thereafter as a source of such families and was overtaken by illegitimacy, separation, and divorce. Women in the latter statuses have virtually no claim on Social Security benefits earned by their former husbands or their children's fathers. Finally, the unstated assumption of the Social Security Act, that persons who are employable can work and earn enough to achieve income sufficiency on their own, has been consistently violated

---

2. In explaining its proposed legislation to President Roosevelt, the Committee on Economic Security said:

"The one almost all-embracing measure of security is an assured income. A program of economic security, as we vision it, must have as its primary aim the assurance of an adequate income to each human being in childhood, youth, middle age, or old age—in sickness or in health. It must provide safeguards against all of the hazards leading to destitution and dependency.

"A piecemeal approach is dictated by practical considerations, but the broad objectives should never be forgotten. Whatever measures are deemed immediately expedient should be so designed that they can be embodied in the complete program which we must have ere long.

"To delay until it is opportune to set up a complete program will probably mean holding up action until it is too late to act. A substantial beginning should be made now in the development of the safeguards which are so manifestly needed for individual security." [*Report of the Committee on Economic Security*, Washington, D.C., Government Printing Office, 1935.]

3. Now OASDHI—Old Age, Survivors, Disability and Health Insurance.

4. *Statistical Abstract of the U.S.*, 1973, table 466.

down to the present time. Many full-time employed persons—
let alone many workers who face periods of unemployment—
have not been able to maintain their families above the poverty
line on the basis of their earnings and their unemployment benefits alone. Avoiding poverty over the last four decades would
have required income supplements for many types of households, not just those without a male breadwinner.

AFDC has borne the brunt of the failure of social policy to
respond to the continuing needs of households for income security. It is not a depression stop-gap run wild, but rather the
opening scene of a social vision let die. The irony is what the
failure to follow through has done to the image, and perhaps the
reality, of AFDC. A program which was originally intended to
strengthen family life is now charged with being a major sub-
verter of the institution of the family among the poor. Is this a
valid charge?

The economics of family life have traditionally been distributional—men transferring resources to women and children
dependents. When men cannot provide and the government can,
the stage is set for a shift from private to public dependency.
To begin our search for evidence of such a shift, we turn now
to a discussion of exactly how welfare discriminates between
family types.

WELFARE ELIGIBILITY ACCORDING TO FAMILY TYPE

Family composition is a critical element in establishing welfare
eligibility for those who are not aged, blind, or disabled. Title
IV Section 406(a) of the Social Security Act defines children
who are to receive AFDC assistance:

> The term child means a needy child who has been deprived
> of parental support or care by reason of the death, con-
> tinued absence from the home, or physical or mental in-
> capacity of a parent, and who is living with his father,
> mother, grandfather, grandmother, brother, sister, step-
> father, stepmother, stepbrother, stepsister, uncle, aunt, first
> cousin, nephew, or niece, in a place of residence maintained
> by one or more of such relatives as his or their own home.

This excludes needy children whose parents are not incapacitated and who live together but are unable to provide support.

Section 407, introduced in 1962, permits the states to grant assistance based on one type of inability to support—the unemployment of the father—but the number of states adopting this provision and the number of families receiving benefits under it has remained small.[5]

The rules barring benefits to intact families are quite explicit, and they have been further elaborated by two recent court rulings. In King v. Smith, 392 U.S. 309 (1968), the Supreme Court found that the man-in-the-house rule employed by 19 states and the District of Columbia was inconsistent with the Social Security Act. As a result of the ruling, states may not deny aid to children of mothers who cohabit with men in or outside their home, since their doing so does not in itself change the status of the children as to their being deprived of parental support. In Lewis v. Martin, 397 U.S. 552 (1970) the Court went further and stated that the resources of men who assume the role of spouse (including nonadopting stepfathers) cannot be considered as available to children unless there is proof of an actual contribution to those children. If a man is not the natural parent of the children or otherwise legally responsible for them, no presumption that he supports them may be made in determining their eligibility for, or the amount of, benefits. Thus, under the Social Security Act and these related rulings, if children in families are in economic need they will be eligible for assistance in virtually every case except where they are living with both natural parents.

Other changes over time have worked to give these distinctions in family make-up even greater impact. Both economic and noneconomic barriers to receiving benefits have been reduced. For example, the one-year-residence requirement employed by many states was ruled unconstitutional in 1969. Income ceilings on eligibility have been raised. Also, the discretionary exclusion of families by welfare administrators appears to have waned as acceptance rates in welfare rose from 56 percent in 1960 to 74 percent in 1971.[6] Thus, exclusion is largely a matter of family structure now. Once a family with few or no earnings or other resources becomes female-headed, acceptance is quite likely.

---

5. The number of states operating these AFDC-UF (UF referring to "unemployed father") programs has moved up and down irregularly since 1962 and currently stands at 23. AFDC-UF recipients were 4 percent of the full AFDC caseload in Feb. 1974. ("Public Assistance Statistics, Feb. 1974," NCSS Report A-2, Social and Rehabilitation Service.)

6. See table 25.

VARIATIONS IN THE MAGNITUDE OF
BENEFITS AND INCENTIVES

If welfare eligibility is becoming increasingly a matter of family composition, the dollar values associated with remaining in a husband-wife family and forfeiting welfare or with splitting up and receiving it seem to be shifting also. Welfare benefits have generally been rising relative to market earnings. Between 1960 and 1970, the average payment per recipient in the AFDC program increased 75 percent while the average earnings of private nonfarm production workers rose 48 percent.[7] The more rapid increase in welfare benefits has outdistanced the earnings ability of a considerable proportion of the population.

Five percent of the work force is currently employed at or below the federal minimum wage of $2.10 an hour.[8] Even if these people were able to work full-time, full-year at the minimum wage, their earnings of $4,368 a year would still be at or below the maximum welfare grant for a family of four in 10 states. On top of the increasing relative attractiveness of cash grants has come an increase in associated in-kind benefits, notably subsidies for food, health care, and housing. In a recent compilation for the Joint Economic Committee,[9] James Storey shows how benefit packages available in 100 U.S. counties favor female-headed families over husband-wife families by allowing them higher net incomes at many different levels of work effort. Table 23 compares net income and benefits for female-headed and husband-wife families with two children, as reported in ten cities located among the 100 counties surveyed. The dollar figures represent annual earnings, excluding federal, state, and local income taxes and Social Security tax, plus annual net benefits from AFDC, General Assistance,[10] food stamps, commodity

---

7. U.S. Dept. of Labor, Bureau of Labor Statistics, "Employment and Earnings," vol. 20, no. 12, June 1974, and Dept. of Health, Education and Welfare, "Social Security Bulletin," vol. 37, no. 9, Sept. 1974. This relationship has turned around recently. Between 1970 and 1973, the average AFDC payment per recipient grew 15 percent while the average earnings of private, nonfarm production workers grew 21 percent. However, even with this recent shift, welfare benefit increases have still outpaced private, nonfarm earnings increases over the entire 1960-1973 period.

8. See tables 1 and 10 in "Minimum Wage and Maximum Hours Standards under the Fair Labor Standards Act," U.S. Dept. of Labor, Jan. 1975.

9. Storey, July 1974.

10. General assistance is the term most frequently applied to public financial assistance to people in need who cannot qualify for help under one of the federal-state public assistance programs. It includes programs variously referred to as "home relief," "outdoor relief," "emergency relief," or "direct relief." It is financed from state or local funds. (John L. Costa, Public Assistance Report no. 39, 1970 edition, "Characteristics of General Assistance in the U.S.")

Table 23

ANNUAL NET CASH INCOME PLUS FOOD AND PUBLIC HOUSING BENEFITS[a] AVAILABLE TO FAMILIES, BY FAMILY TYPE AND WORK STATUS AS OF JULY 1972

	No Work (Includes Unemployment Benefits)		No Work or Benefits		Work 20 Hrs. @ $1.60 (Includes Unemployment Benefits)		Work 20 Hrs. @ $1.60 (No Unemployment Benefits)		Work 40 Hrs. @ $1.60	
	FHF[b]	HWF[c]	FHF	HWF	FHF	HWF	FHF	HWF	FHF	HWF
New York City	$4,665*	$5,121	$4,665*	$5,121	$5,834*	$5,700	$5,834	$5,930	$7,184*	$5,504**
St. Louis	3,869*	2,669	3,477*	1,389	4,382*	4,052	4,174*	3,826	5,134*	4,559
Cleveland	3,885	4,203	3,831	4,194	4,715*	4,654	4,715	4,737	5,536*	4,590**
Chicago	4,542	4,946	4,461	5,081	5,499	5,543	5,499	5,543	6,501*	5,323**
Philadelphia	4,490	4,958	4,497	4,965	5,371	5,590	5,375	5,595	6,250*	5,445**
Detroit	4,413	4,860	4,413	5,074	5,201	5,280	5,201	5,888	5,742*	4,969**
Houston	3,567*	3,255	3,589*	2,737	4,182*	3,696	4,350*	3,294	5,051*	4,307
Los Angeles	4,643	5,405	4,641	5,133	5,758	5,878	5,654	5,858	6,679*	4,978**
Miami	4,186*	4,144	4,032*	3,816	5,161*	4,663	5,093*	4,481	6,034*	5,242
Birmingham	3,184*	3,100	3,006*	2,610	4,089*	3,645	4,087*	3,499	4,916*	4,340

a. See footnote 11.
b. Mother and 2 children.
c. Husband, wife, and 2 children.

* Total income plus benefits is higher for a mother and 2 children than for a husband, wife, and 2 children, despite the presence of an additional adult in the latter family.

** Total income is less for this level of work effort than if the head had worked fewer hours.

Source: *Studies in Public Welfare*, Paper no. 15, "Welfare in the 70's: A National Study of Benefits Available in 100 Local Areas," prepared by James R. Storey, Senior Economist, for the use of the Subcommittee on Fiscal Policy of the Joint Economic Committee of the Congress, July 22, 1974.

distribution programs, school lunches, and public housing.[11]

Entries in table 23 with a single asterisk show net income and benefit levels which are higher for a woman and two children than for a husband, wife, and two children with the same amount of earnings. In the table, there are single asterisks by nearly three out of every five entries for female-headed families. For St. Louis, Houston, Miami, and Birmingham, there is no amount of work effort, up to and including full-time work by one spouse at the minimum wage, which will net the husband-wife family income and benefits equal to what the female-headed family can get with an equivalent amount of work. Furthermore, in every city, without exception, the female-headed family nets more income and benefits than the larger husband-wife family if both have a member who works full time at the minimum wage. The deterioration in the husband-wife family's relative position at higher earnings levels reflects the faster rate of benefit reduction for them as their earnings increase. This is the high cumulative tax rate problem. For example, in New York City female-headed families increase their net income and benefit position by $2,519 as a result of increasing their earnings from zero to $3,200 per year (column 9 minus column 1 in table 23). This is an effective average tax rate on earnings of 21 percent. On the other hand, husband-wife families in New York City increase their net income and benefits by only $383 as a result of increasing their earnings from zero to $3,200 (column 10 minus column 2), an effective average tax rate of 88 percent.

Furthermore, this higher average tax rate for husband-wife families subsumes net income and benefits will actually drop with increased earnings for male heads who move from part-time to fulltime work. This is the so-called notch problem. It is flagged in the table with double asterisks and afflicts husband-wife families in six of the ten cities shown. Interestingly enough, these are the six cities which did not afford higher income and benefit status to female-headed families at zero earnings. Thus some cities favor female-headed families to start, and those which do not initially favor them end up doing so, as earnings rise to the full-year minimum wage level, by imposing actual

---

11. Food benefits equal food stamp bonus values plus the estimated retail values of surplus commodities distributed as free food and school lunches. Public housing refers to housing projects operated by local housing authorities and partially subsidized by federal contributions. The benefit in this table is the difference between the rent tenants pay and the estimated market rent of the unit.

losses in net income and benefits on husband-wife families as the latter increase *their* work effort.

Overall, the picture is one of more favorable income and benefit status for female-headed families in many jurisdictions, and of increasing favor for those families as (1) welfare benefits grow faster than earnings, and (2) female-headed families continue to experience broader categorical eligibility for cash and in-kind benefit programs, and lower tax rates in those programs, than husband-wife families.

THE BEHAVIORAL RESPONSE TO DIFFERENCES IN BENEFITS

The behavioral response to these financial incentives to live in different family types is a matter of great policy consequence and also of great uncertainty. Do characteristics of the welfare system and of its related in-kind programs—notably eligibility criteria and benefit levels—cause families to become female-headed in order to receive assistance?

As can be seen in table 24, female-headed families with children grew considerably in recent years—56 percent between 1960 and 1971. Welfare caseloads also grew dramatically: the number of female-headed families with children served annually by AFDC doubled between 1960 and 1967 and then doubled again by 1971. We know that the numerical increase of female-headed families with children contributed to the growth of welfare caseloads, but we do not know whether the nature of the welfare system itself helped set the whole process in motion by causing female-headed families to form.

It is clear from table 24 that only part of the dramatic caseload growth of the 1967-71 period can be explained by increasing numbers of female-headed families with children. Other factors have also played a significant role. As a first step in analyzing the effect of welfare on female-headed family growth, we wish to sort out the effects of the three major contributors to welfare caseload growth: increasing female-headed families with children, increasing welfare eligibility of female-headed families with children, and increasing welfare participation of eligible female-headed families with children.

Increasing Female-Headed Families with Children. The growth rate and changing composition of female-headed families with children have already been discussed in chapter 2. The figures for 1960-71 are repeated in col. 9 of table 24.

Table 24

TRENDS IN POVERTY, WELFARE, AND FEMALE FAMILY HEADSHIP, 1960-71
(Family numbers in thousands)

	1. NonFarm Poverty Line (Fam. of 4)	2. NonFarm Near Poor Line (125% x1)	3. Income Levels for Welfare Eligibility [a]		4. No. of Poor FHF With Children <18 [b]	5. No. of Near Poor With Children <18 [b]	6. Col. 4 + Col. 5 [b]	7. No. of Welfare Eligible FHF [c]	8. Annual AFDC Caseload FHF	9. Total FHF With Children <18 [b]	10. AFDC Participation Rates (Col. 8 ÷ Col. 7)
			Entry	Exit							
1960	$3022	$3778			1476	266	1742		692	2621	
1961	3054	3818			1505	288	1793		813	2687	
1962	3089	3861			1613	261	1874		844	2701	
1963	3128	3910			1578	303	1881		935	2833	
1964	3169	3961			1439	327	1766		1020	2895	
1965	3223	4029			1499	318	1817		1070	2872	
1966	3317	4146			1410	346	1756		1139	2993	
1967	3410	4623	$3300	$3300	1418	329	1747	2183	1385	3187	63.4
1968	3553	4441	3510	4008	1469	373	1842	2286	1509	3271	66.0
1969	3743	4679	3720	4716	1497	408	1905	2342	1817	3373	77.6
1970	3968	4960	3930	5424	1680	387	2067	2714	2460	3814	90.6
1971	4137	5171	4140	6132	1830	485	2315	3011	2837	4078	94.2
% Increase	37	37	25	85	24	82	33	38	310	56	

a. Irene Lurie, "Legislative, Administrative, and Judicial Changes in the AFDC Program, 1967-71." Madison, Wis.: Institute for Research on Poverty, Reprint 93, 1973.

b. As of March the following year.

c. Barbara Boland, "Participation in the Aid to Families with Dependent Children Program (AFDC)," Wash., D.C.: The Urban Institute, Working Paper 971-02, August 1, 1973.

Sources: "Characteristics of the Low Income Population," P-60, nos. 54, 76, 81, 86, Current Population Reports, Wash., D.C.: U.S. Bureau of Census.

"Reasons for Opening and Closing of Public Assistance Cases," NCSS Reports A-5 & A-9, Wash., D.C. U.S. Dept. of Health, Education and Welfare, Social and Rehabilitation Service, National Center for Social Statistics.

Increasing Welfare Eligibility of Female-Headed Families with Children. The income levels at which female-headed families can qualify for welfare ("entry level"), and those up to which they can earn and still remain eligible for welfare ("exit level") have increased significantly in recent years, as documented by Irene Lurie.[12] From 1967 to 1971, the entry level rose by 25 percent nationwide. Over the same period, the exit level grew by 85 percent. Exit and entry levels are shown in col. 3 of table 24. They were identical in 1967, but diverged thereafter under terms of the welfare amendments of 1967 which incorporated a deduction for work-related expenses and disregarded the first thirty dollars of earned income per month and one-third of remaining earned income—both being intended as work incentives for persons receiving welfare.

The tendency of liberalized eligibility standards to extend welfare coverage to larger numbers of female-headed families is partially offset by increases in nonwelfare family income over time. Such increases would tend to take female-headed families beyond whatever eligibility ceiling is prevailing at any given time. However, for female-headed families, these income increases have been extremely modest, far below the gains experienced by other family types over the 1960s. The proportion of female-headed families with income below the poverty line remained approximately constant over that period—44 percent in 1967 versus 45 percent in 1971. Meanwhile the poverty line moved up 21 percent to allow for cost of living increases. Thus, although the money income of low-income, female-headed families increased somewhat, it was only enough to keep them about as poor as ever in real terms.

The interaction of these effects—liberalized welfare standards and rising incomes—plus the across-the-board increase in female-headed families with children, combine to produce a pool of eligible families which has been increasing since the middle 1960s, with particular spurts in 1970 and 1971, as is shown in col. 7 of table 24.

Increasing Welfare Participation of Eligible Female-Headed Families with Children. A major part of welfare caseload increases in the late 1960s stemmed from increased participation in the AFDC program by eligible families. Careful tabulation of welfare eligibles and participants by Barbara Boland[13] has shown that AFDC participation increased from 63 percent of eligible families in 1967 to 94 percent in 1971 (see col. 10, table 24).

---

12. Lurie, March 1973.
13. Boland, August 1973.

This increase was the result of both client and agency behavior. On the client's end, observers have noted that the 1960s saw a change in both information and attitude on the part of the poor. People were told about the availability of welfare programs and were helped to apply. They came increasingly to see welfare as a right and to know how to exercise it.

The change in agency behavior is reflected in the acceptance rate for welfare. The proportion of applications accepted rose appreciably over the 1960s (see table 25). This was largely a consequence of administrative discretion, although, given the increased information available, it may also have been due in part to a higher proportion of eligibles among applicants. This change in the acceptance rate was very important. Paul Barton[14] has calculated that 40 percent of the caseload growth between 1959 and 1968 was due to this factor alone.

It is interesting to note that the acceptance rate began to climb just about the time Patrick Moynihan[15] observed a divergence in the relationship between welfare openings and the male unemployment rate, which had held until that time in the postwar period. He believed that this divergence signaled a new round of welfare-related deterioration in black family life. However, allowing for the changing acceptance rate would have made the divergence much less dramatic. Indeed, work by Mary Procter[16] shows that through 1968, the last year for which the data she used are available, a significant relationship between welfare *applications* and the male unemployment rate continued to hold. Thus, the break which Moynihan observed was in considerable part a shift in welfare agency behavior rather than a shift in family behavior.

Components Analysis. Using components analysis (see Appendix 5) to apportion caseload growth to each of the three factors identified above, we find that by far the major contributing element has been the increasing participation rate of eligible families, which independently accounts for almost half of the 1967-71 rise. Even if the number of eligible families had not changed at all, their increased rate of participation in AFDC would have accounted for 671,000 families, or 46 percent of the total of 1,452,000 families actually added to the caseload during the 1967-71 period. Another 7 percent of the caseload rise, or 106,000 families, is attributable to the increasing proportion of

14. Barton, March 1969.
15. Moynihan, 1965.
16. Procter, May 1971.

female-headed families with children who were eligible for welfare. The proportion of the caseload increase due independently to increasing numbers of female-headed families with children is 27 percent, or 386,000 families. If we assume, reasonably, that all families which are induced to become female-headed by the welfare system do in fact turn up on the rolls, this estimate of 27 percent of the 1967-71 caseload rise gives us an idea of the scope for possible welfare influence on the growth of female-headed families over that period.

Table 25

ACCEPTANCE RATES FOR AFDC
ALL STATES

1960	55.9
1961	60.2
1962	59.2
1963	57.5
1964	61.5
1965	62.4
1966	63.7
1967	69.7
1968	72.7
1969	74.5
1970	79.5
1971	73.9

Source: "Reasons for Opening and Closing of Public Assistance Cases," NCSS Reports A-5 and A-9, Washington, D.C.: U.S. Dept. of Health, Education and Welfare, Social and Rehabilitation Service, National Center for Social Statistics.

However, this is an unduly static picture which deals only with net changes in numbers of female-headed families eligible for or receiving welfare and ignores the turnover aspect of female-headed family growth emphasized in chapter 2. Welfare may prompt the creation of large numbers of female-headed families who become welfare recipients, but this will not show up in stocks of female-headed families or in welfare cases if commensurately large flows out of welfare and female-headed status are occurring at the same time. Frank Levy [17] reports findings from the Michigan Panel Study of Income Dynamics which indicate that not quite one-third of the persons who were

17. Levy, 1973.

poor in 1967 were also poor consistently during the next four years. Among female-headed families with children, the proportion of persons who were consistently poor was just slightly higher. This suggests appreciable turnover in financial status among poor female-headed families. Indeed such families turn out to be disproportionately represented among all upwardly-mobile poor families—that is, those whose income rose consistently after being poor in 1967 and ended up in 1971 above the poverty line. Applying their upward mobility rate over five years (32 percent) to 1.42 million poor female-headed families with children in 1967 leaves a residual of .96 million poor female-headed families with children in 1971 who had been either consistently or off-and-on poor for five years. This implies that at least .87 million formations of poor female-headed families with children had to occur over that period to make up the observed 1971 total of 1.83 million (see col. 4, table 24). This, of course, is a lower bound since it does not consider families which moved in and out of poverty without any particular pattern between 1967 and 1971 but ended up not poor in 1971. It also does not consider formations of poor female-headed households which may have occurred after 1967 but were followed by dissolutions or upgrading to nonpoverty status before 1971. Even this lower bound estimate of gross formations between 1967 and 1971 is more than double the Census Bureau's figure of .41 million families as the net increase for the period.[18]

It is thus apparent that by allowing for dynamic patterns of change in income and family composition we reach a higher estimate of the possible scope of welfare-induced family instability than can be derived from aggregate static analysis. We also see that it will be a challenging task to isolate the independent effects of welfare on family organization in the midst of change—changes in income levels, in the social and cultural climate with respect to family life and welfare recipiency, and in policy, including welfare policy itself. We now turn to efforts which have been made in this area.

PAST STUDIES

We will consider separately three routes by which welfare may increase its own caseload through the formation or prolonga-

---

18. See chap. 2, fn. 18, for further evidence on the relationship between gross flows into and out of female-headed family status and net increases of families in that status from year to year.

tion of female-headed households—illegitimacy, family dissolution, and delay of remarriage.

Illegitimacy. Some critics of welfare have maintained that women have illegitimate children to become eligible for welfare, to maintain eligibility, or to obtain larger welfare payments. Study of the question shows that the process of deciding to bear and keep an illegitimate child is highly involved. Decisions on sexual behavior and contraceptive use determine exposure to risk of pregnancy. Health status affects probability of successful pregnancy. Decisions on abortion determine whether an otherwise successful pregnancy will be completed. Decisions on marrying before giving birth or giving the child up for adoption have an effect on whether or not a mother-child unit is formed. Decisions on whether that unit lives with relatives or not determine whether a "new family" under the Census definition comes into being, although they need not affect the welfare eligibility of the unit. Further, the changing social and economic climate greatly shifts the environment in which such decisions are made. Chapter 4 has already traced several of the major elements of this process for both black and white women.

What role might welfare play in the process? By shifting the support costs of both children and mothers from private individuals or institutions to the government, it certainly alters the private costs and benefits associated with these decisions. Even if one hesitates to say that conception is planned on the basis of economic considerations, decisions about what follows conception could certainly be open to economic influence.

Phillips Cutright [19] concludes in his work for the Joint Economic Committee that welfare has not had an effect on the illegitimate birth rate, although he notes that illegitimacy has been an increasing source of AFDC recipiency over the postwar period, and currently accounts for 30 percent of total AFDC benefits. He bases his conclusion on two findings: (1) changes in state illegitimacy rates from 1940 to 1960 were unrelated to changes in state welfare benefit levels, and (2) differences in state illegitimacy rates in 1960 were not related to differences in state welfare benefits levels. The same result held for 1970.

His conclusion is a strong one to draw from these facts, however. The comparisons he makes are gross comparisons which do not inquire into the effect of welfare on illegitimacy given that other factors may also be at work, some with off-

19. Cutright, 1973.

setting effects. His comparison shows that welfare is not influencing illegitimate births so strongly that it can be detected without regard to any other factors which may be operating. This is certainly a finding, and one that we might have expected from the preceding overview of the growth of caseloads and female-headed families. But it is not a finding of no welfare effect on illegitimacy.

Fechter and Greenfield [20] attempt to identify the partial effect of welfare on illegitimacy—that is, the effect of welfare after other factors have been allowed for. They develop an economic model of illegitimacy which relates the illegitimacy rate to the level of ADFC benefits; the education, unemployment rate, and earnings of women; region of the country; income of men; and income of intact families. They estimate this equation for blacks and whites separately using state cross-sectional data for 1960 and 1970. Their finding is that the AFDC variable does not significantly affect illegitimacy rates. The significant variables in the model turn out to be region (lower illegitimacy in the South) and education (lower illegitimacy associated with higher education). Their policy conclusion concerns the social benefits of education in reducing illegitimacy, especially for blacks.

Winegarden [21] attempts to analyze the fertility of AFDC women in 50 states and the District of Columbia, using a sample survey of AFDC recipients conducted by the Department of Health, Education and Welfare. He finds that differences in fertility cannot be explained by differences in welfare grant levels but are positively associated with differences in the availability of welfare benefits, as measured by the proportion of poor female-headed families with children who are welfare recipients. He concludes that the size of welfare benefits available to women does not affect their propensity to bear additional children, but that the degree of certainty attached to anticipated benefits may have such an effect.

Cain [22] in an analysis done for the U.S. Commission on Population Growth and the American Future, hypothesizes that new income maintenance laws replacing the current welfare system will encourage fertility, based on three assumptions: (1) families benefiting from increased income will be able to afford more children, (2) families receiving increased cash assistance for increased numbers of children will be encouraged

---

20. Fechter and Greenfield, 1973.

21. Winegarden, 1974.

22. Cain, 1972.

to have more children, and (3) with increased family income and a higher tax rate on earnings as a result of income maintenance, wives may choose not to participate in the labor force and the result could be an increase in their fertility.

Using data from the New Jersey Income Maintenance Experiment two years later, Cain[23] conducted a preliminary analysis of the effect of such laws on fertility and reached a "no effect" verdict, based on observed fertility behavior for the first two and one-half years of the three-year experiment. Receiving experimental cash payments had no significant effect on the rate of pregnancies or births, nor was fertility among experimental families higher in the more generous payment groups than in those groups receiving less generous payments. The wives' educational attainments and wage rates were negatively related to fertility, as were the education, earnings, and ages of the husbands at the start of the experiment. These results indicated that poor, intact families do not experience higher fertility when offered cash transfer payments for additional children during a two-to-three-year period. However, as Cain points out, since fertility decisions involve a parental commitment of approximately 18 years' duration, it is questionable whether the limited information obtained from a three-year experiment would provide reliable estimates of fertility response to national income maintenance plans.

Thus there is virtually no empirical evidence showing that welfare has an independent effect on illegitimacy. Nonetheless, analysts such as Cain and Winegarden are unwilling to reach a final conclusion that no such effect exists, and it is tempting to believe that their reluctance is justified. Illegitimate births and welfare caseloads are both rising, and the former is certainly contributing to the latter. It has been estimated that as many as 80 percent of illegitimate children who are not subsequently legitimated or adopted end up on the AFDC rolls. But whether or not the latter is contributing to the former remains to be convincingly demonstrated.

Family Dissolution. As with illegitimacy, family dissolution through divorce, separation, and desertion has been increasing, and the female-headed families thus formed have contributed to the growing welfare caseload. Female-headed families resulting from family dissolution other than death have been a significant portion of AFDC cases for some time, and between

---

23. Cain, 1974.

1961 and 1971 their caseload percentage has risen from 41 percent to 45 percent.[24]

The question whether welfare contributes to dissolution has been addressed by a number of researchers. Welfare may increase the tendency toward instability by providing women and children with a relatively stable alternative source of subsistence-level income. Hypotheses about exactly how this might occur can be linked to a number of broad explanations for the instability of low-income families—the strains of coping with inadequate and unstable incomes, the depreciation of the role of the male when he cannot provide for his dependents, and the unstable pattern of early marriage and childbearing which characterizes low-income populations. (A full discussion of the determinants of marital instability was given in chapter 3.)

Cutright and Scanzoni[25] have investigated whether welfare in fact causes family dissolution. They report that state AFDC benefit levels in 1950, 1960, and 1970 showed no relationship to the proportion of women married. Higher state AFDC benefits were not associated with higher proportions of children living in other than husband-wife families. They conclude that welfare has not contributed to family splitting but again this is a strong conclusion given their failure to go beyond gross comparisons to isolate the effects of welfare separately.[26]

Marjorie Honig[27] attempts to isolate the independent effects of welfare on family splitting and on AFDC recipiency rates among female-headed families. She uses 1960 cross-section data for 44 metropolitan areas to test her two-equation model. After controlling for female wage and unemployment rates, male earning opportunities, female nonearned, nonwelfare income, and welfare program restrictions which exclude some female-headed families from eligibility, she finds that the size of a metropolitan area's average AFDC benefit does have a significant positive effect on the area's proportion of adult women

24. "Findings" of the 1961 and 1971 (Part III) AFDC Studies, table 12 (1961) and table 4 (1971).

25. Cutright and Scanzoni, 1973.

26. For example, the authors report that urban black children in high AFDC benefit states were more likely to live in husband-wife families in 1970 than were urban black children in low benefit states. They do not cite this finding as evidence that welfare promotes family stability, and presumably they do not believe it does. Rather they probably think some other factor is at work to produce this result. One possibility might be that relatively high AFDC benefit states have relatively high wage structures and that high male earnings promote family stability more than high benefit levels inhibit it. Thus a negative effect of welfare on family stability might be occurring even though the gross comparison shows welfare benefits positively associated with family stability.

27. Honig, 1973.

who are heads of families with children under 18 and on the proportion of adult women who are welfare recipients. Her results suggest that, other things equal, a 10 percent increase in the AFDC stipend will raise the proportion of women who are female family heads 2.6 percent for whites and 3.8 percent for nonwhites,[28] and raise the proportion of women who are welfare recipients 20 percent for whites and 14 percent for nonwhites. These relationships are estimated on 1970 data for the same areas and are found to hold, but more weakly than in 1960.

One important caveat should be borne in mind in interpreting the above findings. Because they are based on cross-sectional data, they tell us little about the process by which welfare benefit levels may or may not influence family structure. For example, if one were to find a positive association between benefit levels and the proportion of women who are separated, it would be impossible to say whether this association was due to higher separation rates in high benefit areas or lower remarriage rates in those areas. As we have noted in previous chapters, both separation *and* remarriage rates affect the proportion of women who are counted as currently separated. For this reason, the Honig study does not necessarily establish a direct link between the welfare system and family *dissolution.* Rather, her research establishes a link between welfare benefits and family *structure.*

One study which addresses more directly the question whether the welfare system affects dissolution was recently completed by Bernstein and Meezan.[29] They asked a sample of 451 welfare mothers in New York City whether the availability of welfare influenced their thinking about separation from a husband or boyfriend. Ten percent of married women and 18 percent of unmarried women answered "yes." Since this is a leading question, the women's answers to it may overstate the influence which welfare actually had on them at the time they made their decision. When asked a more neutral question about the reasons for the break-up of their marriage, none of the women cited welfare although 12 percent mentioned "financial problems." On the other hand, these women were still receiving welfare at the time of the survey and may have been less than candid in acknowledging that welfare influenced them and this

---

28. Although she reports this result separately by race, the racial difference is not statistically significant.

29. Bernstein and Meezan, 1975.

would tend to work in the opposite direction. In fact, since some of the women who disclaimed any welfare influence on their behavior still had reasonably close ties to their ex-husbands, the authors argue that separations, explicitly undertaken for the purpose of maximizing income, are probably somewhat greater than the women's actual responses indicate.

One of the most interesting aspects of the New York study is its documentation of the kinds of conditions which *do* contribute most to high marital dissolution among the poor—particularly alcohol, drugs, competing sexual relationships, and physical abuse. By comparison, welfare and other economic factors appear to play a minor role in the separation decision.[30]

Delay of Marriage or Remarriage. As noted earlier in the discussion, if we consider the flows into and out of female headedness, poverty, and welfare recipiency rather than focus on net changes in families in those statuses, we obtain a larger estimate of the possible scope for welfare effects on family composition. But if female-headed families formed through the influence of welfare are soon transformed into other family types and are moved out of the range of poverty and welfare eligibility, then the influence of welfare is a transitional one. Increasing the flows into and out of welfare may be a problem, if one views the turnover as a bad thing, but it is a much different and certainly less severe problem than creating a class of long-term needy and dependent people.

Nor is the turnover phenomenon necessarily bad. Since women with children have few resources of their own in this economy, there is a high risk that any break, for whatever reason, with men who support or might support them will leave them without adequate income—and in that case the availability of welfare may enable or encourage women to break away if they wish to. They may, subsequently, move back into a more satisfactory family arrangement than the original one

---

30. In comparing the Bernstein and Meezan results to the finding of no welfare effect in chapter 3's analysis of separation, a number of important differences in addition to the issue of question neutrality should be borne in mind. First, their findings relate to a small group of welfare mothers in New York City only. Second, in contrast to chapter 3's analysis, it was the *availability* and not the *amount* of welfare whose influence was investigated in the New York study. Third, it is precisely those women who would end up on welfare for whom the availability of welfare could be expected to have an impact on separation—so that while 10 percent of the married group of welfare mothers said they were influenced by the availability of welfare, the proportion so influenced among the total group of women who separate would be much lower. Finally, our inability to detect a measurable welfare effect in the Michigan data may stem in part from our need to rely, in that analysis, on average AFDC benefit data in each state to estimate the effects of welfare on family splitting.

they left. On the other hand, welfare could help to keep families female-headed once they become so. In a world where family changes are increasingly common at all levels of income, welfare might contribute to female headedness more by maintaining such families than by creating them.

There is evidence that, currently, the most effective way for a female-headed family to get out of poverty and off welfare is to acquire a male head. Levy's analysis of Michigan panel data, as mentioned before, shows female-headed families with children under 18 to be overrepresented among both the upwardly mobile and the consistently poor groups. They are conspicuously underrepresented among the in-and-out-of-poverty group.

Over half of the upwardly mobile group owed their escape from poverty to the acquisition of a male head. This concentration of families with new male heads in the upwardly mobile group may mean either that establishing *any* intact family is likely to make women and children nonpoor, or that women with children look carefully for men who can get them out of poverty before establishing a family tie. Either way, the acquiring of a male head appears to be a key element in determining poverty prospects for female-headed families.

This relation between family composition and poverty prospects may operate differently by race. As noted in chapter 4, Glick and Norton[31] show that blacks have lower remarriage rates than whites, longer separations before divorce, and longer periods of divorce before remarriage. One would expect these demographic facts to be associated with longer tenure on welfare for blacks and this turns out to be the case. Ketron's analysis of AFDC turnover rates[32] shows that for female-headed families on the rolls for two or more years with only one child (their reference group characteristics), whites are twice as likely as blacks to leave the rolls within twelve months if the head's age is less than 26 years, six times as likely if it is between 26 and 35 years, and one-fifth again as likely if it is 36 or more. The gross comparison between black and white discontinuance rates shows the latter half again as likely to leave as the former (average annual probability, .24 versus .16). And as the breakdown by age of head shows, the gross difference would be much greater were it not for the similarity in discontinuance rates for black and white women over 36 who are likely to lose eligibility because their children have reached age 18.

---

31. Glick and Norton, 1971.
32. Ketron, 1973.

The longer duration of welfare recipiency for blacks is an important reason for their higher caseload growth rate, and raises the possibility that the more important welfare contribution to female headedness—at least for black families—is through incentives to continue in female-headed status rather than to enter that status initially. The question is, under a different welfare system would the delays be as long? Perhaps we will have a chance to see, if the new stepfather ruling becomes better known to clients and if its intent is not circumvented by local welfare administration. Already, stepfather cases in AFDC, which accounted for so few units in 1961 that they were not separately listed in the statistics, are growing 85 percent faster than the overall caseload.[33]

SOME ADDITIONAL EVIDENCE

A standard method of testing for the effects of welfare programs on family structure has been to look across jurisdictions—generally states—at a point in time and see whether differences in welfare program features are associated with differences in family living arrangements. This is a useful approach because welfare programs are state operations which, although required by the Social Security Act to meet certain common standards in order to receive federal matching funds, vary significantly from state to state. It is this variation which allows an analysis of behavioral response to a range of different welfare program incentives.

One of the chief variations is in generosity of benefits, with New Jersey providing a maximum monthly grant over four times that available in Alabama. The issue is whether these different amounts of welfare benefits prompt people to live in different kinds of families—specifically, whether higher benefits are associated with more female-headed families. This issue is addressed below, using data on low-income areas of cities from the 1970 Census. The analysis focuses on low-income areas of cities rather than on states, because people in these areas are expected—given their urban location and their low income— to be most open to welfare influence. Since it is not certain that a welfare influence on family structure exists for any group in the population, this is an appropriate place to begin looking for evidence.

---

33. Findings of the 1967 and 1971 AFDC Studies, Part I. "Demographics and Program Characteristics," table 15 (1971), table 22 (1967).

1970 Census Analysis. The Census Employment Survey, taken as part of the 1970 Census of Population and Housing,[34] gathered data on persons living in low-income areas of 60 of the largest U.S. cities and of seven rural counties. The present analysis uses data from 41 of the cities for which sufficient representation of blacks and whites separately was available.[35] Given previous research findings that race is an important variable in explaining family structure and behavior with respect to the welfare system, separate regression analyses were run for blacks and whites.

The objective is to explain the variation across cities in the proportion of women aged 16 to 54 who head families with children. This proportion ranges from a low of 5 percent for white women in Norfolk, Virginia, to a high of 32 percent for black women in Boston, Massachusetts. We are interested in whether, other things equal, this proportion is higher where welfare benefits are more generous and more readily available. As reported in detail in Appendix 6, regression analysis is used to answer this question. The dependent variable—the proportion of women aged 16 to 54 who head families with children—is expressed as a function of a number of independent variables, including three characterizing the welfare system.

Our basic hypothesis is that, other things equal, greater income opportunities for women outside traditional family support arrangements are associated with higher proportions of women heading families. Thus the higher and more readily accessible welfare benefits are, the more likely are women to head families. However, we suspect that it is not the size of the alternative income opportunity—in this case, the welfare grant —alone which has an influence but its size relative to what men can provide. Furthermore, the benefits available to welfare recipients are not confined to cash grants only, but also include a range of in-kind benefits for food, housing, and health care. The values of these benefits to individual families are hard to get data on, and are thought by some not to be legitimately includible as income since they are only available in-kind. However, given the significance and availability of data on one such program—the food stamp program—a measure of its benefit

---

34. 1970 Census of Population and Housing, PHC(3), "Employment Profiles of Selected Low Income Areas."
35. Each of the 41 cities was selected on the basis of whether 5 percent or more of its population, as measured by the 1970 Census of Population and Housing, was white and nonwhite. I.e., where the population of either race was below 5 percent, data by race for that city was considered inadequate for our analysis.

---

value has been included in the income available to welfare recipients. Thus the welfare benefit variable is defined as the average AFDC grant in the state in which the city is located, plus the average food stamp bonus value in the county in which the city is located, divided by the full-time earnings of men in the city's low-income area. As noted above, the value of this welfare benefit variable is expected to vary directly with the proportion of women heading families.

The other two welfare variables are a measure of the prevalence of welfare in the low-income area and an indicator of whether the city has an unemployed parent program. The first variable, defined as the proportion of eligible families who are receiving welfare, measures the availability and acceptability of welfare in the local community and is expected to vary directly with the proportion of women heading families. The second indicates whether a family must split up to receive welfare. The presence of an unemployed parent program allows intact families to be assisted and thus is expected to be associated with fewer women heading families.

Apart from welfare benefits in cash or in kind, another source of income to women outside traditional family support arrangements is their own earnings, and this is included as another independent variable in explaining the proportion of women heading families. Like the welfare benefit variable, it is expressed relative to men's earnings and is expected to vary directly with female family headship. The median income of husband-wife families also appears in the equation as a variable and measures the return to women from living in that type of family. The higher that median income, the lower the expected proportion of women heading families. The final economic variable is a measure of the unemployment experienced by men in the low-income area. This indicates the stability of the most important component of husband-wife family income, men's earnings, and is expected to vary directly with female family headship.

Several additional control variables complete the equation. These are the proportion of the population in the low-income area made up of children under eighteen (expected to vary directly with the dependent variable), the degree of mobility of the area population (also expected to show direct variation), and the region of the country in which the city is located. A location in the South is expected to result in fewer female-headed families.

Regressions were run in both linear and logarithmic form,

the latter to capture some expected non-linearities. Looking at the logarithmic specification and beginning with the white population, we find that none of the three variables characterizing the welfare system significantly affects the proportion of women who head families with children. But other economic variables are significant. The women's economic opportunities hypothesis is supported by the women's relative earnings variable, which is highly significant and has considerable effect. Increasing women's relative earnings by 10 percent increases the proportion of women heading families with children by 11.5 percent. More weeks of male unemployment also raise the proportion of women heading families, while higher husband-wife incomes lower it, indicating that both instability of male earnings and a low level of earnings are associated with female family headship among whites. One control variable, the presence of children, is also highly significant in the expected direction.

For the nonwhite population, the welfare benefit variable is significantly associated with the proportion of women heading families with children. Neither of the other welfare parameters is significant. Women's own earnings relative to those of men are also insignificant.

Welfare benefits appear to play a role for nonwhites similar to the role played for whites by women's relative earnings—an encouraging or enabling factor in the existence of female-headed families with children. But the welfare-income elasticity of female family headship for nonwhites is considerably less than the women's-relative-earnings elasticity for whites. A 10 percent increase in welfare benefits results in only a 2.1 percent increase in the proportion of nonwhite female family heads. However, equal dollar increments to welfare benefits and women's earnings, other things being equal, have roughly similar effects on the percentage point increase in the proportion of nonwhite and white women, respectively, who head families with children. Fifty dollar increases in welfare benefits and women's earnings result in percentage point increases of 1.2 and 1.6, respectively, for nonwhite and white female family headship.

For nonwhites, median husband-wife family income is highly significant and its coefficient indicates an elasticity of female family headship with respect to intact family income which is similar to that for whites. Ten percent increases in intact family income lead to 6.7 percent and 7.2 percent decreases in female family headship for whites and nonwhites, respectively. However, instability of income as measured by male median weeks unemployed does not contribute significantly to female family headship for nonwhites. Among the control variables, only the regional control is significant. Living in the South lowers the proportion of nonwhite women who head families with children by 6.1 percentage points and this effect is not due to different degrees of mobility or to city size.

These results generally support our original hypothesis. They suggest that a similar, economically-based model of family behavior holds for both nonwhites and whites in low-income metropolitan areas. Higher income for intact families results in lower proportions of female-headed families with children, and higher income available to women from other sources results in higher proportions. The major difference is that whites appear more oriented to women's earnings as an alternative source of income, and nonwhites to welfare.

There are several possible reasons for this difference. While women's earnings relative to men's are similar for nonwhites and whites, the mean in both cases being 68 percent, women's absolute earnings, and thus their earnings relative to a common welfare standard, are slightly higher for whites. Women's median full-time monthly earnings are $397 for whites and $368 for nonwhites, the relatively small difference being due to the location of the sample in low-income metropolitan areas. In addition, the average AFDC benefit is likely to be higher for nonwhites than for whites due to the generally larger number of children in nonwhite female-headed family units—an adjustment which could not be accurately made using the present data. Also, nonwhite women are likely to experience more serious unemployment problems than white women, and thus have more difficulty achieving the median earnings of full-time workers of their race and sex, although the women's unemployment variable did not contribute significantly to the equation when it was included.

Other possible explanations are cultural. Eligible nonwhite families show consistently higher participation rates in welfare than eligible white families.[36] Also, poor nonwhite women show slightly lower labor force participation rates than poor white women, and their participation has been dropping recently while that of whites remained roughly constant.[37] Nonwhite families tend to stay on welfare appreciably longer than white families, after controlling for age, education, and number of children.[38]

36. Boland, 1973.
37. U.S. Bureau of the Census, Current Population Reports, Series P-60, "Characteristics of the Low Income Population," nos. 68, 76, 81, 86, 91, and 94.
38. Ketron, 1973.

Underlying Behavior. Our analysis of Census data has indicated a modest upward influence of welfare benefit levels on the proportion of nonwhite women who head families with children. However these data cannot tell us which of the several possible behavioral responses to the welfare system are responsible for this result. Perhaps it is because welfare benefits encourage separation and divorce in intact families, which has been the conventional wisdom. But the analysis of data from the Michigan Panel Study on Income Dynamics in chapter 3 did not find any evidence of such a behavioral pattern. Nor did performing that analysis separately for whites and nonwhites turn up a welfare effect within either racial group separately.

Other possible underlying behavioral responses are, first, the bearing and keeping of illegitimate children, and, second, the setting up of separate households by women and children who would have lived with relatives or other persons were it not for their welfare support. As noted earlier, the existing evidence on these responses is very thin, and we have not been able to add to that stock of knowledge with our present analyses. Of these two responses, the second, or undoubling, effect seems the more likely to be of significance. Cutright and Scanzoni [39] show large historical variations in household membership patterns and conclude that shifts in living arrangements toward less extended family living have been a major contribution to female-headed family growth. However their data indicate that the bulk of such shifts occurred during the 1950s and early 1960s, and our components of growth analysis for the 1960-1970 period in Chapter 2 attributed only a small portion of female-headed family growth to changes in living arrangements.

A final behavioral response of potentially major significance is delay of remarriage. This is a particularly interesting avenue to explore given the fact that the median duration of divorce before remarriage is currently half again as long for nonwhite women as for white women. [40] This might be related to our finding of a welfare influence on the family headship of non-white women, but not of white women.

The Michigan Panel data include some observations on remarriage behavior, and analysis [41] of those data, which we report in detail elsewhere, suggests a significant role for welfare. Women in the sample who headed families with children in

39. Cutright and Scanzoni, 1973.
40. Glick and Norton, 1971.
41. Sawhill, et al., 1975.

1968 had about a 12 percent likelihood of remarrying at some time during the next four years. But that likelihood fell to about 5 percent if the women were welfare recipients. This was true after controlling for such other influences on remarriage rates as female-headed family income, residential location, and number of children and the female head's age, education, race, marital status, and length of time as a female head. On the other hand, these data did not support the hypothesis that welfare affects remarriage for whites and nonwhites differently.

IMPLICATIONS FOR POLICY

What do these results say about the impact of welfare reform on the growth of female-headed families? Broadened income maintenance would be expected to work against such growth by removing the present categorical penalties against remaining in an intact family or forming a new one. The Census analysis can help us put some numbers on the potential magnitude of this countervailing effect. Consider the impact of extending existing AFDC programs at current benefit levels to cover all husband-wife families. This extension of coverage would have no direct effect on the relative value of welfare benefits to women and children, since it would change neither men's earnings nor the amount of welfare benefits available to women and children. But it would raise the income of newly-participating husband-wife families. Strictly speaking, this would raise the median family income variable in the equation very little because most median husband-wife family incomes in the sample are already above the income ceiling for welfare eligibility. However, taking the estimated coefficient of the variable as a general measure of the elasticity of female family headship with respect to intact family income, and making some assumptions about (1) the income distribution of low-income, husband-wife families and (2) the effective tax rates in welfare, we can estimate the stabilizing effect of supplementing the income of eligible husband-wife families.

These estimates for white and nonwhite families are shown in table 26. Also shown in the table are analogous estimates for an alternative welfare reform program which not only extends benefit coverage but also raises average benefit levels —specifically, a universal negative income tax plan with a guarantee at the 1970 poverty level ($3,968 per year for a family of four) and a 50 percent rate of benefit reduction with increases in other income.

Table 26

EFFECTS OF WELFARE REFORM ON FEMALE FAMILY HEADSHIP

	Proportion of H-W Families Eligible for Benefits[c]	Average Pre-Reform Income of Eligible Families[d]	Average H-W Income Increase due to Reform $ (ΔMFI)[e]	(%)	Partial Effect of ΔMFI on Female Family Headship (%)	Average Increase in relative value of welfare benefits to women & children (ΔWL)[f] (%)	Partial Effect of ΔWL on Female Family Headship (%)	Overall Effect of Reform on Female Family Headship (%)
Reform I: Extended AFDC Coverage[a]								
White	.29	4310	428	9.93	−1.95	0.00	0.00	−1.95
Nonwhite	.30	4310	428	9.93	−2.13	0.00	0.00	−2.13
Reform II: Negative Income Tax[b]								
White	.46	5952	992	16.67	−5.18	21.76	0.00	−5.18
Nonwhite	.48	5952	992	16.67	−5.72	21.76	+4.51	−1.21

a. Extension of state AFDC programs at existing benefit levels to cover husband-wife families.

b. Replacement of AFDC and food stamps with a universal negative income tax plan with a guarantee level of $3,968 per year and a tax rate of 50 percent on other income.

c. Assumes that the proportion of families eligible for benefits equals one-half times the ratio of the benefit break-even level to the median family income level for the example. The break-even level for AFDC is calculated assuming monthly deductions of $30 plus $60 for work-related expenses, and a tax rate on additional income of 66⅔ percent.

d. Assumes that the average pre-reform income of eligible families is midway between the guarantee level (guarantee plus deduction level in AFDC) and the benefit break-even level.

e. ΔMFI = increase in the median family income of husband-wife families as a result of reform.

f. ΔWL = increase in the value to women and children of welfare benefits relative to men's earnings as a result of reform.

The table indicates that both of these alternative reform measures will modestly reduce the proportion of women who head families with children. The first reform—extended AFDC coverage at existing benefit levels—raises the income of the approximately 30 percent of white and nonwhite husband-wife families in low-income metropolitan areas who are newly eligible for benefits an average of $428 per year or almost 10 percent. This 10 percent income increase reduces female family headship among recipient families by 6.71 percent for whites and 7.10 percent for nonwhitès, for an overall reduction among all families of 1.95 percent for whites and 2.13 percent for nonwhites.

The second reform, replacement of AFDC and food stamps by a universal negative income tax plan, has a larger stabilizing effect operating through increases in the income of husband-wife families, because those increases are greater than in the first reform due to a nationwide raising of benefit levels. Increased husband-wife income in this case has the overall effect of reducing female family headship by 5.18 percent for whites and 5.72 percent for nonwhites. In the case of whites, this is the total effect on family headship, since no significant impact of higher relative benefit levels for women and children was found for them in the analysis. In the case of nonwhites, the stabilizing effect of greater supplemental benefits for intact families is offset to a degree by the fact that higher benefit levels also mean more income support for women and children, should they become separate households, and this has a destabilizing effect for nonwhites. However, this destabilizing effect increases female family headship by less (4.51 percent) than higher intact family income operates to reduce it (5.72 percent), so that the net result of the reform is to reduce female family headship among nonwhites by 1.21 percent. Thus the net effect of introducing a negative income tax plan, as estimated in this analysis, is a modest reduction in the proportion of women who head families among both whites and nonwhites, even when the tax plan involved provides greater than existing benefits to women and children.

This result assumes that increments to husband-wife family income in the form of supplemental welfare benefits will have the same stabilizing effect on families as equal increments from existing sources of income, primarily earnings. This might not be the case if families discounted welfare income as less de-

sirable than other types of income, or if other income types had
a stabilizing impact stemming not only from the amount but
also from the nature of the income received. For example, earnings might be particularly stabilizing because of their connotations of useful productivity and fulfillment of one's expected
role. There is, however, evidence from an analysis of the Penn-
sylvania-New Jersey Income Maintenance Experiment recently
completed by Gerald Peabody[42] that providing income transfers
to low-income families reduces the rate at which these families
separate, after controlling for experimental status and other factors. Specifically, a $1,000 increase in the level of experimental
payments was found to be associated with a 2 percent reduction
in marital dissolutions.[43]

Using Peabody's findings, together with the set of results
emerging from the Michigan Panel analyses of separation and
remarriage, we can approach from a slightly different angle the
question of how much impact welfare reform might have on
family structure. Using this second approach involves relying on
the elementary demographic model of stocks and flows developed in chapter 2 to calculate the proportion of families headed
by a woman and substituting into this model various estimates
of the policy-induced changes in separation and remarriage rates
associated with various welfare reform proposals. One set of estimates based on this approach is presented in table 27. The
two equations at the top of the table indicate how the incidence
of female headedness would vary with separation and remarriage rates (in a world where illegitimate births, changes in living arrangement, and other sources of female-headed family
growth did not exist). The analysis assumes an initial (pre-
welfare reform) separation rate of 2 percent and a remarriage
rate of 12 percent based on estimates from the data in
chapter 2. Next, the effect of an income maintenance plan
which provides about $1,000 per year to husband-wife families
in poverty is calculated. One consequence of this type of welfare
reform is to reduce separation rates among low-income, husband-wife families, and we have used the Peabody results to
estimate the magnitude of this effect. But an additional change
in family composition occurs because women on welfare are

---

42. Ibid.

43. The elasticity was $-.32$ evaluated at the means. The sample was about
one-third white, one-third black, and one-third Spanish speaking. The payments
coefficient was not significant for the white group.

now assumed to remarry at the same rate as nonrecipient
women with similar characteristics. As the table indicates, the
combined effect of these two separate influences is to lower
the proportion of families headed by a woman from 15 percent
to about 11 percent, or by roughly 25 percent.

This second approach to analyzing the possible changes
in family structure which welfare reform might bring suggests a bigger impact than the Census estimates presented
previously. However, there are reasons for thinking that the
figures in table 27 represent a maximum estimate of this impact.
First, for the reasons outlined in footnote d to the table, it is
likely that the three-to-one ratio between the remarriage rates
of welfare and nonwelfare mothers exaggerates the difference
between the two groups. Second, the calculation assumes that
welfare mothers have personal characteristics which make them
as marriageable as nonwelfare mothers, after controlling for
age, race, income, number of children, and so forth. Third, because a recent Supreme Court ruling (1970) relieves stepfathers
of any presumed financial responsibility for nonadopted children—permitting these children to continue to receive welfare
after their mother remarries—any welfare effect on remarriage
is likely to have become diluted over time. Finally, the calculations in table 27 are based on the premise that the current welfare system would be replaced by a program which approached
neutrality with respect to changes in family composition by providing a benefit schedule tailored to actual economies of scale
in family living and by integrating the negative and positive
tax systems.

The specific numbers coming out of these two analyses can
be taken only as a general measure of the direction and magnitude of welfare effects on family structure. However, they suggest that welfare reform of the sort considered here probably
cannot be viewed as a major policy lever on family organization. While families do appear to be responsive to welfare
program features, that responsiveness is only one component in
the overall dynamic of changing female-headed family stocks
and flows.

The central objective of welfare reform is to provide needy
families and individuals with a more adequate income base, in a
manner which is more equitable across household types and
areas of the country and more conducive to recipients' own
self-support. Providing this greater economic base will expand

Table 27

ESTIMATING THE POSSIBLE EFFECTS OF WELFARE REFORM ON FAMILY STRUCTURE

Demographic Model[a]

F = proportion of families with children headed by a woman

(1 - F) = proportion of families with children headed by a married couple

d = separation rate

r = remarriage rate

t = current time period

t - 1 = previous time period

$$F_t = F_{t-1} + d(1 - F_{t-1}) - rF_{t-1} \tag{1}$$

After all adjustments, the system reaches a "steady state equilibrium in which $F_t = F_{t-1}$ and equation (1) simplifies to:

$$F = \frac{d}{d + r} \tag{2}$$

Calculating the Possible Effects of Welfare Reform

	d	r	F
Under current system[b]	.02	.12	.15
Effect of welfare reform on separation rates[c]	.018	.12	.13
Effect of welfare reform on remarriage rates[d]	.02	.15	.12
Combined effect	.018	.15	.11

a. See Appendix 3 for the development of this model.

b. Estimated from data in chapter 2.

c. Assumes an additional $20 per week of income for poor husband-wife families with children. This would lower their annual dissolution rate by 2 percentage points, and lower the dissolution rate of all husband-wife families with children by about two-tenths of a percentage point (from .02 to .018).

d. Assumes nonrecipients have a remarriage rate which is three times as high as recipients (.15 vs. .05), that recipients are 30 percent of all female-headed families with children, and that welfare reform would raise the remarriage rate of recipients to the nonrecipient level. The estimated annual remarriage rates used here are based on aggregate data from chapter 2. The variation in remarriage rates with recipiency status is taken from the analysis of Michigan Panel data summarized earlier in this chapter and reported fully in Sawhill, et al., 1975. However, because remarriage rates estimated from the Michigan data are so low, percentage differences tend to be large. Thus, the 3 to 1 ratio used here probably overestimates the magnitude of the welfare effect on remarriage.

peoples' options as to family structure, and it appears that this will work in the direction of reducing female-headed families with children, but this effect is slight compared to other influences on family structure and minor compared to the central purposes of welfare reform.

So welfare reform by itself is not likely to reduce dramatically the present trend toward female-headed families. As relative incomes from sources other than welfare, and cultural patterns of thinking and behavior continue to shift, female-headed families will almost certainly continue to grow. This growth is likely to heighten concern among people who believe that female-headed families are, for some reason, socially undesirable. The most frequently cited reason for such undesirability is the assumption that they harm the children who grow up in them. In the next chapter, we will discuss what is known about the effects of female family headship on children.

BIBLIOGRAPHY

Barton, Paul. "The Relationship of Employment to Welfare Dependency." U.S. Department of Labor, March 1969.

Boland, Barbara. "Participation in the Aid to Families with Dependent Children Program (AFDC)." Urban Institute Working Paper 971-02, Aug. 1973.

Bernstein, Blanche, and Meezan, William. *The Impact of Welfare on Family Stability.* Center for New York City Affairs, New School for Social Research, June 1975.

Cain, Glen G. "The Effect of Income Maintenance Laws on Fertility in the U.S." In vol. 6, *Aspects of Population Growth Policy*, of the Commission on Population Growth and the American Future, 1972.

_____. "The Effect of Income Maintenance Laws on Fertility: Results from the New Jersey-Pennsylvania Experiment," Part D, chapter 7 of *Final Report of the New Jersey Graduated Work Incentive Experiment*, 1974.

Cutright, Phillips. "Illegitimacy and Income Supplements." In Paper no. 12, *Studies in Public Welfare*, prepared for the use of the Subcommittee on Fiscal Policy of the Joint Economic Committee of the Congress, 1973.

Cutright, Phillips, and Scanzoni, John. "Income Supplements and the American Family." In Paper no. 12, *Studies in Public Welfare*, prepared for the use of the Subcommittee on Fiscal Policy of the Joint Economic Committee of the Congress, 1973.

Dupont, Robert L. "Where Does One Run When He's Already in the Promised Land?" D.C. Department of Human Resources, Narcotics Treatment Administration (mimeo), March 1973.

Durbin, Elizabeth. "The Vicious Cycle of Welfare: Problems of the Female-Headed Household in New York City." In Cynthia B. Lloyd, ed., *Sex, Discrimination, and the Division of Labor*. Columbia University Press, 1975.

"The Family, Poverty, and Welfare Programs: Household Patterns and Government Policies." In *Studies in Public Welfare,* Paper no. 12 (Parts I and II) prepared for the use of the Subcommittee on Fiscal Policy of the Joint Economic Committee of the Congress, 1973.

Fechter, Alan, and Greenfield, Stuart. "Welfare and Illegitimacy: An Economic Model and Some Preliminary Results." Urban Institute Working Paper 963-37, Aug. 1973.

Glick, Paul C., and Norton, Arthur J. "Frequency, Duration, and Probability of Marriage and Divorce." *Journal of Marriage and the Family,* May 1971, pp. 307-17.

Honig, Marjorie. "Do Welfare Payment Levels Influence Family Stability?" In Paper no. 12, *Studies in Public Welfare,* prepared for the use of the Subcommittee on Fiscal Policy of the Joint Economic Committee of the Congress, 1973.

Joint Economic Committee of the Congress. "The Family, Poverty, and Welfare Programs: Household Patterns and Government Policies." In *Studies in Public Welfare,* Paper no. 12 (Parts I and II) 1973.

Ketron, Inc. "Estimates of Annual Natural Turnover Rates from 1969 and 1971 AFDC National Survey." Wayne, Pennsylvania (mimeo), Aug. 1973.

Levy, Frank. "The Demographics of Low Income Households." Dept. of Health, Education, and Welfare (mimeo) summer 1973.

Lurie, Irene. "Legislative, Administrative, and Judicial Changes in the AFDC Program." Madison, Wis.: Institute for Research on Poverty, Reprint 93, 1973.

Moynihan, Daniel P. "The Negro Family: The Case for National Action." Washington, D.C.: Office of Planning and Research, U.S. Dept. of Labor, 1965.

National Center for Social Statistics. "Findings of the AFDC Studies," 1961, 1967, 1969, 1971, and 1973. Washington, D.C.: Department of Health, Education and Welfare, Social and Rehabilitation Service.

Procter, Mary E. "The Demand for Welfare, 1953-1968." Princeton University (mimeo) May 1971.

Report of the Committee on Economic Security. Washington, D.C.: Government Printing Office, 1935.

Storey, James R. "Welfare in the 70's: A National Study of Benefits Available In 100 Local Areas." In Paper no. 15, *Studies in Public Welfare,* prepared for the use of the Subcommittee on Fiscal Policy of the Joint Economic Committee of the Congress, July 1974.

Sawhill, Isabel; Peabody, G.; Jones, C.; and Caldwell, S. *Income Transfers and Family Structure.* Urban Institute Working Paper 979-03, 1975.

U.S. Bureau of the Census. *Employment Profiles of Selected Low Income Areas,* Series PHC(3), 1972.

U.S. Department of Labor, Employment Standards Administration. "Minimum Wage and Maximum Hours Standards Under the Fair Labor Standards Act," January 1975.

"Welfare in the 70's: A National Study of Benefits Available in 100 Local Areas." In Paper no. 15, *Studies in Public Welfare,* prepared for the use of the Subcommittee on Fiscal Policy of the Joint Economic Committee of the Congress, July 22, 1974.

Winegarden, C. R. "The Welfare 'Explosion': Determinants of the Size and Recent Growth of the AFDC Population." *The American Journal of Economics and Sociology,* July 1973, pp. 245-56.

_____. "The Fertility of AFDC Women: An Econometric Analysis." *Journal of Economics and Business,* vol. 26, no. 3, spring 1974.

Chapter 6

WHAT HAPPENS TO CHILDREN IN FEMALE-HEADED FAMILIES?

INTRODUCTION

The rise in family headship by women has been mirrored by an even more dramatic shift in the living arrangements of children. Children living with only one parent increased twelve times as rapidly as children living with both parents between 1960 and 1970. Indeed, over that period, the absolute increase in numbers of children in single-parent homes exceeded the increase in children in two-parent homes. Furthermore, this greater absolute increase among single-parent children occurred for both whites and nonwhites.

Table 28 gives an overview of these changing family patterns of children. It appears from the table that part of the increase in children in single-parent homes is related to a significant decline for both whites and nonwhites in the number of children in institutions and in families where they are unrelated to the family head. Among single-parent families with children, those with a male head have been growing faster than those with a female head, especially among whites, but the numbers are still quite small. Table 29 indicates that, despite this growth, 84 percent of all children in single-parent homes were living with a female parent in 1970.

Table 28

CHILDREN UNDER AGE 18, BY RACE AND LIVING ARRANGEMENT

(Numbers in thousands)

	All Races			Nonwhite			White		
	1960	1970	Percent Change	1960	1970	Percent Change	1960	1970	Percent Change
Total No. of Children <18 (Percent)	64,298 (100)	69,880 (100)	9	8,738 (100)	10,475 (100)	20	55,560 (100)	59,405 (100)	7
in 2-Parent Families (Percent)	57,299 (89)	59,912 (86)	5	6,337 (73)	6,877 (66)	9	50,962 (92)	53,035 (89)	4
in 1-Parent Families (Percent)	6,080 (9)	9,700 (14)	60	2,134 (24)	3,556 (34)	67	3,946 (7)	6,144 (10)	56
in Other Arrangements* (Percent)	919 (1)	268 (.4)	-71	267 (3)	42 (.4)	-84	652 (1)	226 (.4)	-65

* These figures are residuals, comprising children living in institutions, foster homes, and other arrangements where the children are unrelated to the person(s) with whom they live.

Source: U.S. Census of the Population 1960, Subject Report "Families," PC (2) - 4A, table 6. Washington, D.C.: U.S. Bureau of the Census.

U.S. Census of the Population 1970, Subject Report "Family Composition," PC (2) - 4A, table 8. Washington, D.C.: U.S. Bureau of the Census.

Table 29

CHILDREN UNDER AGE 18 IN ONE-PARENT FAMILIES, BY RACE
(Numbers in thousands)

	All Races			Nonwhite			White		
	1960	1970	% Change	1960	1970	% Change	1960	1970	% Change
No. of Children in 1-Parent Families	6,080	9,700	60	2,134	3,556	67	3,946	6,144	56
in Male-Headed Families	873	1,566	79	229	388	69	644	1,178	83
in Female-Headed Families (Percent)	5,207 (100)	8,134 (100)	56	1,905 (100)	3,168 (100)	66	3,302 (100)	4,966 (100)	50
Widowed (Percent)	1,870 (36)	2,161 (26)	16	624 (33)	717 (23)	15	1,246 (38)	1,444 (29)	16
Divorced (Percent)	1,088 (21)	2,334 (29)	115	210 (11)	534 (17)	154	878 (27)	1,800 (36)	105
Separated (Percent)	1,333 (25)	2,266 (28)	70	729 (38)	1,244 (39)	71	604 (18)	1,022 (21)	69
Single (Percent)	252 (5)	706 (9)	180	180 (9)	490 (15)	172	72 (2)	216 (4)	200
Other* (Percent)	664 (13)	667 (8)	.5	162 (9)	183 (6)	13	502 (15)	484 (10)	−4

* This Census category refers to married persons with spouse absent. It comprises married persons whose spouses are employed and living away from home or in the armed forces, immigrants whose spouses remained in other areas, or wives of inmates in institutions.

Source: U.S. Census of the Population 1960, Subject Report "Families," PC (2) - 4A, table 6. Washington, D.C.; U.S. Bureau of the Census.

U.S. Census of the Population 1970, Subject Report "Family Composition," PC (2) - 4A, table 8. Washington, D.C.; U.S. Bureau of the Census.

Table 29 also shows that, among female-headed families, the living arrangements of children by marital status of the head have been shifting over the last decade. In 1960, more children (36 percent) lived in families headed by widows than in any other female-headed family type. By 1970, children of both divorced (29 percent) and separated (28 percent) heads outnumbered those of widowed (26 percent) heads, and marital instability had become the source of single parentage for the majority of children living in that status. Almost identical proportions of white children and nonwhite children in female-headed families were living with a separated or divorced parent—57 percent and 56 percent respectively—but the bulk of the white children had a divorced parent while the bulk of the nonwhite children had a separated parent. For both whites and nonwhites, by far the fastest increasing group of children in female-headed families were those with a single (never married) parent. They grew over three times as rapidly as all children in female-headed families, with whites showing the largest percentage increase.

Thus a few basic Census data give a picture of considerable shifts in the living arrangements of children:

1. More children are living in families where they are related to the family head.
2. More children in related families are living with a single parent, usually the mother.
3. More children in female-headed families are living with a parent who is unmarried, separated, or divorced.

The central element of these shifts is that children are living increasingly without a father present at home. It has long and widely been thought that this sort of family arrangement is damaging to children—not only when they are young but also later in their adult life—and that this, in turn, hurts society, which must cope with the damaged children's antisocial behavior or impaired abilities to achieve. The issue faced in this chapter is whether we should indeed anticipate adverse consequences for children and society from the shifts in children's living arrangements now under way.

EVALUATING EXISTING KNOWLEDGE

The following pages are devoted to a review of existing knowledge about the effects of female family headship on children. Our purpose is to determine whether or not female-headed families per se can be shown to entail negative consequences for children of such seriousness that a case might exist for thwarting the preferences of the people involved and discouraging the formation of such families through public policy.

The literature on family structure and child well-being is extensive, although it turns out to be quite narrow in its focuses (principally on female single parents and male children, rather than on both female and male single parents and children of both sexes) and in its selection of hypotheses for testing, its theoretical underpinnings, and its research methods.[1] Here we will draw together the particularly important and influential work in the field, confining our inquiry to measures of adverse consequences which affect the socioeconomic well-being of individuals and society. These consequences are divided into those which appear during childhood, and those which affect the child's adult life. Looking at the child directly, we shall review literature dealing with juvenile delinquency and school achievement. Looking at the child as an adult, we will focus on his or her later socioeconomic status and family stability.

This review does not deal directly with the extensive literature on the psychological effects of single parentage (mostly father absence), including studies of such matters as schizophrenia and the confusion of sex roles.[2] This is not to say that such matters are unimportant, but rather that they achieve particular social and policy significance when they result in objective problems of antisocial behavior or socioeconomic impairment.

NEGATIVE CONSEQUENCES FOR CHILDREN

Juvenile Delinquency. The public and many criminologists have linked broken homes with juvenile delinquency, apparently believing that children from broken homes are more likely to become youthful offenders than children from intact homes.

The review of existing literature exposes two major difficulties which can seriously undermine the analysis of such a linkage: first, not enough attention has been given to the presence and role of important intervening variables; and, second, there is a strong bias in the collection of juvenile delinquency

---

1. For a comprehensive review of the literature on children in fatherless homes, see Elizabeth Herzog and Cecilia Sudia, 1970.

2. Brandwein, et al., 1974; Biller, 1970; and Hetherington and Duer, 1971.

counts. Regarding the first problem, the interaction between family structure and such potential factors in delinquency as low income, inadequate parental care and supervision, and marital strife, is highly complex, and the analysis of it requires careful research design and execution. Unless income, the age of the child at separation, parental characteristics, and a host of other variables are controlled, the independent effects of family structure cannot be successfully isolated.

The second problem is systemic in all studies of juvenile delinquency. To what extent do official statistics represent the differing incidence of juvenile delinquency in different population groups? In the official counts of children who have been apprehended for some offense, there seems to be a bias directly related to the offender's home background. As reported in *Welfare in Review*, the "stability of the child's family and his potential for receiving proper parental supervision seemed to be the most common basis for dismissals."[3] It is also likely that a black child or a child from a lower-class home will be treated differently in the reporting of an offense. Black children and lower-class children are much more likely to come from single-parent homes.

These doubts about the accuracy of data on juvenile delinquency having been voiced, what do research studies actually show? The best known work on juvenile delinquency is a study by Eleanor and Sheldon Glueck of adolescent boys in the greater Boston area. The study used a sample of lower-class youth committed for juvenile delinquency and a control group matched by age, IQ, race and ethnic background, and area of residence. The Gluecks isolated 41 home factors which they found to be significantly associated with juvenile delinquency; one of those 41 factors was the absence of a father. In the delinquent group, 61 percent of the boys had absent fathers compared with 34 percent in the matched control group.

However, sixteen other home factors were found to be more significantly related to juvenile delinquency, in the sense that for these factors the measured differences between delinquent and nondelinquent groups exceeded the 27 percentage-point difference shown above for father absence. Foremost among these other factors were "unsuitable discipline of boy by mother" (96 percent in the experimental group as compared with 34 percent in the control group), and "unsuitable super-

---

3. *Welfare in Review*, 1965, p. 19.

vision of boy by mother" (64 percent as compared with 13 percent). This implies that although the absence of the father was associated with juvenile delinquency, other factors played a greater causal role. A re-analysis by Maccoby[4] of some of the Glueck data strongly suggested that the mother's supervision held the key to whether a child would become a delinquent or not, rather than the presence or absence of a father.

Two other studies of note also analyzed data on samples of male youths and focused on the quality of home life in searching for a meaningful association between family instability and juvenile delinquency. McCord, et al.,[5] compared boys from permanently broken homes and those from united homes. The united homes were divided between those judged as tranquil and those characterized by conflict. The study population included about 200 boys and their families from lower-class, relatively deprived areas in Cambridge and Somerville, Massachusetts. The boys were studied over a five-year period and were between 10 and 15 years of age. When defining delinquency as membership in a delinquent gang, McCord found that there was "little support for the theory that paternal absence led to delinquent gang activities."[6] In fact, there was a significantly higher proportion of gang delinquents among boys whose parents lived together in spite of considerable overt conflict than there was either among boys whose parents had little conflict or among those whose fathers were absent from the home. The study further found that parental absence tended to result in gang delinquency if the absence occurred when the boys were older, suggesting to the authors that the absence was less crucial than the extended time during which the child presumably experienced conflict and hostility between his parents. The percentages designated *delinquent* shifted, however, when actual convictions were used as a measure of antisocial behavior. "Tranquil homes produced a significantly lower proportion of criminals than did the father-absent homes or the conflictful homes."[7]

The authors conclude that the onset of delinquency cannot reasonably be attributed to father absence, but rather to "certain parental characteristics—intense conflict, rejection, and deviance—which occur more commonly in broken families."[8]

---

4. Maccoby, 1958.
5. McCord, *et al.*, 1962.
6. Ibid., p. 367.
7. Ibid., p. 367.
8. Ibid., p. 368.

Of father-absent boys whose mothers and fathers were judged
to be nondeviant (that is, they adhered to the established norms
of society), none had become criminals. Juxtaposed to this result, McCord found that "9 of the 10 father-absent boys whose
mothers were both rejecting and deviant had been convicted for
felonies."[9]

Nye[10] compared selected characteristics, including delinquency companionship and delinquency behavior, of 780 youths
of high school age in the state of Washington. Comparisons were
made between groups of children in the following categories:
happy unbroken families, unhappy but unbroken families, and
several types of broken families. The study concluded that
adolescents in broken homes showed less delinquency behavior
than children from unhappy unbroken homes.

Thus these sample-based studies found some evidence that
broken homes were associated with delinquency, but stressed
the importance of the quality of home life—how appropriately
parents related to each other and to children—as an underlying
causal factor, from which family instability and juvenile delinquency were both outcomes instead of themselves being linked
in a causal relationship. Keeping an unhappy intact family together was no way to improve the home life of children or to
ward off delinquency.

Other authors have used Census and other aggregate data to
explore the socioeconomic determinants of juvenile delinquency.
In an effort to determine whether low income is a cause of delinquency, Fleisher[11] developed an economic model of delinquency which included family structure along with income, unemployment, mobility, race, and region as independent variables. He applied the model to three different data samples: (1)
74 subdivisions of the city of Chicago, (2) 45 Cook County
suburbs of Chicago with populations over 10,000, and (3) 101
U.S. cities with populations over 25,000. His dependent variable
for samples (1) and (2) was the annual average number of court
appearances during the years 1958-1961 of males, aged 12
through 16, per thousand males in the population of that age.
For sample (3), the dependent variable was the annual average
number of arrests during 1960-1962 of males, aged less than 25
years, per thousand males of that age.

---

9. Ibid., fn 14, p. 368.
10. Nye, 1957.
11. Fleisher, 1966b.

As his family structure variable, Fleisher used the proportion of females over 14 years of age in the locality who were separated or divorced, which he took to represent the proportion of broken families in the community. This, of course, is a crude measure, in that it includes some childless women and excludes families where break-up has already been followed by remarriage or where the female head has never married. These are sizable numbers of people, but their inclusion or exclusion need not harm the analysis if they are distributed across sample communities in ways which are not correlated with other variables in the analysis.

He gave three arguments on how family structure might influence delinquency: (1) female heads will probably have to work and will thus have less time for supervision of children; (2) fatherless boys are deprived of the opportunity to observe their father's connection with the economic system and thus find it difficult to develop the long time-horizon needed to appreciate legitimate activity; and (3) attitudes of broken families are oriented less toward legitimate behavior and more toward delinquent behavior. Fleisher did not attribute these arguments to anyone in particular, and made no effort to document their correctness.

His results as to the independent effect of family structure on delinquency are inconsistent. Regression analysis for the 101 city sample showed family structure as the most important explanatory variable in the model. Its measured effect on juvenile delinquency was larger than that of any other variable (a one percent increase in the proportion of separated and divorced women led to a one percent increase in the proportion of males under 25 arrested for crimes against property) and was highly significant statistically. However, the size of the effect was smaller for males under 17, although still significant; it became insignificant when the dependent variable was proportion of males under 25 arrested for crimes of violence. Furthermore, the family structure variable was always insignificant in regressions using the Chicago and Chicago suburbs samples and in some cases had the wrong sign (more separated and divorced women associated with lower delinquency).

Fleisher concluded that "the erratic behavior of the family structure variable is not strong evidence of its appropriateness in the regressions"[12] but that the model nonetheless gave rea-

12. Ibid., p. 133.

sonable estimates of the effect of economic conditions. Picking
the regression showing the highest income effect, and throwing
in a number of free-hand adjustments for income effects operating through the stabilization of families, he decided that "a 10
percent rise in income may be expected to reduce delinquency
rates by between 15 and 20 percent when the income occurs in
highly delinquent areas and is of the type that will reduce the
number of broken families as well." [13]

In a 1967 paper, Willie [14] used Census data and Juvenile
Court statistics for Washington, D.C., to address the relative
contribution of family status and economic status to juvenile
delinquency. From among 1960 Census tracts in the District, he
took those which were predominantly (two-thirds or more)
white and predominantly nonwhite and ranked them as to economic status (a composite index based on occupation and education of adults, and soundness and value of housing units) and
family status (the percent of children not living with both
parents). The economic status variable took on two levels (affluent and poor) and the family status variable two levels (few
broken homes and many broken homes). For each racial group
separately, he calculated a mean juvenile delinquency rate for
Census tracts cross-classified by economic status and family
status. The delinquency rates were average annual numbers of
youths from each Census area referred to the District of Columbia Juvenile Court for other than traffic offenses or dependency
during a 33-month period between 1959 and 1962, per 1,000
persons aged 10-17 living in those areas according to the 1960
Census. The results are shown in table 30.

Table 30
JUVENILE DELINQUENCY RATE PER 1,000 YOUTHS[15]

	Few Broken Homes		Many Broken Homes	
Nonwhites				
affluent	19.7	(6)*	20.9	(2)
poor	26.5	(5)	42.4	(38)
Whites				
affluent	10.6	(32)	30.4	(4)
poor	19.6	(4)	44.3	(1)

*   Numbers in parentheses show numbers of Census tracts in each cell.

---

13. Ibid., p. 135.
14. Willie, 1967.
15. Ibid., pp. 331 and 332.

It appears that juvenile delinquency decreases with increased income and with increased family stability for both nonwhites and whites. However, there is no way of telling from the reported data whether any of these differences by race, by family status, or by economic status are significant. Some of them very likely are and some surely are not, but failure to provide information on which ones are significant makes interpretation difficult.

Willie concluded that the most and least favorable combinations of family and economic status were the same for blacks and whites and produced similar delinqency consequences for the two groups. Affluence and few broken homes led to low delinquency rates for both groups. However "in between these most and least favorable circumstances, whites were more affected by family composition while nonwhites were more affected by economic circumstances." [16] He drew this conclusion from the fact that the measured delinquency rate dropped more with increasing family stability than with increasing economic status for whites, and vice versa for nonwhites. While stating that "because of the kinds of data and methods used in this analysis, these differential effects cannot be stated with certainty," [17] he went on to speculate that nonwhites would be able to deal with the family instability source of juvenile delinquency only after their economic status had improved considerably. From his data, it is not clear that affluence will buy as much family stability for nonwhites as for whites, at least in the short run, and it is the family stability that accompanies affluence which most forcefully reduces the delinquency rate for whites. However, once nonwhites have achieved affluence, they do not gain much in terms of lower delinquency from family stability, so affluence, regardless of how it is translated into family stability, is the key to reduced juvenile delinquency for nonwhites. Thus, with the caveat that none of the reported differences may be significant, Willie's final policy conclusion—that juvenile delinquency in large urban minority populations should be attacked by increasing the economic status of these populations—seems correct.

School Achievement.   Another indicator often used to weigh the effect of father absence is the level of school performance or intellectual ability demonstrated by children whose fathers are

16. Ibid., p. 333.
17. Ibid., p. 333.

absent compared to those whose fathers are present. The validity of IQ tests has been questioned in dealing with poor and black children, the group in which the proportion of father absent families is highest. However, although absolute test readings may be questionable for this population, the relative scores between groups of children within the population who differ only by the presence or absence of a father may give us some insight into the possible negative consequences of father absence for children. Furthermore, performance in a school setting may in many cases be a good proxy measure for adjustment in society. We review below the findings of nine studies, selected because they span a wide range of research addressing the issue of association between father absence and school performance.

The often-discussed Equal Opportunity Survey, or Coleman Report[18] tried to relate resource inputs into schools to school outputs as measured by student scores on standardized achievement tests. The results emphasized the strong association between pupil achievement and socioeconomic background. Student achievement also was found to be strongly related to the educational backgrounds and aspirations of other students in the school. Subsequent analysis of the Coleman report results by Hanushek[19] suggests that father absence per se was not associated with school performance. That is, when control for family socioeconomic status was introduced, the father's absence was not significantly related to test scores. Another re-analysis by Tabler[20] found that father-absent children did more poorly than father-present children but that the difference vanished when a control for race was introduced.

A more refined effort to control for economic levels was made by Deutsch and Brown.[21] They studied the intelligence test scores of 543 urban public school students stratified by race (white, Negro), grade level (first and fifth grades) and socioeconomic status (three levels). They found that IQ scores did not differ significantly between grade levels but did differ very significantly between races and socioeconomic status (SES) levels. The pattern they found was that Negro children at each SES level scored lower than white children and that scores increased for both racial groups as SES increased, but less for Negroes than for whites, so that Negro-white differences in-

18. Coleman, 1966.
19. Hanushek, 1972.
20. Tabler, et al., 1968.
21. Deutsch and Brown, 1964.

creased as SES rose. They hypothesized that race becomes more important in reducing test scores as SES rises because blacks and whites are both effectively limited by lower-class status but blacks are unable to convert higher SES into equal participation with whites in the social mainstream.

They went on to explore social background data to address this hypothesis of differential participation. Looking at the two lowest SES groups, they observed that children coming from fatherless homes scored significantly lower than children from intact homes. However, after controlling for race, grade level, and SES, they found that father absence did not have a significant effect on test scores. Nevertheless, observing that father absence was associated with lower (albeit not significantly lower) scores for Negro children of both sexes, in both grades, and in every SES classification but one, they termed this a pattern worthy of attention. They further noted that test scores deteriorated between first and fifth grade for virtually every sex, SES, and father-presence category, and even though, again, these differences were not significant and occurred for both the father-present and father-absent groups, the authors speculated that they might be tapping the effect of cumulative fatherless years in these declining scores. Alternatively they raised the possibility that tests at the fifth grade level might call more for responses which relied on verbal interaction experienced in an intact family setting. All these speculations about the effects of family structure are seriously undermined by the lack of statistically significant supporting results.

The authors continued with an analysis of the effects of preschool experience on student test scores and concluded: "The present data on family cohesion and preschool experience represent two possible environmental modifiers of intelligence test performance that would seem to account for a portion of differences found between ethnic, class or experiential groups. If these are influential variables, a positive implication is that they are amenable to social intervention and change."[22] The mechanism for intervening in family cohesion is not laid out, and the question whether the family cohesion variable is influent or not is still very much open following their research.

In a separate effort, Deutsch[23] studied approximately 400 students in grades 4, 5, and 6 in two urban schools—one 99

22. Ibid., p. 34.
23. Deutsch, 1960.

percent black, which he called the experimental group, and one 94 percent white but of approximately comparable socioeconomic make-up, which he called the control group. In the experimental group, 55 percent of the students came from broken homes, while in the control group 9 percent did. Overall, children in the experimental group did worse on achievement tests than children in the control group, but this was true when the analysis was confined to children in both groups who came from intact families, and the author concluded that broken homes were not the basic determinant of lower test scores for the experimental group.

Looking at differences by family status for children within the experimental group, Deutsch found that the responses of children from broken homes were not more negative with respect to self-image or family atmosphere, but that they did score significantly lower on general, reading, and mathematics achievement tests. After doing a cluster analysis of factors potentially associated with reduced test scores, he concluded that specific deprivations—such as broken homes—do contribute to poor school performance, but that they are only a modest part of the total negative influences on deprived children and that it is "objective social conditions which are associated with poor school achievement, rather than the more specific individual and familial factors, although these last, in turn, are of course influenced by the objective life conditions." [24]

Two further studies looked at preschool children. Hess, et al.,[25] found little difference in the intellectual capacity of four-year-old children who lived with their fathers and those who did not. Looking at a group of 60 preschool low-income black children, Mackie [26] found that those children from families with a father present did better on IQ tests than those from father-absent homes. Although all children were from black low-income homes, those with fathers present had twice the per capita income of those in father-absent homes. Mackie nevertheless concluded that the effect of father absence was greater than could be accounted for by the difference in income.

Mackler [27] studied lower-class children from Harlem and classified them as failing, average, or successful in their school performance. His data on father presence or absence in the

24. Ibid., p. 18.
25. Hess, et al., 1968.
26. Mackie, et al., 1967.
27. Mackler, 1969.

home showed no significant differences between the three performance rankings. Of those failing, 27 percent had absent
fathers; 22 percent of the average students were without fathers;
and 20 percent of the successful students' fathers were not
present. Although the number of children in this study was
small, the direction of the percentages was toward lower
achievement with father absence. Mackler did not conclude that
father absence was critical since in both white and Negro homes
he found the father either weak or unimportant for the children
who achieved in school. Through interviews accompanying
these data, Mackler judged that what counted in achievement
was the "real quality of home life"—the ways in which the parent or parents expressed their concerns over children's performance.

Kriesberg cited a number of studies giving evidence that
children in fatherless families "have lower IQs, are retarded in
school, and complete fewer years of study than do children of
complete families."[28] He then cited another group of studies
where the evidence was either equivocal or showed no difference
between children in father-absent and father-present homes.

Against this mixed background, he looked at the concern
which women with and without husbands exhibited toward
their children's educational achievement. He concluded that
among married mothers, aspirations were related to income
variables, with the lower-income levels expecting less from
their children. In fatherless families, mothers were generally
more, rather than less, concerned about the educational achievement of their children. Husbandless mothers did not relax the
"pressure for academic achievement when married mothers
might."[29] Kriesberg suggested that perhaps these mothers clung
to what they felt they could influence and urged their children
on to greater academic achievement.

Russell[30] studied 174 children from broken and intact
homes, matched by age, sex, race, and intelligence. In addition,
insofar as could be determined, he included only those intact
homes where there was no parental strife. The incidence of
educational retardation between the broken and intact groups
was not significant. However, he found that children of homes
broken by death were more likely to have academic problems

28. Kriesberg, 1967, p. 288.
29. Ibid., p. 288.
30. Russell, 1967.

than those children whose homes were broken by divorce or separation.

Looking at school achievement as measured by the number of school years completed, Duncan[31] found modest differences between males who had grown up in an intact family and those who had not. In multiple regressions explaining the additional years of school completed, the net effects of family stability (after allowing for the education and occupation of the head of the family of origin and for the number of siblings in that family) are as shown in table 31.

Table 31

ADDITIONAL YEARS OF SCHOOL
ATTRIBUTABLE TO GROWING UP IN AN INTACT FAMILY[32]

Age	All races	White	Nonwhite
27-36	0.7	0.7	0.8
37-46	0.7	0.6	0.7
47-61	1.1	1.2	0.4

Growing up in an intact family increased school years by between .6 and 1.2 years for whites and between .4 and .8 years for nonwhites, with the greatest effects occurring for older age groups among whites and for younger age groups among non-whites. Whether these differences are significant or not is not clear, but Duncan, Featherman, and Duncan in a later publication indicate that "it is difficult to distinguish true changes from sampling and other errors in this analysis."[33]

Data for the analysis came from a special supplement, "Occupational Changes in a Generation," to the March 1962 Current Population Survey and pertained to noninstitutional males aged 25 to 64 of native nonfarm background. Growing up in an intact family meant living with both parents most of the time until age 16. In a later section, we will come back to further steps in their analysis which trace the effects of this possible educational impairment on the adult socioeconomic status of men raised in female-headed families.

We have briefly summarized nine studies looking at academic achievement, measured in different ways, as it has or has

31. Duncan, 1967.
32. Duncan, et al., 1972, p. 64.
33. Ibid., p. 64.

not been found to be associated with father absence. The findings are clearly mixed. Our impression, and that of many of the researchers whose work has been reviewed, is that if there is an association between school performance and father absence, the explanation must go beyond the mere fact of the father's absence and consider elements in the general quality of the children's home life, including adult interaction with children and attitudes toward children's success in school. In addition, careful and refined measures of socioeconomic class need to be developed before interpretations of the findings can proceed with any confidence—and, of course, appropriate school achievement test materials must be used.

Occupational Achievement and Later Family Stability. Both occupational achievement and later family stability may be partly the consequence of childhood experiences. If individuals who grow up in female-headed families are found to suffer a loss in adult socioeconomic status relative to individuals from intact homes, they may be considered disadvantaged by their childhood experience in a broken home. If they in turn form unstable marriages as adults, this could also be considered a disadvantage, although the basis for such a judgment is much less clear than in the case of lower socioeconomic achievement.

Using the Occupational Changes in a Generation data mentioned earlier, Duncan and Duncan [34] determined that the mean socioeconomic status of occupations currently or most recently held by men from intact family backgrounds was "slightly higher" [35] than that of occupations held by men from families headed by women. The mean socioeconomic status scores of those occupations for men currently married and living with their wives are seen in table 32.

Table 32

MEAN SOCIOECONOMIC STATUS SCORES [36]

Family Background	Negro	Non-Negro
All	20.00	44.20
Both parents	21.80	45.12
Female head	17.93	40.28

34. Duncan and Duncan, 1969.
35. Ibid., p. 276.
36. Ibid., p. 277.

The lower scores for men from female-headed families were due partly to fewer years of schooling (reported above, p. 144) and partly to an impaired ability to translate formal education into occupational achievement. Both of these effects were modest, as was the total differential shown above. The significance of the differences was not reported by the authors, although in the one case where a calculation of significance from tabular data was possible (ability to translate education into occupational achievement), the difference between men of different family backgrounds was significant. An extra year of schooling resulted in 1.6 more occupational status points for Negro men from intact families than for Negro men from broken families, and .9 more points for whites. These are small numbers, especially when compared to the status differences caused by race, independent of family structure. In table 32, an intact family background adds 3.87 status points to Negro males' occupational achievement, but such males still suffer a 23.32 status point disadvantage relative to white men from intact families.

In their 1969 article, the Duncans placed considerable weight on these family background differences, saying that "For Negroes as for non-Negroes . . . the indication that an intact family background facilitates occupational success is quite compelling" and that "efforts directed to maintenance of family units which include a man and his wife cannot be dismissed as misguided." [37]

However, in their book, Duncan, Featherman, and Duncan[38] interpret these results in a somewhat different light. "Rearing in a broken family (headed by a female) is somewhat unfavorable for occupational achievement for both blacks and whites. Contrary to the import of some discussion on this topic, however, family stability is not a major factor in the explanation of racial differences in occupational success. Comparatively, number of siblings is more important than stability of the family of origin in accounting for occupational achievement. However, color alone is the major source of differences in the educational, occupational, and economic achievements of the races, overshadowing in import the color differentials in family size and stability." [39] They conclude that "efforts directed solely to

37. Ibid., p. 285.
38. Duncan, et al., 1972.
39. Ibid., p. 67.

the strengthening of family structure are likely to have substantially less impact on the equalization of racial socioeconomic differentials than efforts applied to the elimination of racial discrimination." [40]

A further aspect of Duncan and Duncan's 1969 analysis bears reporting. In regressions explaining men's current occupational status as a function of background characteristics, having had a female head who worked undid much of the damage in current status attributable to growing up in a female-headed family. In fact, for Negroes, a working female head resulted in status scores for men from those families higher than the mean score for all men who grew up in intact families. "If the figures can be believed," as the authors put it,[41] this might support hypotheses of the positive effects on children of extra money in the family, of having an adult role model who is attached to the labor force, or of having a female parent who has learned to cope successfully with single-parent status.

Finally, in a separate tabulation, Duncan and Duncan address the issue, whether family instability is transmitted from one generation to another. Arraying the current marital status and family background of their usual population—noninstitutional males, age 25 to 64, of native nonfarm background, they get the results presented in table 33.

Table 33

MARITAL STATUS BY RACE AND FAMILY BACKGROUND [42]

Race and Family Background	Percent Never Married	Percent Ever Married Spouse Present	Other
Negro — All	11.7	72.7	15.6
Both parents	13.2	70.8	16.0
Female head	11.5	73.3	15.2
Non-Negro — All	9.5	85.7	4.9
Both parents	9.7	85.3	5.0
Female head	9.6	86.7	3.7

They ask the question "Does the experience of growing up in a broken family increase the probability that a man will be found

---

40. Ibid., p. 68.
41. Duncan and Duncan, 1969, p. 284.
42. Ibid., p. 275.

unmarried or living apart from his wife in adulthood?"[43] and answer it *no*. For both non-Negroes and Negroes, having a female-headed family background does not reduce the likelihood that a man will be currently married and living with his wife (column 2: percent ever married, spouse present).

There are two points to be made about this study. The first is that the measure of family stability being used here includes never married men as implicitly unstable and, more importantly, considers only the stability of the current or most recent marriage rather than the stability of all marriages to date. The authors point out that it is impossible to determine stability of the latter sort with their data, but this is an important gap. The current marital status of a population is not generally a good measure of the stability of families within that population. Further, to compare the family stability of two populations by contrasting their current marital status can be misleading. For example, Cutright's[44] tabulation of 1960 Census data for ever-married nonwidowed males of age 45 to 54 showed that 87 percent of nonwhites and 96 percent of whites were currently living with a wife, a racial difference of nine percentage points. However, the proportion of ever-married males of age 45 to 54 who were living with their first wife—i.e., who had never been involved in family breakup—was 56 percent for nonwhites and 78 percent for whites, a racial difference of 22 percentage points. The use of "current marital status" might similarly understate the true difference in family stability associated with growing up in broken versus intact families. It might be argued that, for some purposes, current marital status is a preferred measure of family stability, but that does not seem to be appropriate where conclusions are to be drawn about the intergenerational transmission of family instability. On the other hand, the stability of family of origin in this analysis is so defined that families which were female-headed for as long as eight years while male respondents were growing up in them could be counted as stable. It is clear that getting a consistent definition of stability for intergenerational comparisons is not a simple task, especially given the limitations of generally available statistics.

The second point is that the data presented in this study show a consistent pattern of higher marital stability, as defined by the authors, for men from female-headed families, but they

---

43. Ibid., p. 275.
44. Cutright, 1971.

do not choose to comment on this, confining themselves to the statement that broken family background is not associated with higher instability. It is not likely that the differences are significant and that some important finding is being overlooked here. But given the authors' willingness to cite small differences elsewhere in the text and to speculate, sometimes at considerable length, as to their origin and meaning, it is an interesting omission.

Kriesberg[45] compared the performance of adult males in the population at large with the performance of the now adult sons of families who had received Aid to Families with Dependent Children (AFDC)—the latter families being female-headed. Although the populations obviously are not strictly comparable, he concluded that the matured "sons of ADC families are as likely to have a higher occupational status than their fathers as are males in the population at large,"[46] implying that family form is not a significant contributor to occupational achievement.

Herzog and Sudia[47] reviewed eight studies which examined the question whether growing up in a broken home led to later marital disruption. They concluded that even if the probability of later marital split-up was greater among people from broken homes, there was no way of knowing from these studies whether this was due to the father's absence, to the stress which usually precedes the father's departure, or to other events that occurred after his departure.

CONCLUSIONS

Despite the fragmentary nature of the evidence, there are some important general conclusions to be drawn from the existing literature. The first is that the relationship between single parenthood and child development is so complex—and arises in enough distinctively different situations—that although it can sometimes be detected in aggregate cross-section data, such as the data of Fleisher and Duncan, it cannot generally be isolated in a way that makes the direction of causality clear or clarifies our understanding of the mechanisms at work. For these purposes, panel-type survey data on individual families and children are necessary—although, as the foregoing review suggests, they

45. Kriesberg, 1970.
46. Ibid., p. 180.
47. Herzog and Sudia, 1970.

are not necessarily sufficient. Most useful will be interview data which follow family members over time.

The key prerequisite for using panel data to explore successfully the issue of father absence and children's welfare is a carefully developed model of child development with special attention to the independent and joint roles of parents and parent figures. Such a model would specify expected relationships and interrelationships and offer hypotheses on the effect of father absence for empirical testing. No such model presently exists.

The purpose of the model would be to explore causal links rather than simply document associations. We know that family instability is associated with low income and with parental conflict and that both of these are generally poor environments for children. But this does not establish a causal relationship between father absence and child welfare; indeed, it complicates the isolation of such a relationship.

The model would have to recognize the wide range of both the father's and the mother's potential involvement in the rearing of children, rather than focus on simply the presence or absence of one or the other. For example, research reported here [48] and elsewhere [49] has found that the father's participation in the raising of children, particularly young children, is often minimal, implying that loss of his personal attention may not amount to very much directly. Indeed, some analysts, such as Ruth Brandwein, et al.,[50] have speculated that children of female family heads suffer not from father absence but from maternal deprivation, because women who become single parents are forced to spread their energies beyond their prior child-rearing tasks.

In analyzing the consequences for children of separations which have occurred, considerable descriptive information must be obtained for each family in question. Data on race and socioeconomic status are clearly essential. Also important is information on any decline in family income associated with loss of a husband. Other pertinent factual information includes the reasons for family-breakup, the age of a child when single-parent status began, the presence of siblings and father substitutes, the degree of contact with the absent father, and how long the child lives in a single-parent family.

---

48. Mackler, 1969.
49. Brandwein, et al., 1974.
50. Ibid., p. 7.

Effort must also be made to get measures of true family and kinship relations which standard data such as U.S. Census statistics do not provide. The official statistics are developed according to conventions which may not accurately portray relationships between household members, and have no ability to reflect relationships between people in different household units. These latter relationships can often be particularly important for children's well-being—e.g. informal ties with a father who lives nearby and is seen often, with a father who is not nearby but keeps in touch on some regular or irregular basis, or with an absent father's immediate or extended family which accepts the children as part of its network of kinship and mutual assistance. Identifying and determining the effect on children of these relationships are difficult tasks on which little research headway has been made. This is so despite general acknowledgment of the prevalence and significance of informal, not readily visible, kinship ties, especially in the black population.

The dynamic aspects of the situation are also important, as pointed out by Hugh Heclo, *et al.*[51] in a working paper prepared for the HEW Office of Child Development. Children of nonintact families are often shifted around between parents, relatives, foster homes, and other institutions, although the frequency with which such children live consistently with their mothers has been rising steadily for several decades.[52] The authors also distinguish a transitional period of entry into female-headed status, lasting from two to four years, from a later period of functioning in that status,[53] and they stress the role of uncertainty and expectation as to the duration of single parenthood in the adjustment of both mothers and children. All of these dynamic aspects are essentially unresearched.

But beyond the wealth of objective factual detail looms an issue of even greater significance—the quality of home life. This can be broken down into two major elements—the quality of family functioning before a separation or divorce occurs and the ability of the new family unit, particularly the head, to cope with its new status afterwards. Literature reviewed here—for example, Glueck and Glueck, McCord, *et al.*, Nye, and Mackler [54]

51. Heclo, et al., 1974.

52. Ibid., p. 4.

53. Ibid., p. 23.

54. Glueck and Glueck, 1962; McCord, et al., 1962; Nye, 1957; and Mackler, 1969.

—document the prominence of the quality-of-life variables in children's development. A particularly cogent review of the social, economic, and psychological issues involved in women and children coping with the transition to—and the sustaining of—single-parent family life is given by Robert Weiss in "Single Parent Families: Issues and Policies."[55] Such issues include those connected with the amount of practical hardship to be faced, the self-image of the family members, their psychological attitudes, and the availability of community support.

Although there is fragmentary evidence indicating the importance of the various factors cited above, no research that takes into account all or most of these elements has yet been attempted. This is why clear-cut answers on the effect of father absence on child development are not available and why new research efforts are warranted. A further reason is that the relationships in question are shifting over time, tending to outdate even the best-executed research. Probably the most important shift is the accelerating divorce rate and concomitant growth in female-headed families. What once might have been considered deviant simply by virtue of its rarity has now become commonplace. This has almost certainly changed the character of the people involved in female-headed family units by drawing in a broader cross-section of society. It may also have reduced the psychological strains on those who experience marital dissolution and have increased the level of community acceptance and support somewhat. The growing proportion of female family heads who are not widows has tended to shorten the duration of single-parent status [56] and, on balance, to reduce the income available to single-parent families, because single and separated women have particularly low incomes.[57] Also, it seems plausible that the emotional strains on women and children from marital break-up and illegitimate status could be different from those of losing a husband or father through death, but little systematic exploration of these differences has been done.

Without a better understanding of what contributes to the well-being of children, policy prescriptions are hard to make. We do know that an increasingly familiar pattern for children is marital dissolution while they are fairly young, a transitional

---

55. Heclo, et al., 1974, pp. 17-29.
56. See Appendix I, table 1–I. The duration of female-headed status is approximately the reciprocal of the remarriage rate.
57. Heclo, et al., 1974, p. 13.

period in a female-headed family, and then membership for some period in a new intact family following their mother's remarriage. It seems likely that public policy should be updated to reflect these significant changes in children's living arrangements, but exactly what policy response is called for is not clear. Should efforts at keeping families together be undertaken; efforts to make female-headed family life less isolated and deprived; or efforts to facilitate remarriage and the formation of new husband-wife families? What acceptable, effective policy devices are there to promote any of these objectives?

Given the paucity of evidence that marital mobility and single-parent headship harms children, the genuine social and economic hardships faced by female-headed families, and the general lack of existing policy other than subsistence-level public assistance to deal with their needs, there is a presumption that the pressing policy need is to make life less difficult for female-headed families. Furthermore, some of the policy options in this area—for example, improved day care, social services, and child support arrangements—are better defined and more within the range of accepted public policy than are devices to influence private decisions on marriage and family.

But there is still a tremendous need to know more. And there is an opportunity now to develop the needed knowledge, not as part of a continuing search for pathology in the female-headed family, but in connection with a fast-developing public debate on the general sharing of responsibilities for children both within the private sector and between the public and private sectors. A modest first step is to stop the overstatement of results which has characterized much of the previous literature on father absence and child well-being—an overstatement which has undermined further inquiry by making people think they know much more than they do, and which has undermined public understanding by fostering images of failure and irresponsibility that do not fit the facts today, and perhaps never did.

BIBLIOGRAPHY

Aldous, Joan. "Children's Perceptions of Adult Role Assignment: Father Class, Race and Sex Influences." *Journal of Marriage and the Family*, vol. 34 (February 1972) pp. 55-56.

Bell, Robert R. "The One-Parent Mother in the Negro Lower Class." Paper presented at Eastern Sociological Meeting. New York, April 1965.

Bernard, Sydney. "Fatherless Families: Their Economic and Social Adjustment." *Papers in Social Welfare Number 7.* Waltham: Florence G. Heller Graduate School for Advanced Studies in Social Welfare, Brandeis University, 1964.

Biller, Henry B. "Father Absence and the Personality Development of the Male Child." *Development Psychology,* vol. 2, no. 2 (March 1970), pp. 181-201.

_____. "A Note on Father-Absence and Masculine Development in Young Lower-Class Negro and White Boys." *Child Development,* vol. 39, no. 9, Sept. 1968, pp. 1003-1006.

Billingsley, Andrew, and Giovannoni, Jeanne M. "One Parent Family," pp. 362-73 in Robert Morris, ed., *Encyclopedia of Social Work,* 16th Issue. New York: National Association of Social Workers, vol. 1, 1971.

Brandwein, Ruth A.; Brown, Carol A.; and Fox, Elizabeth Maury. "Women and Children Last: The Social Situation of Divorced Mothers and Their Families." *Journal of Marriage and Family,* Aug. 1974, pp. 498-514.

Burchinal, Lee G. "Characteristics of Adolescents from Unbroken, Broken, and Reconstituted Families." *Journal of Marriage and the Family,* vol. 26, no. 1, Feb. 1964, pp. 44-51.

Carlsmith, Lyn. "Effect of Early Father Absence on Scholastic Aptitude." *Harvard Educational Review,* vol. 34, 1964, pp. 3-21.

Clark, Vincent. *Unmarried Mothers.* New York: Free Press, 1961.

Coleman, James, *et al. Equality of Opportunity.* National Center for Educational Statistics. Washington, D.C.: Government Printing Office, 1966.

Cutright, Phillips. "Income and Family Events: Marital Stability." *Journal of Marriage and The Family,* vol. 33, no. 2, May 1971, pp. 291-306.

Deutsch, Martin. "Minority Group and Class Status as Related to Social and Personality Factors in Scholastic Achievement." *The Society for Applied Anthropology,* Monograph, no. 2. Ithaca, N.Y.: Cornell University, 1960.

Deutsch, Martin, and Brown, Bert. "Social Influences in Negro-White Intelligence Differences." *Journal of Social Issues,* vol. 20, no. 2, April 1964.

Duncan, Beverly. "Family Factors and School Dropout, 1920-1960." Final Report Submitted to the U.S. Office of Education. Ann Arbor: University of Michigan, 1965.

_____. "Education and Social Background." *American Journal of Sociology,* vol. 72, no. 4, January 1967.

Duncan, Beverly, and Duncan, Otis Dudley. "Family Stability and Occupational Success." *Social Problems,* vol. 16, winter 1969.

Duncan, Otis Dudley; Featherman, David L.; and Duncan, Beverly. *Socioeconomic Background and Achievement.* New York: Seminar Press, 1972.

Eisner, Victor. "Effect of Parents in the Home on Juvenile Delinquency." *Public Health Reports,* vol. 81, no. 10, October 1966, pp. 905-910.

Fleisher, Belton M. *The Economics of Delinquency.* Chicago: Quadrangle Books, 1966a.

_____. "The Effect of Income on Delinquency." *American Economic Review,* vol. 56, no. 1, March 1966b, pp. 118-37.

George, Victor, and Wilding, Paul. *Motherless Families.* London: Routledge and Kegan Paul, 1972.

Glasser, Paul, and Navarre, Elizabeth. "Structural Problems of the One-Parent Family." *Journal of Social Issues,* vol. 21, January 1964, pp. 89-109.

_____. "The Problems of Families in the AFDC Program." *Children,* vol. 12, no. 4, July-August 1965, pp. 151-56.

Glueck, Sheldon, and Glueck, Eleanor. *Delinquents and Nondelinquents in Perspective.* Cambridge: Harvard University Press, 1968.

_____. *Unraveling Juvenile Delinquency.* New York: The Commonwealth Fund, 1950, Cambridge, Mass.: Harvard University Press, 1951.

_____. *Family Environment and Delinquency.* Boston: Houghton Mifflin, 1962.

Gregory, Ian. "Anterospective Data Following Childhood Loss of a Parent., I. Delinquency and High School Dropout." *Archives of General Psychiatry,* vol. 13, no. 2, August 1965, pp. 99-109.

_____. "Anterospective Data Following Childhood Loss of a Parent., II. Pathology, Performance and Potential among College Students." *Archives of General Psychiatry,* vol. 13, no. 2, Aug. 1965, pp. 110-20.

Hanushek, Eric. *Education and Race.* Lexington, Mass.: D. C. Heath, 1972.

Hansen, Donald A., and Hill, Reuben. "Families Under Stress." In Harold T. Christensen, ed., *Handbook of Marriage and the Family.* Chicago: Rand McNally, 1964.

Heclo, Hugh; Rainwater, Lee; Rein, Martin; and Weiss, Robert. "Single-Parent Families, Issues and Policies." Unpublished draft manuscript, 1974.

Herzog, Elizabeth, and Sudia, Cecelia E. "Fatherless Homes." *Children,* Sept.-Oct. 1968, pp. 177-82.

_____. "Family Structure and Composition." In R. R. Miller (ed.), *Race, Research and Reason: Social Work Perspectives.* New York: National Association of Social Workers, 1969, pp. 145-64.

_____. *Boys in Fatherless Families.* Office of Child Development, Children's Bureau, U.S. Department of Health, Education and Welfare. Washington, D.C.: 1970.

Hess, Robert D.; Shipment, Virginia C.; Brophy, Jere E.; and Bear, Roberta Meyer. *The Cognitive Environments of Urban Preschool Children.* The Graduate School of Education, University of Chicago, November 1968.

Hetherington, E. Mavis. "Effects of Paternal Absence on Sex-Typed Behaviors in Negro and White Preadolescent Males." *Journal of Personality and Social Psychology,* vol. 4, no. 1, July 1966, pp. 87-91.

_____. "Girls Without Fathers." *Psychology Today.* Feb. 1973.

Hetherington, E. Mavis, and Deur, Jan I. "The Effects of Father Absence on Child Development." *Young Children,* March 1971, pp. 233-48.

Jacobsen, Gary, and Ryder, Robert G. "Parental Loss and Some Characteristcs of the Early Marriage Relationship." *American Journal of Orthopsychiatry,* vol. 39, no. 5, Oct. 1969, pp. 779-87.

Kadushin, Alfred. "Single Parent Adoptions—An Overview and Some Relevant Research." *Child Welfare,* 1969.

Koch, Margaret Body. "Anxiety in Preschool Children from Broken Homes." *Merrill-Palmer Quarterly,* vol. 7, no. 4, Oct. 1961, pp. 225-31.

Kotelchuck, Milton. "The Nature of the Child's Tie to His Father." Unpublished Doctoral Dissertation. Cambridge: Harvard University, 1972.

Kriesberg, Louis. "Rearing Children for Educational Achievement in Fatherless Families." *Journal of Marriage and the Family,* vol. 2, no. 2, May 1967, pp. 288-301.

_____. *Mothers in Poverty.* Chicago: Aldine, 1970.

Landis, Judson. "The Trauma of Children When Parents Divorce." *Marriage and Family Living,* vol. 22, Feb. 1960, pp. 7-13.

_____. "A Comparison of Children from Divorced and Non-divorced Unhappy Marriages." *Family Life Co-ordinator,* vol. 2, July 1962, pp. 61-65.

Lewis, R. L. "The Unmarried Parent and Community Resources." *Child Welfare*, vol. 47, Nov. 1968, pp. 487-614.

Maccoby, Eleanor E. "Effects upon Children of Their Mothers' Outside Employment." In National Manpower Council, *Work in the Lives of Married Women*. New York: Columbia University Press, 1958.

Mackie, James B.; Maxwell, Anabel D.; and Rafferty, Frank T. "Psychological Development of Culturally Disadvantaged Negro Kindergarten Children: A Study of the Selective Influence of Family and School Variables." Draft of paper presented at American Orthopsychiatric Association Meeting, March 1967.

Mackler, Bernard. "The Little Black School House." Report prepared for the U.S. Department of Health, Education and Welfare, 1971.

McCord, Joan; McCord, William, and Thurber, Emily. "Some Effects of Paternal Absence on Male Children." *Journal of Abnormal and Social Psychology*, vol. 64, no. 5, March 1962, pp. 361-69.

Marsden, Dennis. *Mothers Alone: Poverty and the Fatherless Family*. London: Penguin, 1969.

Nye, F. Ivan. "Child Adjustment in Broken and in Unhappy Homes." *Marriage and Family Living*, vol. 19, no. 4, Nov. 1957, pp. 356-61.

Pollack, Otto. "The Broken Family." In Nathan E. Cohen, ed., *Social Work and Social Problems*. New York: National Association of Social Workers, 1964.

Rose, Lawrence. "The Broken Home and Male Delinquency." In M. Wolfgang, N. Johnson and L. Savitz, eds., *The Sociology of Crime and Delinquency*, pp. 489-95. New York: John Wiley, 1970.

Russell, Ivan L. "Behavior Patterns of Children from Broken and Intact Homes." *Journal of Educational Sociology*. Nov. 1967, pp. 124-29.

Schlessinger, Benjamin. *The One-Parent Family: Perspectives and Annotated Bibliography*. Toronto: University of Toronto Press, 1969.

Siegman, Aron Wolfe. "Father Absence During Early Childhood and Antisocial Behavior." *Journal of Abnormal Psychology*, vol. 71, 1966, pp. 71-74.

Slocum, Walter L., and Stone, Carol L. "Family Culture Patterns and Delinquent Type Behavior." *Marriage and Family Living*, vol. 25, no. 2, May 1963, pp. 202-208.

Sprey, Jetse. "The Study of Single Parenthood: Methodological Considerations." *Family Life Coordinator*, vol. 16, nos. 1 and 2, Jan. and April 1967.

Tabler, Kenneth A.; Hixson, Eugene E.; and Collins, Elmer F. "Elementary and Secondary Student Characteristics." Analytic Note no. 81. Washington, D.C.: National Center for Educational Statistics, Office of Education, March 1968.

Tennyson, Ray. "Family Structure and Delinquent Behavior." In *Juvenile Gangs in Context: Theory, Research and Action*, ed. Malcolm Klein. Englewood Cliffs, N.J.: Prentice-Hall, 1967.

Thomes, Mary Margaret. "Children with Absent Fathers," *Journal of Marriage and Family*, Feb. 1968, pp. 89-96.

Trunnel, Thomas L. "The Absent Father's Children's Emotional Disturbances." *Archives of General Psychiatry*, vol. 19, Aug. 1969, pp. 180-88.

Walters, James, and Stinnett, Nick. "Parent-Child Relationships: A Decade Review of Research." In Carlfred B. Broderick, ed., *A Decade of Family Research and Action, 1960-1969*. Minneapolis: National Council on Family Relations, 1971.

Weiss, Robert S. "The Contributions of an Organization of Single Parents to the Well-Being of Its Members." *The Family Coordinator*, July 1973, pp. 321-26.

Welfare in Review. "Juvenile Court Cases in 1963." Vol. 3, no. 5, May 1965.

Westman, Jack C.; Cline, David W.; Swift, William J.; and Kramer, Douglas A. "The Role of Child Psychiatry in Divorce." *Archives of General Psychiatry,* vol. 23, Nov. 1970, pp. 416-20.

Willie, Charles V. "The Relative Contribution of Family Status and Economic Status in Juvenile Delinquency." *Social Problems,* vol. 14, no. 3, winter 1967, pp. 326-34.

Wynn, Margaret. *Fatherless Families.* London: Michael Joseph, 1964.

Chapter 7

THE FAMILY IN TRANSITION

We have seen that, for most women, single parenthood is a "time of transition" between living in one nuclear family and another, that the prevalence of female-headed families cannot be viewed as a rejection of marriage or family living on the part of the individuals involved. Yet, at a more aggregate level, mushrooming divorce rates, an increasing number of out-of-wedlock births, a rising age at first marriage, and a declining birth rate are all indicators of the kinds of change that call for further explanation. Thus, one is quite naturally led to inquire whether social institutions and values themselves are going through a "time of transition," and if so, why?

This chapter is devoted to such an inquiry. It begins with a summary of the findings from previous chapters and then moves on to consider the larger social and historical context in which recent changes might be viewed, as well as their possible implications for the future. It concludes with a discussion of policy actions which our work suggests are appropriate responses to the growth of female-headed families. This is a much more speculative chapter than its predecessors and is infused with some ideological currents which seem to us to be the sustaining, if not the driving, force behind much that is new and which cast a more interesting and coherent light on the meaning of these events.

A SUMMING UP

In the preceding chapters, the purpose has been to trace the growth and changing composition of single-parent families, most of which are headed by women; to sort out both the immediate and underlying causes of this growth; and to review the evidence on what happens to children who grow up in these families. What has been learned thus far?

In chapter 2, we found that over the past decade the number of families headed by a mother increased almost ten times as rapidly as the number of two-parent families, with the result that the proportion of all families headed by a mother now stands at 15 percent, up from 9 percent in 1960. The growth of such families has been substantial among all segments of the population although it has been particularly pronounced among younger women and among those who are black.

As dramatic as this numerical growth has been, it seriously underestimates the number of women who have experienced headship status during this period, for it represents only the net excess of newly formed female-headed families over those who have left this status through marriage, remarriage, or children leaving home. For most women and their children, living outside a traditional family is a transitional rather than a permanent state, an experience which typically lasts no more than 5 or 6 years. Thus, the major contribution of chapter 2 was to measure the size and composition of the flows into and out of single parenthood and to provide some indication of the dynamics and the duration of this experience.

One important conclusion which emerged from this analysis was that rising divorce rates are the major cause of the observed increase in female-headed families. Rising illegitimacy rates among teenagers, and a greater tendency for women to establish independent households rather than live with relatives, have also played a role, but it is the increasing number of divorced and separated women with young children which accounts for the greatest share of the growth. The probability of divorcing after, say, 6 to 9 years of marriage has more than doubled in the postwar period, with the result that almost one out of every three marriages among younger couples is predicted to end in divorce. This finding led to the decision to explore the underlying causes of marital instability in greater detail in chapter 3.

Chapter 3's review of the literature on divorce revealed a certain empirical regularity in previous research findings but little in the way of either a consistent framework to guide further analysis or a commonly accepted interpretation of existing results. Some attempt to deal with these lacunae in an eclectic and interdisciplinary manner led us to emphasize both declining role specialization and growing role conflict within marriage as possible reasons for rising instability. Add to this the growing social acceptance of divorce (and the lower tolerance for unhappy marriage, which is undoubtedly its correlate) and one has at least a plausible explanation of recent trends. This should not be interpreted to mean that there has been a rejection of marriage as a life style. Rather, our contention is that the social and economic constraints which may have once inhibited the dissolution of a less-than-satisfactory marriage operate less strongly now than was true in the past. Empirical validation of this thesis has proved difficult, and further work on the subject is continuing. To date, the most significant finding to emerge from the analysis of a national sample of about 2500 families whose marital behavior and other characteristics were monitored for 5 years is that two important predictors of marital instability are employment problems for the husband and the availability of alternative means of support for the wife in the form of her own earnings. Unlike previous studies on this topic, we did not find a positive correlation between family income and family stability. In fact, high-income families, or those in which the husband was highly successful, appeared to be more unstable than those with moderate incomes. Couples who marry young, who have few assets, who live in the West or in large cities and who attend church infrequently are also more likely to divorce.

Chapter 4's discussion of race and family structure dealt with some of the factors which may account for a disproportionately high and continually growing rate of female headedness in the black community. Relatively high rates of illegitimacy among black teenagers and relatively low remarriage rates among black women generally contribute to this situation, but marital disruption (typically separation rather than divorce) is the primary reason for a higher incidence of single parenthood among black women. Greater marital instability among blacks than among whites is, in turn, related to differences in socioeconomic status.

Although previous research has not been able to show that all of the white-nonwhite difference in marital instability is related to the greater economic and social deprivation of black families, in our analysis of the Michigan data we found that black families were generally as stable as white families with the same economic and demographic characteristics. Explaining the continued high growth rates of female heads in the black population is more difficult, especially in the light of this last finding, but we speculate that it may be due to the continued urbanization of this group, rising illegitimacy rates among teenagers, high unemployment and underemployment among the youngest and least well-educated black men, and perhaps the more rapid economic gains of black women relative to black men in recent years, especially among those with the least education.

The question raised in chapter 5 is whether or not the current welfare system contributes to the growth of female-headed families. A critical review of the literature on this topic, along with several new pieces of research, indicates that welfare does indeed have an impact on family structure, not so much because it encourages separation but rather because it inhibits remarriage. We could find no evidence that welfare has a measurable influence on separation rates, but the remarriage rates of women on AFDC are much lower than the remarriage rates of other women in similar circumstances, including other poor women. In addition, our analysis suggests that providing additional transfer income to low-income, husband-wife families would help to stabilize their marriages. In combination, these two sets of findings suggest that a broadened income maintenance program which provided benefits to all poor families with children would both increase the remarriage rate and reduce the separation rate. As a result, there would be fewer women heading families than there would be in the absence of such reform.

Our concern with the growth of female-headed families stems from a belief that life is not easy for those who live in such families. We know that many are poor, and that their poverty often necessitates state intervention in the form of income support for the mother and her children. But there remains the question, whether children who live in single-parent homes face problems in addition to the obvious economic ones. In chapter 6, we reviewed a large number of studies dealing with this issue, focusing primarily on the effects which father absence may have on school performance, juvenile delinquency, and the child's later socioeconomic status and family stability as an adult. The evidence on adverse consequences for children is mixed, and the interpretation of this evidence hangs on an understanding of the methodological difficulties encountered. The nature, timing, and duration of a father's absence, the current and past family environment of the child, and the process by which the quantity and quality of parental attention affects child development, all need to be better understood and measured before any sound conclusions can be drawn from research in this area. It is especially critical to keep in mind the less favorable economic position of one-parent families if we are to avoid the error of attributing the effects of poverty to the absence of a parent. It is also essential to remember that the alternative to separation may be a tension-ridden environment for the child. Thus, until the facts are better established, it is our judgment that a healthy skepticism about the putative pathology commonly attributed to "broken homes" is warranted.

DIRECTIONS FOR FURTHER RESEARCH

Thus far our research on female-headed families has not even asked all the relevant questions much less provided all of the answers. Accordingly, this report should be viewed as a way station in continuing work on this topic, a summarizing of what is known to date. In fact, one of the chief values of this effort has been to identify research gaps and to provide some sense of the kinds of analysis useful in advancing our understanding.

Since the value of this work depends in part on its relevance for public policy, it may be useful to begin this discussion by stressing the need to build more careful links between the policy environment extant at any point in time and the costs and benefits of engaging in different sorts of family behavior, including marriage, divorce, remarriage, childbearing, and choice of living arrangements. This means asking who has an incentive to do what under existing legislation, judicial interpretations of that legislation, and current administrative practice. How, for example, have recent Supreme Court rulings relating to the man-in-the-house rule and the financial responsibilities of stepfathers changed the financial consequences of marrying vs. choosing a more informal tie? How frequently, given current administrative practice, does a woman on welfare lose the benefits going to her children once she remarries? What kinds of penalties (negative incentives) do child-support laws impose on parents who fail in their financial responsibility toward their children? How do changes in the tax treatment of married vs.

single individuals shift the costs and benefits of marriage compared to its alternatives?

Knowing something about these incentives, the next task is to estimate their actual impact on people's behavior. In chapter 5, for example, we dealt with the extent to which welfare affects separation and remarriage. But more work needs to be done before we will have confidence that the effects of welfare have been accurately isolated from the effects of other variables. Moreover, because any income maintenance plan affects not only the level of family income, but also the stability and source of that income and its distribution among family members, more thought needs to be given to the process by which income affects marital stability. Does it matter whether income is in the form of earnings, government transfers, or a return on savings or other assets; whether it is husband's income or wife's income; whether it is higher or lower than what one would expect as a member of a certain social class; whether it is temporarily or permanently lower than expected? Without answers to these kinds of questions, it is impossible to judge accurately the impact of various types of welfare reform on family structure.

If policy does elicit and shape behavior, then it would be helpful if one could predict the implications of this behavioral response for the growth and composition of different family types. In chapter 2, we attempted to deal with this question by relating the stock of female-headed families to various demographic events. But a more sophisticated model of the relationship between stocks and flows needs to be developed and given empirical content. Once accomplished, this would provide a tool for judging the relative contribution which various types of demographic change distributed among various subgroups in the population make to the overall growth of female-headed families. It could be, for example, that policies aimed at helping people bring their actual fertility in line with their desired fertility, or policies encouraging remarriage, would have a rather large impact on the number of female-headed families with children, but at present we have no rigorous means of analyzing the relative importance of these different types of change.

Finally, we have given little attention to the consequences of the trends we have been studying for individual welfare. We have noted the economic problems which a large proportion of single-parent families face and have reviewed some of the outcomes for children, but we have not delved into how people cope with this situation in their daily lives, the possible psychological trauma involved, and the need for community support and for specific new initiatives in public policy to deal with the hardships that single-parent families often face.

This completes the summary of previous chapters and an overview of a continuing research agenda in this area. But having assembled the facts and subjected them to some scrutiny, one is left with a great deal of uncertainty about what it all means. Is the growth of female-headed families a mere "blip" in the data, reflecting relatively short-term demographic events, problems associated with the accuracy of reported information on marital status, relatively insignificant changes in living arrangements, and the like? Or, is this growth an indicator of a more fundamental shift in values and behavior, perhaps related to other social trends? To provide some context for answering these questions, we now offer some less guarded speculations about the events we have been describing.

THE FAMILY: PAST, PRESENT, AND FUTURE

In every society there are individuals who are too young, too old, or too incapacitated to engage in significant productive activity and who, to one degree or another, must be supported by the work of others. The relative size of the dependent population varies with economic, demographic, and cultural factors. Casual observation of different societies reveals a good deal of variation with respect to the age at which children are assigned productive tasks, the age at which the elderly retire from the world of work, and the economic contribution expected of women.

Turning to the way in which industrialized societies organize to support their dependent populations, there are essentially three institutions which transfer funds from individuals who work in the market to those who do not: the family, the government, and private philanthropy. The study of these one-way transfers has been called "grants economics" by Kenneth Boulding, and, as he points out, the family is by far the largest donor in the grants system, accounting for $313 billion of transfers in 1970, as compared to $74 billion for the public sector and $20 billion for private charity.

The family stands out as the overwhelmingly important sector of the grants economy. Many of the needs of the public grants economy arise at the point where the family grants economy breaks down, as in the case of female heads of households. A great part of the poverty problem in this country is a result of the failure of the family grants economy. Unless you look at the problem in terms of grants economics, you just don't think this way. The family perhaps isn't as important in the exchange economy and you're apt to miss its significance.[1]

So, in our present culture, families are the major way of resolving the problem of dependency. Children require care and support during their formative years. And most women, as well, have traditionally relied on their position within a family to provide them with economic security. It is not that women are unproductive. In fact, much has been made of the implicit value of a married woman's services as a housewife or mother. But the fact remains that these services can be "bartered" for the necessities of life only within the context of the family so, from a practical point of view, such women are almost as dependent on the paid work of others as are children or other nonproductive individuals. They have little status or bargaining power within an exchange economy. But why has this particular division of labor between husband and wife been so common?

One answer comes from the work of economists whose recent interest in marriage and the family has yielded valuable insights. They emphasize that the family can be viewed as an economic subsystem that uses the paid and unpaid time of productive members to provide both market and home-produced goods and services for all members. Decisions must be made about (1) how to allocate the time of individual family members to a variety of paid and unpaid tasks, and (2) what combination of goods and services should be consumed, with particular importance attached to the choice between market and home-produced commodities.

Given the fact that women tend to be at least as productive as men within the home and that their earnings and job opportunities are less than those of men, an economically rational division of labor between the sexes requires that women specialize in home work and men in market work. Of course, there is a vicious circle here since it is this very specialization that limits the market productivity of women and increases their domestic productivity. Biological and technological constraints which may have once confined women to hearth and home are

---

1. Boulding, 1973.

no longer operative in most industrialized nations, yet their cultural correlates persist. However, as the market opportunities of women improve relative to those of men, this particular division of labor is likely to change, although probably only slowly, given the strength of deeply ingrained attitudes and patterns of behavior.

With respect to the proportion of goods and services produced in the market vs. the home, the choice depends on the relative cost of each—where the cost of home goods includes the value of the time of those individuals producing them. Families with relatively high-earning adult members will tend to minimize the allocation of time to home production. Thus, either a reduction in home-centered activities or a substitution of purchased goods and services will tend to occur where the time of the housewife is highly valuable in alternative occupations and where there are relatively inexpensive market substitutes for her domestic production.

None of this is meant to imply that the family is strictly an economic unit in the narrow sense—that is, pursuing ever higher standards of living by whatever means. Rather the emphasis is on the allocation of time—time which may be devoted to love and leisure, companionship and consumption, as well as to various kinds of productive work both in and out of the home. As the constraints and rewards affecting this allocation shift, so will the character of marriage and the shape of the family. However, it is clear that, at least for the recent past, an important source of the family's stability as an institution has been its more economic or utilitarian functions. Whether one relies on Maslow's argument that there is a hierarchy of needs in which physical survival and economic security are more basic than interpersonal relationships and individual fulfillment, or on the findings of sociologists that utilitarian marriages are more stable than those emphasizing affective values, or on the relationships between family stability and economic variables discussed earlier in this volume—one is inevitably led to the conclusion that the family is, at least in part, an economic unit. As such, it has three distinct functions: production, distribution, and consumption. It may produce goods and services within the household, it may buy them with the paid labor of one or more family members and redistribute them to nonworking members, and it may (even in the absence of redistribution) pool the total resources of its individual members for maximum efficiency or satisfaction in consumption.

Looking at the family over the long sweep of history, it is clear that its economic functions have been both changing in character and diminishing in importance.

In an early preindustrial stage, technology was limited and unchanging, most economic activity took place within the household, and production and distribution were organized by custom and tradition. High mortality rates and low productivity meant that life was short and living conditions were harsh—an existence which was accepted fatalistically. In this type of society the family (although not in its modern home-centered form) played a central role, since economic and social status were defined by birth, family ties, and social custom. Most importantly, the family was a productive unit, and physical strength—typically a male attribute—was an essential element in survival.

In a later, industrial stage of development, new technology and the benefits of specialization caused production to shift from home to factory. Living standards rose, death rates fell, and individuals were more imbued with a sense of control over their environment and their social institutions. Status was determined increasingly by one's position in the market and less and less by membership in a particular family. To some extent, the family itself became a more specialized unit whose major responsibility was the creation and socialization of children. But because it had been stripped of some of its earlier functions, the family was no longer the central institution in society. Declining fertility, the loosening of kinship ties, and the streamlining of the extended family into its present nuclear form may be viewed as adaptations to industrialization. Children are no longer needed to help on the farm or to provide for one's old age. Smaller families are more mobile and less costly for the breadwinner to support. At the same time, as a vestige of an earlier, preindustrial era, the household remains an economically primitive organization and family relationships and roles continue to be somewhat dominated by custom and tradition—examples being the often arbitrary division of tasks between men and women and the continued authority of the male head of household in spite of the diminishing functional importance of specifically-male and specifically-female attributes.

During this stage of development, although there is little market production within the home, the family continues to play a crucial economic role in redistributing resources from one group of individuals (primarily male breadwinners) to another group (primarily market-dependent women and children)—a situation which helps to maintain the superior status of the former vis-à-vis the latter.

The third stage of development is still unfolding and lies mostly in the future. We may speculate that its inception came with the extension of technology to those responsibilities which have remained rooted in the family—especially control over reproduction—and that its fruition will be marked by equality between the sexes, companionate marriages, and families operating largely as consumption (income-pooling) units. Already, contraceptive technique has advanced to the point where decisions about family size and spacing can be controlled and this, together with an emerging concern about overpopulation, appears to be changing values about the desirability of numerous children and about the status of women in society. In other words, population control is possible, is viewed as desirable, and, to be effective, requires new options for women. If this vision of the future is correct, a time will come when women will no longer be "market dependents" and there will be no need to socialize them to perform only their "traditional role." At the same time, men will have been freed from the full burden of family support. Children will still entail costs in both time and money just as do other consumption activities, but there will be fewer of them and they will have been freely chosen for whatever intrinsic satisfactions they bring. The care of children will be a shared activity rather than the exclusive responsibility of women. In this world of the future, the family's major raison d'être will be to meet the expressive or psychological needs of individuals—its more utilitarian functions having been eliminated or transferred to other institutions.

The shift from the productive to the distributive household is now a matter of history and is of interest only because it places recent trends in some perspective. Futurologists have made it fashionable to speculate about a further shift, but it is difficult to substantiate these projections. What is the basis for thinking that the family is in transition?

The present distributive family will become at least partially obsolete if and when (1) fertility declines to the point where a large proportion of families contain few or no children, (2) women's market opportunities increase to the point where the present division of labor has little economic justification, and (3) child care and other household tasks are increasingly turned over to more specialized institutions, or living and working arrangements change the focus of such activities. These would appear to be closely related events. Fertility and a general orientation toward home-centered activities are linked to the alternatives available to women in the market. But a woman's ability and desire to compete effectively in the working world depends on her own and everyone else's expectations about her responsibilities within the home. In the past, this nexus has operated as a vicious circle, constraining women's freedom to choose. In the future, loosened by both technological and ideological developments, the breaking up of this nexus may become a force for cumulative change.

It is clear that women's economic position has been changing rapidly. The proportion of women in the labor force increased from 25 percent in 1950 to 43 percent in 1970. Currently, more than half of married women with school-age children are working, and each cohort of women is spending an increasing proportion of the family life cycle in paid employment. In addition, there is evidence that over the longer run women's earnings have risen relative to men's. Although there was some reversal of this historical trend during the postwar period, it still remains true that far more women are financially independent than ever before because of their increased labor force experience. Along with these labor force trends, we find that younger women are planning much smaller families than in the past, and the fertility rate has dropped from 3.6 children per family in 1961 to about 2.0 ten years later.

Economic research to date suggests that the increased employment of women is largely due to an expansion of job opportunities in predominantly "female occupations" (e.g., white collar work) and that decisions about family size are, in turn, closely related to the market opportunities available to women, which are an important determinant of the "cost" of children. Moreover, as the market earnings of women increase, a demand is created for day care, prepared foods, commercial laundries, and other market substitutes for those services currently provided within the home. It also provides the basis for a reallocation of tasks between men and women, although there is little evidence to date that men are taking on child care and other domestic responsibilities as women enter the world of paid work and this has undoubtedly contributed to the strains which modern marriages face, as suggested in chapter 3.

Although these appear to be the underlying social trends most likely to shape the future character of the family, once set in motion these changes may set up a dynamic and partially self-generating reaction which also needs to be considered. For example, as multiple-earner families become increasingly the norm rather than the exception, two things are likely to happen. First of all, society will adjust to their existence with changes in hours of work, living arrangements, availability of supportive services, attitudes, and the like, making the pattern itself a more attractive one. Second, there will be strong economic pressures on the remaining single-earner families who will find themselves increasingly at a competitive disadvantage in terms of standards of living. It is difficult enough to keep up with the Joneses under normal circumstances but when both of them are working it becomes virtually impossible. In 1974, the median income in younger families with a working wife was $15,000, compared to $12,000 where there was only one earner, in spite of the fact that female participation rates are negatively correlated with husband's income and that women earn only about 60 percent of what men do. In general, it may be that more and more families are discovering that their economic welfare is tied up as much with the ratio of earners to nonearners in the household as with wage levels, and that decisions about family size and employment for the wife allow a good deal of control over the former. This doesn't mean that all families will necessarily forfeit the luxury of children and fulltime homemaking—in fact, affluence could by itself enable an increasing proportion of families to opt for these "luxuries." But it has been shown that people make such decisions on the basis of their *relative* not their absolute income position so that the keeping-up-with-the-Joneses effect can be expected to play an important role. Thus, one might predict that single-earner families will be most prevalent at the top of the income distribution, provided that the relatively well-educated women in these families remain content with their homemaking role—perhaps a dubious assumption. If the latter do insist on working, they will set a social and economic standard for other families which will be difficult to ignore.[2]

In sum, the economic status of women is very much in flux, and the distributive family appears to be slowly becoming obsolete. Women have an increasing number of economic op-

2. See Moore and Sawhill for a more extended discussion of these issues.

tions outside traditional family arrangements, and men, as a result, have fewer economic responsibilities within them. Along with these economic changes—perhaps even partly because of them—cultural norms and personal aspirations appear to have been shifting. What we find then is that people are moving in and out of marriage more freely than in the past because it is less and less bound up with social and economic status and is increasingly a means to personal fulfillment. Rising divorce rates may be viewed as an indicator of rising expectations coupled with greater economic opportunities.

The future of the family will be shaped by how people respond to these changing circumstances. The increase in female-headed families which this book documents and describes appears likely to continue in the near future, and their representation among all families will probably reach new, and permanently higher, levels. The growing independence of women will certainly affect decisions pertaining to marriage, childbearing, and family formation, which will likely result in further growth of female-headed families. However, at some point in the future this growth is likely to level off. Once women have achieved a greater measure of economic independence and family roles and responsibilities have adjusted to these new economic realities, then those husband-wife families which continue to form and endure will be based more on the personal satisfactions they provide and less on economic needs. Thus, although lifelong marriages may be less prevalent than at present, they are likely to entail greater personal happiness for the individuals involved.

The particular patterns of family composition and living arrangements which will emerge as sex role equality and income-pooling families become more prevalent is not clear. It is clear, however, that in the meantime there will be strains and stresses as social institutions attempt to adapt to the changes which are already under way. In all likelihood, there will be, for example, more divorce, and more sexual activity among women who have been liberated from social controls and the double standard but are not yet fully autonomous, and the result of both will be more female-headed families. Many of the women in these families—caught between the old order and the new—will be unable to support themselves and their children, raising difficult questions for public policy. The answers will require sensitivity to the simultaneous existence of traditional and modern attitudes and to the transitional character of both female-headed families and the larger society in which they live. In the next section, we address the question of how public policy might respond to these changes.

NEW DIRECTIONS FOR PUBLIC POLICY

The growth of female-headed families presents a number of challenges to policy. Perhaps the most pressing, and the one to which we have paid most attention in our work, is the problem of inadequate income. We know that most women who become single parents through divorce or widowhood experience a sharp drop in income—a drop which is much greater than that experienced by men in similar circumstances.[3] Many of these women have lived in middle-class circumstances before becoming single parents and many will eventually improve their economic position by acquiring a new spouse.[4] But, in the interim, most remain clustered near the bottom of the income distribution. Of course a great deal of poverty exists independent of these changes in family structure. But female-headed families run an exceptionally high risk of being poor and are currently a majority of poor families with children. The weakening of distributive family ties is occurring before most women are economically strong.

There is a major need, then, to develop opportunities for women to earn an adequate income and to make young women aware of the risks and responsibilities which they are likely to face in their adult years. But in the meantime, there will be a need for other kinds of social support: income maintenance programs which do not unwittingly exacerbate family instability, and private transfers similar to current alimony and child-support payments but placed on a new and more equitable basis. Female-headed families will be major beneficiaries of these policies, but the policies themselves will not be directed solely at these families.

Economic Opportunities for Women. Existing research on the labor market handicaps and discrimination with which women workers must contend[5] strongly suggests that it is the *kinds* of jobs at which women work that are the major cause of their relatively low income. Occupations in which women traditionally work pay much lower wages than occupations in which

3. *Five Thousand American Families,* vol. 4, chap. 2.
4. Ibid., chap. 3.
5. See Sawhill, 1973.

men traditionally work, even after taking into account educational requirements, experience, and other factors. An analysis of Census data [6] shows that women high-school graduates between the ages of 25 and 34 are able to earn enough working full-time to keep a family of three children out of poverty in 80 percent of all "traditionally male occupations" but in only 46 percent of all "traditionally female occupations." Since most women work in these traditionally female occupations, it is not surprising that so many female-headed families are poor. Thus, new policies are needed to insure that women are welcome in traditionally male jobs and that encourage younger women to enter these occupations. Bus drivers earn more than bank tellers, and auto workers do better than elementary school teachers, but women have too often chosen— or been forced to accept—the less well-paid alternative.

Another factor which limits the success of women in the job market is the less continuous attachment to the work force which their family responsibilities necessitate. Here again policy must be sensitive to the transitional nature of sex role expectations within the family. Although women are working in large numbers, men are not as yet sharing in the care of children in any meaningful way, and in 90 percent of all divorce cases, custody is still awarded to the mother. As a result women must often handle two jobs rather than one, putting them at a competitive disadvantage in the labor market. These considerations suggest that day care facilities, after-school programs, or subsidization of informal child care arrangements, which most parents appear to prefer, might help some women to plan for, and engage in, more continuous employment. At the same time, social planners need to bear in mind that no amount of day care is likely to improve the economic status of women if there are no decent jobs available. An analysis of the potential earnings of female-headed families on welfare shows that only one-fourth of nonworking mothers had a reasonable chance of increasing their income by as much as $1,000 per year by going to work full-time.[7] If these same women, on the other hand, had been able to earn as much as men with similar levels of education, job experience, and other characteristics, more than half of them could have improved their economic status significantly by working. So job opportuni-

6. Sawhill, 1976.
7. Ibid.

ties are critical and should, in our opinion, be one cornerstone for policy directed at the needs of these families.

Less tangible, but perhaps equally important, is the need to change women's own attitudes. Women at all economic levels continue to marry and have children on the assumption that someone else will provide for the children. About one-third of these women face the prospect of divorce at some point in their lives. If more young women were made aware of this risk, they might make a different set of decisions about their own education, work experience, marriage, and child bearing. They might postpone marriage, as many young women are currently doing, and make a wiser choice of husband. They might also become more aggressive about insisting on their fair share of the better-paid jobs, which they have been led to believe they are not qualified for or are not welcome to enter. In the meantime, some social protections in the form of private and public transfers will be required to ease the transition to a new division of responsibility between men and women. Women and children are especially vulnerable as these changes occur. How can society respond?

Private Transfers. The inadequate incomes of most female-headed families stem from the loss of a male earner, the mother's continuing responsibility for the care of young children, and the inability of most women to earn enough to support a family. However, the loss of a male earner within the household need not mean the loss of all of the father's income. Alimony and child support payments as well as more informal gifts of money and other items help to maintain women and children living on their own. But indications are that the flow of these private transfers is somewhat smaller than is commonly believed. They are certainly inadequate to the task of keeping many women and children out of poverty.

In 1973, only 22 percent of court-ordered payments to AFDC families were being met in full and in about half the cases there was no compliance at all.[8] Furthermore, data collected by the General Accounting Office in 1974 indicate that there is little relationship between a father's ability to pay and either the amount of the payment agreed to or his compliance with the law.[9] Some low-income men are paying substantial proportions of their income to support their children while

8. Findings of the 1973 AFDC study, table 7.
9. *Congressional Record.*

many who are more affluent have failed to comply at all. Finally, a study by Robert Hampton, using University of Michigan Panel survey data, shows that of all the married couples in his sample who separated between 1968 and 1973, 35 percent of the ex-wives, but only 19 percent of their former husbands, fell into the bottom 30 percent of the income distribution, after adjustment for family size and any child support or alimony obligations of the husband.[10] These admittedly skimpy data call into question the often-heard assertion that absent fathers are already paying as much as they can afford.

Establishing the principle and fact of adults supporting their own children is a desirable policy goal. A number of European countries, particularly in Scandinavia, have through the exercise of social policy made considerable progress toward this goal. They have achieved a level of what might be called support morality far beyond what we are now experiencing in this country, where even the idea of a federal role in establishing and enforcing support obligations is still very controversial.

A large part of the current controversy is focused on the father-tracking debate in welfare. But the need for a regular, orderly transfer of income from parents to children who no longer live with them goes far beyond the welfare population, and is of social concern for much more than the welfare dollars it might save.

As long as mothers bear major responsibility for the physical care and custody of children, fathers will need to bear major responsibility for their financial support in or out of marriage. The danger is that male responsibility will die long before women have sufficient economic independence to share more equally in the support of children. When and if fathers come to participate more in the primary care of children, and are more frequently awarded custody in divorce proceedings, some adjustment in support responsibilities will be appropriate as women are freed for new career opportunities which give them the same lifetime earning potential as men. Both for the future and for our present transitional society, a more equitable and effective system for sharing child support costs needs to be developed—a system which takes into consideration both the income position and child care responsibilities of each parent but which is not tied to any particular set of assumptions about

---

10. *Five Thousand American Families*, vol. 3, chap. 4.

these matters, which operates more independently of any adversary proceedings and which is not subject to the whims of individual judicial decisions.

Since little attention has been given to these issues to date, this is an area where further research could be particularly illuminating. This research might provide a basis for the design of a national child support program. How should such a program be structured? How cost effective can it be? How much income will it provide to economically hard pressed single-parent families, almost all of whom are currently headed by women? How can it best protect civil liberties? Will it further disrupt the family life of an already separated family and thereby harm the individuals involved? Will it seriously hamper the ability of people to form and support new families? These are questions about which very little is known. But we have the opportunity now to address them in the context of a broad ongoing debate on the appropriate split between public and private responsibilities in the areas of child rearing and maintenance. This discussion of social versus individual responsibility for the well-being of an upcoming generation is the appropriate arena for consideration of private support obligations, not the narrow arena of special, often punitive, welfare rule-making.

Public Transfers.   The traditional response to the poverty of female-headed families has been welfare, specifically **Aid to Families with Dependent Children.** Realistically, there will always be a role for public income maintenance, since there will always be some families, whatever their composition, that are unable to maintain themselves on their earned income or private transfers alone. But major changes in the current welfare system are badly needed and overdue.

One key change is the removal of existing rules which discriminate against husband-wife families by denying them federally supported assistance in most instances. In chapter 5, we saw that this discrimination has a modest upward influence on the number of female-headed families, and that an overhaul of the system so as to extend benefits to all low-income families, whether headed by one or two parents, would likely result in a shift of family structure back toward husband-wife family units. The current welfare system is a particularly clear-cut case of policy which presents undesirable incentives to alter family structure, but there are other such cases which need attention

throughout the range of public policy. Examples which are beginning to receive attention at the federal level are the differential treatment of married and unmarried people in the social
security and personal income tax systems.

The proper objective in structuring public policy with respect to family organization is neutrality. Policy should not
attempt to promote one family living pattern over another, and
policy directed at other purposes should be structured with an
eye to minimizing incentives for people to live or appear to
live in any particular family arrangement. True neutrality, in
the sense of no distorting influence on private choice, is difficult
and often impossible to achieve in the complex, multi-purpose
web of public policy, but we have found no evidence that it is
not the proper standard for such a policy. Research has not
demonstrated convincingly, for example, that children who grow
up in female-headed families are harmed by this experience.

In the case of income maintenance policy, the goal of reform should be a universal program which provides a comparable base of support to all families and individuals who have
no other income, and reduces that amount gradually as they
have increased income of their own, merging smoothly into the
positive income tax at some breakeven level of income. This
type of plan can provide a coherent, equitable, and adequate
system of support across the full range of family and household
types. Female-headed families will be among the gainers from
such reform for several reasons. The new program will provide
a more adequate, nationally-uniform, base of support. It will not
require women and children to form female-headed families to
obtain benefits, nor will it lock them into female-headed status
to continue receiving benefits. It will not single them out as a
unique and controversial dependency problem. And it will encourage them to increase their earnings through lower tax rates
than those statutorily imposed under present law.

The lower tax rates are an essential feature of the reform
program if it is not to conflict with the primary strategy of
increasing women's own earnings. Lower rates also reduce the
incentive to underreport income and misrepresent family structure. The situation posed here is one which points up the difficulties of achieving neutrality in family-related policy. For
purposes of determining transfer income eligibility and calculating transfer benefits, it is desirable for all persons in an income-
pooling unit to be considered together and their income ade-

quacy measured jointly. Otherwise, for example, nonearning members of well-to-do families would be eligible for assistance. But this approach means that families can maximize their public support by separating out their dependent members into an assistance-eligible group containing no earners. This may cause some families to separate, or at least appear to separate. Thus, living arrangements become a key policy criterion. Policy becomes trapped between presumptions of support within household units which drive some people out and drive others to conceal their true living arrangements, and investigations to establish an actual flow of income within or among households which may be very ineffective, costly, and privacy-invading. This will remain a dilemma in income maintenance policy and a testimony to the impossibility of a completely family-neutral policy. A similar dilemma may exist in attempting to achieve neutrality with respect to family size. Can the benefits paid to an unwed mother or to a couple upon the birth of a child be generous enough to provide adequately for that child's needs without at the same time increasing child-bearing at public expense? These dilemmas in policy design will require more careful attention as the demise of social controls and the increasing fragility of marital and family ties make private behavior more susceptible to policy influence.

Conclusion.   We have identified three major areas where public policy must make strides in response to the growth of female-headed families. They are: policy directed at increasing the work opportunities and earnings levels of women; policy directed at increasing and facilitating the flow of income support payments within the private sector from parents to their own children; and policy directed at reforming and extending the system of public income maintenance.

Social policy in the United States has a long way to go to catch up with the changing behavior of people and families. As traditional husband-wife families become less dominant features of the social order, the demands on policy, and also the leverage of policy to influence behavior, become greater. In this situation, social decision-making must consider both its ends and means carefully. Among the greatest challenges to that decision-making, and among the greatest beneficiaries of its wise exercise, are those women and children who will spend some part of their lives in female-headed families.

BIBLIOGRAPHY

Bell, Daniel. *The Coming of Post-Industrial Society: A Venture in Social Fore-casting.* New York: Basic Books, 1973.

Bernard, Jessie. *The Future of Marriage.* New York: World Publishing Co., 1972.

Boulding, Kenneth. "Love, Fear and the Economist." *Challenge,* vol. 16, no. 3, July-Aug. 1973, p. 32.

Congressional Record. House of Representatives, U.S. Congress, Dec. 4, 1974.

Findings of the 1973 AFDC Study, Part II A. Washington, D.C.: DHEW National Center for Social Statistics.

Five Thousand American Families—Patterns of Economic Progress, vols. 1-3 (vol. 4 in preparation). Institute for Social Research, University of Michigan, 1973-75.

Goode, William J. *World Revolution and Family Patterns.* New York: The Free Press, 1963.

Maslow, A. H. *Motivation and Personality.* New York: Harper, 1954.

Moore, Kristin A., and Sawhill, Isabel V. "Implications of Women's Employment for Home and Family Life." In Juanita Kreps, ed., *Women in the American Economy,* "The American Assembly Series." Prentice-Hall, forthcoming.

Rainwater, Lee. *What Money Buys: Inequality and the Social Meanings of Income.* New York: Basic Books, 1974.

Sawhill, Isabel V. "The Economics of Discrimination Against Women: Some New Findings." *Journal of Human Resources,* Summer 1973.

———. "Discrimination and Poverty Among Women Who Head Families," *Signs: Journal of Women in Culture and Society* (forthcoming, Spring 1976).

Young, Michael and Peter Willmott. *The Symmetrical Family.* London: Routledge and Kegan Paul, 1973.

Appendices

APPENDIX 1

The Stocks and Flows of Female-Headed Households and Families

This appendix contains a detailed documentation of the growth and changing distribution of the household and family types summarized in chapter 2. It begins by reviewing the evidence on changing stocks of female-headed households and then presents some basic data on demographic flows.

STOCKS

1. Households

Arraying Census data over time provides a useful place to start this analysis. Table 1-A shows that total households have grown 100 percent between 1940 and 1974 and that the slowest increasing component of that growth (except for male-headed primary families, which have been a trivial proportion of total households throughout the period) has been households headed by a husband and wife, which grew 76 percent. By far the greatest growth has been among households headed by a primary individual. These households grew by 332 percent between 1940 and 1974, more than doubling their share of total households over that period. The other evident trend is one toward greater household headship by women—increasing from 15 percent of all households in 1940 and 1950 to 23 percent in 1974.

2. Primary Individuals

Primary individuals have been the greatest source of increasing household headship by women, so a look at their characteristics is in order, although the degree of detail in published data on primary individuals is not great. A general picture of changes in the primary individual population by age and living arrangements can be seen in tables 1-B and 1-C. Table 1-B shows that although the fastest growth among female primary individuals has been in the 20-34 age group, the total population has become increasingly dominated by aged women. The latter were 45 percent of female primary individuals in 1960, and 51 percent in 1974.

By way of contrast, table 1-B also shows the numbers and age distributions of male primary individuals, which have a different pattern. The greatest growth here has also been in the youngest age group, but the over-65 component has dwindled from its modest early share of 34 percent in 1960 to 24 percent in 1974.

Table 1-C indicates that the overwhelming majority of primary individuals have lived by themselves in recent years, and that the proportion of women who live this way has been edging up and now stands at 93 percent. Although female primary individuals currently exceed female heads of families in both numbers and rates of growth (see table 1-A), their households contribute many fewer persons to the stock of total persons in female-headed households. According to

183

Bureau of Census data for March 1974 (U.S. Census, Series P-20, no. 276, tables 4 and 16), female-headed families had on average twice as many members as did households headed by female primary individuals so that 68 percent of all persons in households headed by women at that time were in female-headed families. We now turn to a discussion of those families.

3. Families

Table 1-D shows the household status of female-headed families and the marital status of the family head. In recent years virtually all female-headed families have been primary families, and the trend for the relatively small number of secondary families appears to have been downward until the economic reverses of 1970 and 1971 forced some women to forego their own households. The greatest increases in headship have been among separated and divorced women, who accounted for 29 percent of female family heads in 1960, and 47 percent in 1974. These two components both appear to be growing rapidly. The data, however, may be misleading for two reasons:

First, the increase in single female heads of families during most of the 1960s is not sufficient to encompass the rapid increase in unwed mothers (indicated by rising illegitimacy rates) during the same period. One possibility is that many of these mothers live with relatives, but the data on subfamilies do not give much weight to this explanation. There were 528,000 female-headed subfamilies in March 1960, and their number has moved erratically around that level since then, ending up with 602,000 in March 1974 (U.S. Census, Series P-20, nos. 106 and 276, tables 6 and 12). Another possibility is that women put their illegitimate children up for adoption, or for some other reason do not have the children living with them.

Second, there are always many fewer men than women reported as separated. In March 1974, twice as many women as men in the 14-54 age group were reported separated, a discrepancy which can in no way be accounted for by different mortality rates. Part of this is certainly due to the undercounting of separated men, higher remarriage rates among men, and the misreporting of their marital status. On the other hand, it appears that "separated" is a status which is overreported by women, particularly by single women with children. The growth rates of separated women have probably been increased by many of these unwed women, an effect which is only partially offset by greater openness about extralegal living arrangements in recent years.

Finally, it should be noted that "widowed" is still the most common marital status among female family heads, but that this dominance has been decreasing dramatically over the 1960s and 1970s.

Tables 1-E and 1-F show the growth patterns of female-headed families by age and race of the head. Since 1960, the fastest rate of growth has been in the youngest age group, and this result is not changed when one adjusts for the fact that the number of 14-24 year-olds has been growing faster than have other population groups.

In general, the rate of growth of female-headed families has been higher the lower the age of the head.

Nonwhite female-headed families have grown about three times as fast as white female-headed families over the 1960s and have increased their share of the total female-headed family population from 21 percent in 1960 to 29 percent in 1974. Similarly, nonwhite female-headed families with children have grown slightly over twice as fast as white female-headed families with children, increasing their share of such families from 28 percent in 1960 to 35 percent in 1974. Among both racial groups, female-headed families with children have been increasing faster than female-headed families as a whole, with a particular spurt in the early 1970s. The overall result is that female-headed families increasingly have children and nonwhite heads.

We have seen that female-headed families are growing two and a half times as fast as husband-wife families (table 1-A), and that female-headed families with children are growing over half again as fast as all female-headed families (table 1-F), which suggests that the living arrangements of children may be shifting considerably. To see whether this is true, we must include in the picture the changing patterns of child rearing in husband-wife families. Table 1-G shows that the proportion of all husband-wife families which have children present (and this includes children other than their own) has dropped considerably during the period—from 61 percent in 1960 to 56 percent in 1974—a drop attributable entirely to the decrease in white families with children present. The result is that 15 percent of all families with children are now female-headed, up from 9.4 percent in 1960 (U.S. Census, P-20, nos. 106 and 276, tables 4 and 1). If we use "own children" these proportions drop slightly.

Turning to the economic status of female-headed families, the data demonstrate some pronounced disparities both by race and in contrast to other family types. In 1960, there were 40 million poor persons; by 1974 this number had fallen to 23 million.[1] But virtually the entire decline was accounted for by persons in husband-wife families. Meanwhile, the number of poor persons in female-headed families rose by 1,164,000. This has resulted in a substantial swing in the composition of poor families.

In 1960, 1,916,000 female-headed families were living in poverty; by 1974, the number had climbed to 2,193,000, an increase of 14 percent. During the same period, poor husband-wife families declined by 59 percent. Focusing on families with children, the shift is even more dramatic, revealing that the majority of poor families with children are now female-headed (see figure 1-A).

In a racial breakdown of poor female-headed families with children the growth of nonwhite families (57 percent) far outdistances that of white families (11 percent) between 1960 and 1974. On the

1. The criterion for determining poverty is the average low-income threshold for a non-farm family of four. In 1960 this was $2,973, and in 1973, it was $4,540. All of the statistics in this appendix referring to the poverty population were derived from U.S. Census, Series P-60, no. 98, "Characteristics of the Low-Income Population: 1973," tables 1, 4, and 24; and P-60, no. 68, table 3.

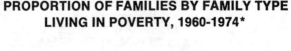

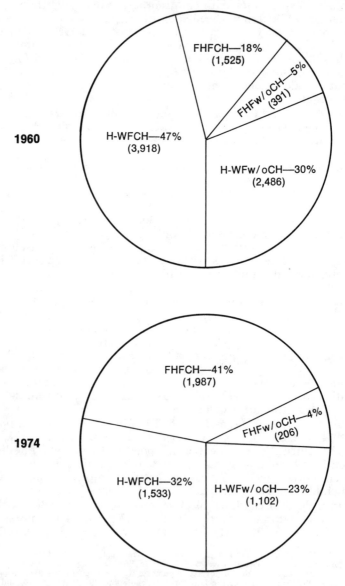

Figure 1-A

PROPORTION OF FAMILIES BY FAMILY TYPE LIVING IN POVERTY, 1960-1974*

*Actual number of families in thousands in parentheses.
FHFCH   = Female-Headed Families with Children under 18.
H-WFCH = Husband-Wife Families with Children under 18.
w/oCH   = without Children.

other hand, poor husband-wife families with children, of both races, experienced a decline over the same period: 65 percent for non-whites and 61 percent for whites.

FLOWS

Evidence of major flows into and out of female-headed house-hold status comes from Vital Statistics on demographic events such as divorce, death of spouse, birth of child, and remarriage. As observed in the previous tabulation of marital status of female heads, the predominant source of female-headedness is absence of husbands from former husband-wife families. This may occur through separation, divorce, or death, but since there is no reporting associated with separation and therefore no standard compilation of statistics on it, we are limited here to data on death and divorce. Separation and divorce are, of course, closely associated, but separation may occur without divorce. When they do occur jointly, the elapsed time between separation and divorce may vary widely.

Table 1-G presents data on termination of marriages through death and divorce. The termination rate per thousand marriages from both causes has been quite stable over the century covered, but this has been the net result of significant offsetting trends up-ward and downward in divorce and death, respectively. These data surely understate the role of divorce in creating female-headed households, since death here signifies the death of either spouse, and the death of the wife seldom has any potential for creating female-headed households, while every divorce does have such potential. On the other hand, since women's longevity has been increasing faster than men's, marital deaths which leave a surviving wife have probably not dropped as rapidly as marital deaths in general.

Table 1-H, which expresses divorces as a proportion of married women 14 to 44 years old, shows much the same pattern as table 1-G. There is a gradual upward drift in divorce rates until World War II and a peak in the immediate postwar period, followed by relative stability during the 1950s and early 1960s and a sharp upturn beginning in 1965, leading to this century's highest divorce rates in the most recent period.

Table 1-I also shows the trends in marriage rates for women. The overall marriage rate declined from a postwar high during 1945-47 of 173 per 1,000 unmarried women 15-44, to a low in 1960-62 of 144 per 1,000, which was still considerably above the prewar level. Since then there has been a gradual upward turn. But this overall measure disguises some recent divergent trends. In particular, the recent upward turn is due entirely to a marked increase in re-marriage rates for widowed and divorced women since the middle 1960s. The first marriage rate for single women 14-44 has been dropping steadily since the late 1940s and stands, in the most recent period, at the level of the late depression years.

The lower first marriage rates are consistent with women either marrying later or marrying less. Table 1-J suggests that it is the former, since the median age at first marriage for women has been moving up gradually since 1962. Other suggestions that marriage is delayed but not rejected come from table 1-K. The proportion "ever married" at young ages is less in 1974 than in 1960, especially for women, but the proportion ever-married at older ages (30-54) is generally higher. That is, more women are marrying later, and they are marrying more often—at least as of 1974.

Whether these developments will continue or not we cannot know until we have observed the marriage experience of today's young women directly over time. Meanwhile, later ages at marriage extend the length of exposure to female-headed household creation of another sort—the bearing of an illegitimate child.

Table 1-L shows that illegitimate births as a proportion of all births have been rising steadily in the postwar period, and account for one of every 8 births in the latest year available. This overall ratio subsumes very different proportions by race. About 2 out of every 5 nonwhite births were illegitimate in 1973, while nearly 1 in 16 white births were illegitimate. The absolute number of nonwhite illegitimate births has exceeded the number of white illegitimate births for the full period recorded.

However, the rate of increase of the illegitimacy ratio has been smaller for nonwhites, starting from their higher base, than for whites. Furthermore, as can be seen in table 1-M, the general illegitimacy rate—that is, the number of illegitimate births per 1,000 unmarried women 15-44—appears to have peaked in the middle sixties for nonwhites and is presently declining. The illegitimacy rate for whites showed an upward trend until 1971 and has tapered off subsequently. The reason that the declining illegitimacy rate for nonwhites has not resulted in a lower illegitimacy ratio for nonwhite births is that general fertility for nonwhites has been dropping even faster than illegitimate fertility. For whites, the rising illegitimacy ratio has been a result not only of increasing illegitimate fertility, but also of declining legitimate fertility. For both nonwhites and whites, general fertility began to fall in the early 1960s and has been dropping significantly ever since.

Table 1-A

TOTAL HOUSEHOLDS, 1940-1974

(Numbers in thousands)

	TOTAL	PRIMARY FAMILY HOUSEHOLDS						OTHER HOUSEHOLDS			
		Husband-Wife		Male Head		Female Head		Male Primary Indv.		Female Primary Indv.	
		No.	% of Total HH	No.	% of Total HH	No.	% of Total HH	No.	% of Total HH	No.	% of Total HH
July 1940	34,949	26,571	76.0	1,510	4.3	3,410	9.8	1,599	4.6	1,859	5.3
March 1950	43,554	34,075	78.2	1,169	2.7	3,594	8.3	1,668	3.8	3,048	7.0
April 1951	44,656	34,378	77.0	1,161	2.6	3,974	8.9	1,731	3.9	3,438	7.7
April 1952	45,504	35,138	77.2	1,138	2.5	3,959	8.7	1,756	3.9	3,543	7.8
April 1953	46,334	35,560	76.7	1,205	2.6	3,753	8.1	1,892	4.1	3,952	8.5
April 1954	46,893	35,875	76.5	1,313	2.8	3,751	8.0	1,904	4.1	4,028	8.6
April 1955	*47,874	36,251	75.7	1,328	2.8	4,153	8.7	2,059	4.3	4,083	8.5
March 1956	*48,902	37,067	75.8	1,418	2.9	4,157	8.5	2,058	4.2	4,250	8.7
March 1957	*49,673	37,702	75.9	1,242	2.5	4,322	8.7	2,038	4.1	4,374	8.8
March 1958	*50,474	37,906	75.1	1,262	2.5	4,240	8.4	2,329	4.6	4,718	9.3
March 1959	*51,435	38,422	74.7	1,286	2.5	4,269	8.3	2,449	4.8	5,015	9.8
March 1960	*52,799	39,254	74.3	1,228	2.3	4,435	8.4	2,716	5.1	5,179	9.8
March 1961	*53,464	39,531	73.9	1,226	2.3	4,541	8.5	2,832	5.3	5,333	10.0
March 1962	54,652	40,339	73.8	1,265	2.3	4,581	8.4	2,927	5.4	5,540	10.1
March 1963	55,189	40,838	74.0	1,296	2.3	4,679	8.5	2,845	5.2	5,531	10.0
March 1964	55,996	41,257	73.7	1,202	2.1	4,819	8.6	2,961	5.3	5,757	10.3
March 1965	57,251	41,588	72.6	1,168	2.0	4,964	8.7	3,271	5.7	6,260	10.9
March 1966	58,092	42,060	72.4	1,165	2.0	4,944	8.5	3,292	5.7	6,631	11.4
March 1967	58,845	42,489	72.2	1,185	2.0	5,117	8.7	3,408	5.8	6,646	11.3
March 1968	60,446	43,267	71.6	1,194	2.0	5,273	8.7	3,661	6.1	7,049	11.7
March 1969	61,805	43,818	70.9	1,217	2.0	5,381	8.7	3,893	6.3	7,496	12.1
March 1970	62,875	44,408	70.6	1,209	1.9	5,493	8.7	3,971	6.3	7,794	12.4
March 1971	64,374	44,704	69.4	1,250	2.0	5,869	9.1	4,385	6.8	8,166	12.7
March 1972	66,676	45,724	68.6	1,331	2.0	6,108	9.1	4,839	7.3	8,674	13.0
March 1973	68,251	46,297	67.8	1,432	2.1	6,535	9.6	5,129	7.5	8,858	13.0
March 1974	69,859	46,806	67.0	1,397	2.0	6,706	9.6	5,659	8.1	9,291	13.3
% Change since 1960:	32.3	19.2		13.8		51.2		108.4		79.4	

*Revised in 1965 for consistency with revised estimates of the population.

Sources: "Household and Family Characteristics." Series P-20, nos. 233, 246, 258, and 276. *Current Population Reports,* Population Characteristics. Washington, D.C.: U.S. Bureau of the Census.

Abbott L. Ferriss, "Indicators of Trends in Status of American Women," New York: Russell Sage Foundation, 1971.

Table 1-B
PRIMARY INDIVIDUALS BY AGE, 1960-1974
(Numbers in thousands)

Year	Male 20-34	Male 35-64	65 and over Number	65 and over %	Female 20-34	Female 35-64	65 and over Number	65 and over %
1960	427	1282	904	34.6	377	2425	2304	45.1
1962	580	1441	896	30.7	524	2312	2700	48.8
1967	746	1527	1097	32.5	545	2678	3370	51.1
1971	1180	1907	1247	28.8	941	2962	4207	51.9
1972	1588	1943	1276	26.5	1116	3028	4510	52.1
1973	1727	2023	1315	26.0	1124	3090	4568	52.0
1974	2133	2087	1331	24.0	1361	3128	4667	51.0
% change since 1960	399.5	62.8	47.2		261.0	29.0	102.6	

Sources: 1960, 1971 CPR P-20, no. 233, Table D
1967 CPR P-20, no. 173, Table F
1962, 1972 CPR P-20, no. 242, Table A
1973 CPR P-20, no. 255, Table 2
1974 CPR P-20, no. 271, Table 2

Table 1-C
LIVING ARRANGEMENTS OF PRIMARY INDIVIDUALS
(Numbers in thousands)

Year	All Primary Individuals Number	Living Alone Number	Living Alone %	Female Primary Individuals Number	Living Alone Number	Living Alone %	Male Primary Individuals Number	Living Alone Number	Living Alone %
1962	8475	7443	87.8	5536	4949	89.4	2939	2494	84.8
1967	10,054	9139	90.9	6646	6130	92.3	3408	3009	88.3
1972	13,504	12,169	90.1	8678	8072	93.0	4826	4097	84.9
1973	13,986	12,636	90.3	8856	8239	93.0	5130	4397	85.7
1974	14,942	13,368	89.5	9288	8626	92.9	5654	4742	83.9

Sources: 1967 CPR P-20, no. 173, Table F
1962, 1972 CPR P-20, no. 242, Table A
1973 CPR P-20, no. 255, Table 6
1974 CPR P-20, no. 271, Table 6

Table 1-D

FEMALE-HEADED FAMILIES BY HOUSEHOLD STATUS AND MARITAL STATUS OF HEAD, 1955-1974

(Numbers in thousands)

	HOUSEHOLD STATUS					MARITAL STATUS OF HEAD										
	Total Female-Headed Families	Primary Families		Secondary Families		MARRIED						WIDOWED		DIVORCED		SINGLE	
						Separated		Husband in Armed Forces		Other							
		No.	%	No.	%	No.	%	No.	%	No.	%	No.	%	No.	%	No.	%
March 1955	4234	4153	98.1	81	1.9	576	13.6	131	3.1	389	9.2	2147	50.7	538	12.7	453	10.7
1960	4507	4422	98.1	85	1.9	595	13.2	104	2.3	406	9.0	2330	51.7	694	15.4	379	8.4
1961	4616	4541	98.4	75	1.6	679	14.7	83	1.8	351	7.6	2354	51.0	752	16.3	396	8.6
1962	4643	4581	98.7	62	1.3	696	15.0	121	2.6	432	9.3	2284	49.2	757	16.3	353	7.6
1963	4741	4679	98.7	62	1.3	678	14.3	109	2.3	460	9.7	2280	48.1	825	17.4	384	8.1
1964	4882	4819	98.7	63	1.3	790	16.2	103	2.1	381	7.8	2309	47.3	879	18.0	425	8.7
1965	5006	4964	99.2	42	.8	851	17.0	75	1.5	466	9.3	2308	46.1	901	18.0	405	8.1
1966	4992	4944	99.0	48	1.0	809	16.2	140	2.8	449	9.0	2296	46.0	924	18.5	366	7.5
1967	5171	5117	99.0	54	1.0	869	16.8	129	2.5	429	8.3	2384	46.1	1034	20.0	331	6.4
1968	5333	5273	99.0	59	1.0	928	17.4	133	2.5	229	4.3	2453	46.0	1051	19.7	539	10.1
1969	5439	5381	98.9	58	1.1	984	18.1	141	2.6	261	4.8	2366	43.5	1110	20.4	582	10.7
1970	5579	5493	98.4	87	1.6	939	16.8	141	2.5	244	4.4	2389	42.8	1258	22.5	608	10.9
1971	5948	5869	98.7	81	1.4	1128	19.0	114	1.9	254	4.3	2323	39.0	1417	23.8	712	12.0
1972	6191	6108	98.7	83	1.3	1256	20.3	58	.9	307	5.0	2370	38.3	1487	24.0	713	11.5
1973	6607	6535	98.9	72	1.1	1289	19.5	76	1.2	214	3.2	2468	37.4	1712	25.9	848	12.8
1974	6804	6709	98.6	95	1.4	1288	18.9	40	.6	233	3.4	2505	36.8	1884	27.7	854	12.6
% change since 1960:	51.0	51.7		11.8		116.5		−61.5		−42.6		7.5		171.5		125.3	

Revised in 1965 for consistency with revised estimates of the population.

Sources: "Marital Status and Living Arrangements," Series P-20, nos. 225, 242, 255, and 271. *CPR Population Characteristics*, Washington, D.C.: U.S. Bureau of the Census.
"Marital Status and Family Status." Series P-20, nos. 62, 105, 114, 122, 135, 144, 159, 170, 187, 198, and 212, *CPR Population Characteristics*, Washington, D.C.: U.S. Bureau of the Census.
"Household and Family Characteristics," Series P-20, nos. 106, 116, 125, 139, 153, 164, 173, 191, 200, 218, 233, 258, and 276. *CPR Population Characteristics*, Washington, D.C.: U.S. Bureau of the Census.

Table 1-E

FEMALE-HEADED FAMILIES, ALL RACES, BY AGE GROUPS, 1960-1974
(Numbers in thousands)

	Age 14-24	*	Age 25-44	*	Age 45-64	*	Age 65+	*	Total FHF	*
March 1960	166	166	1,568	1,568	1,730	1,730	1,028	1,028	4,492	4,492
1961	207		1,570		1,815		1,023		4,615	
1962	204		1,668		1,781		991		4,644	
1963	213		1,701		1,759		1,065		4,738	
1964	258		1,740		1,803		1,083		4,884	
1965	228		1,873		1,815		1,089		5,005	
1966	239		1,805		1,820		1,125		4,989	
1967	250		1,894		1,905		1,123		5,172	
1968	309		1,957		1,940		1,126		5,332	
1969	319		2,081		1,898		1,140		5,438	
1970	434		1,995		2,032		1,115		5,576	
1971	464		2,314		2,153		1,015		5,946	
1972	564		2,473		2,131		1,017		6,185	
1973	609		2,683		2,144		1,170		6,607	
1974	606	485	2,903	3,338	2,158	2,342	1,136	1,082	6,804	7,247
Percent change since 1960:	265.1	192.2	85.1	112.9	24.7	35.4	10.5	5.3	51.5	61.3

*Standardized for age using 1960 population.

Sources: "Marital Status and Living Arrangements," CPR, Series P-20, nos. 225, 242, 255, and 271, Washington, D.C.: U.S. Bureau of the Census.
   "Marital Status and Family Status," CPR, Series P-20, nos. 105, 114, 122, 135, 144, 159, 170, 187, 198, and 212, Washington, D.C.: U.S. Bureau of the Census.

Table 1-F

FEMALE-HEADED FAMILIES, BY RACE AND PRESENCE OF CHILDREN, 1960-1974
(Numbers in thousands)

	ALL RACES			WHITE			NONWHITE		
	Total	With Members <18 No.	%	Total	With Members <18 No.	%	Total	With Members <18 No.	%
March 1960	4,492	2,542	56.6	3,543	1,834	51.8	949	708	74.6
1961	4,618	2,620	56.7	3,682	1,921	52.2	936	699	74.7
1962	4,641	2,687	57.9	3,605	1,922	53.3	1,036	765	73.8
1963	4,743	2,700	56.9	3,628	1,846	50.9	1,115	854	76.6
1964	4,878	2,830	58.0	3,793	1,960	51.7	1,085	870	80.2
1965	5,005	2,896	57.9	3,879	2,020	52.1	1,126	876	77.8
1966	4,990	2,874	57.6	3,858	2,007	52.0	1,132	867	76.6
1967	5,177	2,960	57.2	4,014	2,073	51.6	1,163	887	76.3
1968	5,332	3,191	59.8	4,008	2,147	53.6	1,324	1,044	78.9
1969	5,440	3,272	60.1	4,053	2,193	54.1	1,387	1,079	77.8
1970	5,580	3,374	60.5	4,185	2,263	54.1	1,395	1,111	79.6
1971	5,950	3,813	64.1	4,386	2,519	57.4	1,564	1,294	82.7
1972	6,191	4,078	65.9	4,489	2,665	59.4	1,702	1,413	83.0
1973	6,607	4,324	65.4	4,672	2,750	58.9	1,935	1,574	81.3
1974	6,804	4,598	67.6	4,853	2,989	61.6	1,951	1,609	82.5
Percent change since 1960	51.5	80.9		37.0	63.0		105.6	127.3	

Sources: 1960-1967, "Poverty in the U.S. 1959-1968," *Current Population Reports, Consumer Income*, Series P-60, no. 68, Washington, D.C.: U.S. Bureau of the Census. 1968-1974, "Household and Family Characteristics," Series P-20, nos. 191, 200, 218, 233, 246, 258, and 276. *Current Population Reports, Population Characteristics*, Washington, D.C.: U.S. Bureau of the Census.

Table 1-G

FAMILIES WITH CHILDREN BY RACE AND HEADSHIP, 1960 and 1974
(Numbers in thousands)

	1960	1974	Percent Change
Nonwhite Families			
Husband-Wife			
Total	3,193	3,918	22.7
Total with related members <18	2,079	2,567	23.5
Total with own children <18	1,839	2,390	30.0
Female-Heads			
Total	950	1,951	105.4
Total with related members <18	712	1,609	126.0
Total with own children <18	528	1,349	155.5
White Families			
Husband-Wife			
Total	36,464	42,894	17.6
Total with related members <18	22,243	23,416	5.3
Total with own children <18	21,636	22,888	5.8
Female-Heads			
Total	3,543	4,853	37.0
Total with related members <18	1,834	2,989	63.0
Total with own children <18	1,499	2,732	82.3
All Races—Families			
Husband-Wife			
Total	39,657	46,812	18.0
Total with related members <18	24,310	25,983	6.9
Total with own children <18	23,475	25,278	7.7
Female-Heads			
Total	4,493*	6,804	51.4
Total with related members <18	2,546	4,598	80.6
Total with own children <18	2,026	4,082	101.5

* Total FHF prior to revision of 1965

Sources: "Household and Family Characteristics: March 1974," Series P-20, no. 276, *Current Population Reports, Population Characteristics,* Washington, D.C.: U.S. Bureau of the Census.
1960 Census of Population, Subject Report "Families," PC(2)-4A, tables 3 and 4, Washington, D.C.: U.S. Bureau of the Census.

Table I-H

ANNUAL MARITAL DISSOLUTIONS BY DEATH AND LEGAL DIVORCE, AND RATES PER 1000 EXISTING MARRIAGES, 1860-1970

	DISSOLUTIONS PER YEAR		PER 1000 EXISTING MARRIAGES[a]			DIVORCES AS PER CENT OF TOTAL DISSOLUTION
	Deaths[b]	Divorces[c]	Deaths	Divorces	Combined	
1860-64	197,200	7,170	32.1	1.2	33.3	3.5
1865-69	207,000	10,529	31.1	1.6	32.7	4.8
1870-74	226,400	12,417	30.3	1.7	32.0	5.2
1875-79	238,600	15,574	28.7	1.9	30.6	6.1
1880-84	285,400	21,746	30.6	2.3	33.0	7.1
1885-89	290,400	27,466	27.6	2.6	30.2	8.6
1890-94	334,800	36,123	28.3	3.1	31.3	9.7
1895-99	328,800	45,462	24.9	3.4	28.4	12.1
1900-04	390,800	61,868	26.5	4.2	30.6	13.7
1905-09	427,400	74,626	25.4	4.4	29.8	14.9
1910-14	453,600	91,695	23.7	4.8	28.5	16.8
1915-19	551,000	119,529	26.0	5.6	31.6	17.8
1920-24	504,200	164,917	21.9	7.2	29.0	24.6
1925-29	573,200	193,218	22.6	7.6	30.3	25.2
1930-34	590,800	183,441	21.9	6.8	28.7	23.7
1935-39	634,600	239,600	21.9	8.3	30.2	27.4
1940-44	656,400	330,557	20.4	10.3	30.7	33.5
1945-49	681,200	485,641	19.2	13.7	32.8	41.6
1950-54	692,400	385,429	18.2	10.0	28.3	35.9
1955-59	733,600[d]	385,385	18.3	9.2	27.8	34.2
1960	790,400	393,000	18.9	9.4	28.3	33.2
1961	789,200	414,000	18.7	9.8	28.6	34.4
1965	820,800	479,000	18.5	10.8	29.4	36.9
1970	908,200	715,000	19.3	15.2	34.5	44.0

a.　Existing marriages 1860-1949 from Paul H. Jacobson, *American Marriage and Divorce*, New York: Rinehart, 1969, tables A6-A9, A22 (number of married *men*) 1950-60, from *Historical Statistics of the United States*; 1961 and 1965 from *Statistical Abstracts of the United States*; 1970 from 1970 Census, United States Summary, p. 311.

b.　Deaths to married persons, 1860-1959 from Jacobson, op. cit., p. 178; 1960-61 from National Office of Vital Statistics, Mortality (A) for relevant years; 1965 and 1970 estimated by present writers.

c.　Divorces 1860-1954, from Jacobson, Table 42; 1955-69, from NCHS, "Divorce Statistics, 1969," *Monthly Vital Statistics Report*, vol. 20, no. 4, Supplement 2 (July 22, 1971); 1970 from NCHS, "Annual Summary for the United States, 1970," ibid., vol. 19, no. 13, September 21, 1971.

d.　Average for 1955 and 1959 only.

Source: U.S. Commission on Population Growth in the American Future. *Demographic and Social Aspects of Population Growth*, Charles F. Westoff and Robert Parke, Jr., eds., vol. 1 of Commission Research Reports, Washington, D.C.: GPO, 1972, p. 256.

Table 1-I

MARRIAGE AND DIVORCE RATES PER 1000 WOMEN, 1921-1971

	Divorce Rates Married Women [a] 14-44	Marriage Rates Unmarried Women [b] 15-44	First Marriage Rate Single Women [a] 14-44	Remarriage Rate Widowed/ Divorced [a] 14-54
1921-23	10	—	99	98
1924-26	11	—	95	99
1927-29	12	—	94	84
1930-32	10	—	81	61
1933-35	11	—	92	69
1936-38	13	—	98	83
1939-41	14	133	106	103
1942-44	17	135	108	139
1945-47	24	173	143	163
1948-50	17	166	134	135
1951-53	16	163	122	136
1954-56	15	160	120	129
1957-59	15	151	112	129
1960-62	16	144	116	133
1963-65	17	145	110	139
1966-68	20	146	110	150
1969-71	26	149	107	168

a. Paul C. Glick and Arthur J. Norton, "Perspectives in the Recent Upturn in Divorce and Remarriage." *Demography* 10:3 (August 1973).
b. "Marriages, Trends and Characteristics: U.S.," Series 21, no. 21, NCHS Vital and Health Statistics, Rockville, Md. September 1971, T. 1, p. 23.

Table 1-J

MEDIAN AGE AT FIRST MARRIAGE, BY SEX, 1890-1974

	Male	Female
1890	26.1	22.0
1900	25.9	21.9
1910	25.1	21.6
1920	24.6	21.2
1930	24.3	21.3
1940	24.3	21.5
1950	22.8	20.3
1960	22.8	20.3
1961	22.8	20.3
1962	22.7	20.3
1963	22.8	20.5
1964	23.1	20.5
1965	22.8	20.6
1966	22.8	20.5
1967	23.1	20.6
1968	23.1	20.8
1969	23.2	20.8
1970	23.2	20.8
1971	23.1	20.9
1972	23.3	20.9
1973	23.2	21.0
1974	23.1	21.1

Sources: "Marital Status and Living Arrangements" and "Marital Status and Family Status," Series P-20, *Current Population Reports, Population Characteristics,* Washington, D.C.: U.S. Bureau of the Census.
"Historical Statistics of the U.S., Colonial Times to 1957," Washington, D.C.: U.S. Bureau of the Census, 1960.

Table 1-K

POPULATION PERCENTAGES EVER MARRIED, BY SEX AND AGE

	Percentage Ever Married		
Sex and Age	**1910**	**1960**	**1974**
Females			
14-17		5.4	3.4
18	12.1 [a]	24.4	18.1
19		40.3	31.1
20-24	51.7	71.6	60.4
25-29	75.1	89.5	86.9
30-34	83.9	93.1	93.2
35-44	88.6	93.9	95.2
45-54	91.5	93.0	95.8
Males			
14-17	—	1.0	.6
18	—	5.4	4.6
19	—	12.9	12.6
20-24	25.1	46.9	43.0
25-29	57.2	79.2	77.4
30-34	74.0	88.1	89.2
35-44	83.3	91.9	91.7
45-54	88.9	92.6	94.1

a. Ages 15-19

Sources: 1910—U.S. Commission on Population Growth in the American Future, *Demographic and Social Aspects of Population Growth,* ed. C. F. Westoff and Robert Parke, Jr., vol. I of Commission Research Reports, Washington, D.C.: GPO, 1972, p. 243.
1960 and 1974 "Marital Status and Living Arrangements: March 1974," Series P-20, no. 211, table C. *Current Population Reports, Population Characteristics,* Washington, D.C.: U.S. Bureau of the Census.

Table 1-L
ILLEGITIMACY STATISTICS, 1940-1973

	ALL RACES			WHITE			NONWHITE		
	Total Births (000)	Illegitimate Births (000)	Percent Illegitimate	Total Births (000)	Illegitimate Births (000)	Percent Illegitimate	Total Births (000)	Illegitimate Births (000)	Percent Illegitimate
1940	2,599	90	3.5	2,199	40	1.8	360	49	13.6
1945	2,858	117	4.1	2,471	56	2.3	388	61	15.7
1950	3,632	142	3.9	3,108	54	1.7	524	88	16.8
1955	4,104	183	4.5	3,488	64	1.8	617	119	19.3
1960	4,258	224	5.3	3,601	83	2.3	657	142	21.6
1961	4,268	240	5.6	3,601	91	2.5	667	149	22.3
1962	4,167	245	5.9	3,394	93	2.7	642	147	22.9
1963	4,098	259	6.3	3,326	102	3.1	639	151	23.6
1964	4,027	276	6.9	3,369	114	3.4	658	161	24.5
1965	3,760	291	7.7	3,124	124	4.0	636	168	26.4
1966	3,606	302	8.4	2,993	132	4.4	613	170	27.7
1967	3,520	318	9.0	2,923	142	4.9	598	176	29.4
1968	3,502	339	9.7	2,912	155	5.3	589	184	31.2
1969	3,600	361	10.0	2,994	164	5.5	607	197	32.5
1970	3,731	399	10.7	3,091	175	5.7	640	224	35.0
1971	3,556	401	11.3	2,920	164	5.6	636	238	37.4
1972	3,258	403	12.4	2,656	161	6.1	603	243	40.3
1973	3,137	407	13.0	2,551	163	6.4	586	244	41.6

Sources: 1940-1968 data—"Vital Statistics of the U.S. 1968," vol. I "Natality," tables 1-2 and 1-24, National Center for Health Statistics, Rockville, Md. 1967-1973 births—"Summary Reports Final Natality Statistics," NCHS *Monthly Vital Statistics Reports*, vol. 22, no. 7; vol. 22, no. 12; vol. 23, no. 3; vol. 23, no. 8; and vol. 23, no. 11 (tables 1 and 11), Rockville, Md.

Table 1-M

FERTILITY AND ILLEGITIMACY RATES, 1940-1973

	Fertility Rates [a]			Illegitimacy Rates [b]		
	All Races	White	Nonwhite	All Races	White	Nonwhite
1940	79.9	77.1	102.4	7.1	3.6	35.6
1945	85.9	83.4	106.0	10.1		
1950	106.2	102.3	137.3	14.1	6.1	71.2
1955	118.5	113.8	155.3	19.3	7.9	87.2
1960	118.0	113.2	153.6	21.6	9.2	98.3
1961	117.2	112.2	153.5	22.7	10.0	100.8
1962	112.2	107.5	148.8	21.9	9.8	97.5
1963	108.5	103.7	144.9	22.5	10.5	97.1
1964	105.0	99.9	141.7	23.0	11.0	97.2
1965	96.6	91.4	133.9	23.5	11.6	97.6
1966	91.3	86.4	125.9	23.4	12.0	92.8
1967	87.6	83.1	119.8	23.9	12.5	89.5
1968	85.7	81.5	114.9	24.4	13.2	86.6
1969	86.5	82.4	114.8	25.0	13.5	86.6
1970	87.9	84.1	113.0	26.4	13.8	89.9
1971	81.8	77.5	109.5	25.6	12.5	90.6
1972	73.4	69.2	100.3	24.9	12.0	86.9
1973	69.2	65.3	94.3	24.5	11.9	84.2

a. Fertility rate is the number of births per 1000 women aged 15-44.

Source: 1940-1968—"Vital Statistics of the U.S. 1968," vol. I "Natality," National Center for Health Statistics, (NCHS), Rockville, Md.
1969-1971—"Summary Report Final Natality Statistics, 1971," NCHS, Monthly Vital Statistics Report, vol. 23, no. 3, Supplement (3) June 7, 1974.

b. Illegitimacy rate is the number of illegitimate births per 1000 unmarried women aged 15-44.

Source: 1940-1950—"The Social and Economic Status of the Black Population in the U.S., 1971," Series P-23, no. 42, Washington, D.C.: U.S. Bureau of the Census, Table 88.
1955-1965—"Trends in Illegitimacy U.S. 1940-1965," Series 21, no. 15, table 2, NCHS, Rockville, Md.
1966-1968—"Vital Statistics of the U.S. 1969," vol. I "Natality," NCHS, Rockville, Md.
1969-1971—"Summary Reports Final Natality Statistics," NCHS, vol. 23, no. 3: vol. 22 no. 12; vol. 22 no. 7; vol. 23, no. 8 (1972); and vol. 23, no. 11 (1973), table 11, Rockville, Md.

APPENDIX 2

Definitions of Variables Used in Analysis of Stocks and Flows: Derivation and Sources

FC = Stock of female-headed families with own children under 18; includes subfamilies; excludes female-headed families where a woman was married and her husband was absent for reasons other than marital discord.

	1960	1970
Total	2,012,000	3,230,000
White	1,450,000	2,199,000
Nonwhite	562,000	1,031,000

Sources: 1970 Census of Population, Subject Reports, "Family Composition," PC(2)-4A, tables 20 and 25, and "Marital Status," PC(2)-4C, table 1.

1960 Census of Population, Subject Reports, "Families," PC(2)-4A, tables 6 and 21, and "Marital Status," PC(2)-4E, table 1.

Also, see table 4-B, Appendix 4, below.

d = Divorce rate for husband-wife families with children

	1960	1970
Total	8.9	14.4
White	8.7	14.06
Nonwhite	10.9	17.62

Source: *1960* total divorce rate for families with children—from National Center for Health Statistics (NCHS) Series 21, no. 18, "Children of Divorced Couples: U.S., Selected Years," Feb. 1970.

The separate white and nonwhite rates were derived with ratios (1960-1966) calculated from Current Population Reports (CPR), Series P-20, no. 223, "Social and Economic Variations in Marriage, Divorce, and Remarriage: 1967" (assuming all second dissolutions are divorces).

White $= 8.9_T \times 8.3_w/8.5_T = 8.7$
Nonwhite $= 8.9_T \times 10.4_{nw}/8.5_T = 10.9$

1970 figures were derived from aggregate divorce rates from Table 1-H, Appendix 1, and 1960 ratio of divorce rate for families with children to the aggregate rate.

$$15.2 \times 8.9/9.4 = 14.4$$

White, nonwhite figures derived as above.

White $= 14.4 \times 8.3_w/8.5_T = 14.06$
Nonwhite $= 14.4 \times 10.4_{nw}/8.5_T = 17.62$

md = Death rate for male heads of families with children. Derived from death rates for males (Vital Statistics) weighted by age distribution of male-headed families with children under 18 (Census).

	1960	1970
Total	5.0	5.0
White	4.9	5.0
Nonwhite	10.8	10.8

Source: NCHS, HSM 73-1121, vol. 21, no. 13, "Annual Summary for U.S. 1972," table 5, June 27, 1973.

1960 Census of Population, Subject Reports, "Families," PC(2)-4A, table 8.

1970 Census of Population, Subject Reports, "Marital Status," PC(2)-4C, table 1.

MC = Stock of intact husband-wife families with children; includes subfamilies.

	1960	1970
Total	24,006,321	24,947,597
White	22,301,976	22,615,801
Nonwhite	1,704,345	2,331,796

Source: 1960 Census of Population, Subject Reports, "Families," PC(2)-4A, tables 6 and 21.

1970 Census of Population, Subject Reports, "Family Composition," PC(2)-4A, tables 8 and 20.

p = Proportion of out-of-wedlock births not adopted after one year.

	1960	1970
Total	.61	.69
White	.34	.38
Nonwhite	.95	.93

Source: Robert B. Hill. *The Strengths of Black Families,* New York: Emerson Hall Publishers, 1971, table 5. 1960 proportions are 1962 data, 1970 proportions are 1968 data.

b = First birth illegitimacy rates per 1,000 single women 15-44.

	1960	1970
Total	10.6	16.2
White	5.9	9.7
Nonwhite	40.0	49.1

Source: 1960 rates taken directly from NCHS Series 21, no. 15, "Trends in Illegitimacy, U.S. 1940-1965," Feb. 1968.

1970 rates derived by dividing numbers of all illegitimate first births by total illegitimate births in 1970 and multiplying by the 1970 illegitimacy rate.

First birth data from unpublished NCHS data; totals and rates from NCHS *Monthly Vital Statistics Report,* "Summary Report Final Natality Statistics, 1970," vol. 22, no. 12, March 20, 1974.

F = Stock of single women 14-44.

	1960	1970
Total	10,185,000	15,345,000
White	8,806,000	12,972,000
Nonwhite	1,379,000	2,373,000

Source: 1960 Census of Population, Subject Reports, "Marital Status," PC(2)-4E, table 1.
1970 Census of Population, Subject Reports, "Persons by Family Characteristics," PC(2)-4B, table 2.

r^w = Remarriage rates for widows with children under 18. Use 30.8 (calculated from CPR P-20, no. 223, "Social and Economic Variations in Marriage, Divorce, and Remarriage: 1967") for 1960, 1970, totals, white and nonwhite. Use 30.8 for 1960 and 1970 because aggregate remarriage rates for widows show little change over decade. Use 30.8 for white and nonwhite because aggregate widow remarriage rate does not differ much by race.

r^d = Remarriage rates for divorcees with children under 18. Use rate for divorcees with children under 18 calculated from CPS data on 1960-66 annual averages. Adjust for race by aggregate white-nonwhite ratios calculated from CPS. Adjust for trend with Glick and Norton remarriage series for all divorced and widowed women 14-54.

153.6 = 1960-66 annual average remarriage rate for divorced women with children under 18 calculated from CPS.

Glick and Norton remarriage series for divorced and widowed women 14-54 increased 4.5 percent from average of 1960-62 to average of 1963-65.

1960 = 149.76
1970 = 188.6 (149.75 × 1.26) [increase in rates 1960-1970 from Glick and Norton series]

Ratios by race calculated from CPS 1960-66 are

w/T = 1.01   nw/T = .92

	1960	1970
Total	149.76	188.6
White	151.3	190.5
Nonwhite	137.8	173.5

Source: Paul C. Glick and Arthur J. Norton, "Perspectives on the Recent Upturn in Divorce and Remarriage," Demography, vol. 10, no. 3, August 1973.

r^{dts} = Remarriage rate when the stock of separated women who eventually divorce is added to the denominator in calculating the remarriage rate of divorcees. It is based on the assumption that such women spend an average of one year between separation and divorce and equals $\frac{1}{1 + 1/r}$ or $\frac{r}{1 + r}$.

fd = Death rate for female-headed families with children under 18. Use female death rates weighted by age distribution of female-headed families with children under 18.

	1960	1970
Total	4.2	3.2
White	3.1	2.1
Nonwhite	6.5	5.1

Source: NCHS, HSM 73-1121, vol. 21, no. 13, "Annual Summary for U.S. 1972," table 5, June 27, 1973.

1960 Census of Population, Subject Reports, "Families," PC(2)-4A, table 8.

1970 Census of Population, Subject Reports, "Marital Status," PC(2)-4C, table 1.

APPENDIX 3

The Dynamics of Family Formation and Dissolution

The number of female-headed families observed at any point in time is no more than a snapshot of a situation which is very much in flux. People marry, have children, divorce, die, remarry, grow older, and change their living arrangements. Unless we are able to trace the impact of these various demographic flows on the stock of female-headed families, we will not be able to analyze the under-lying behavior which may be giving rise to the recent increase in families of this type. We begin with the very simplest kind of demographic model and then suggest how it might be modified gradually to simulate the complexity of the real world.

Consider a world in which everyone lives in a male-headed or a female-headed family, where the only route by which the latter can be created is divorce, and the only route by which it can disappear is remarriage. Then, the stock of female-headed families in a given year (F_t) depends on (1) the probability that an existing male-headed (i.e., husband-wife) family (M_{t-1}) will become female-headed through divorce (P_{mf}) and (2) the probability that an existing female-headed family (F_{t-1}) will remain female-headed (P_{ff})—i.e., not remarry. More succinctly,

$$F_t = P_{mf} M_{t-1} + P_{ff} F_{t-1}$$

Similarly, the stock of male-headed families depends on the relevant stocks the preceding year and the transitions into and out of that status, or

$$M_t = P_{mm} M_{t-1} + P_{fm} F_{t-1}.$$

We can call P_{mf} the "divorce rate" and P_{fm} the "remarriage rate." Note that all existing female heads must either remarry or not marry (remain female-headed) so that $P_{ff} + P_{fm} = 1$. Analogously, all existing male-headed families either remain male-headed or become female-headed so that $P_{mf} + P_{mm} = 1$. Moreover, if F_t and M_t are defined as the *proportion* of all households which are female- or male-headed respectively, then $F_t + M_t = 1$ as well. Finally, if there is no change in population or in divorce and remarriage rates, the stock of female- or male-headed households would, after a certain period of time, reach a "steady-state equilibrium" (i.e., no further changes in these proportions would be observed). In this case, $M_t = M_{t-1}$ and $F_t = F_{t-1}$. We now have

$$F_t = P_{mf} (1 - F_t) + (1 - P_{fm}) F_t$$

and solving this equation, we obtain

$$F_t = \frac{P_{mf}}{P_{mf} + P_{fm}}.$$

Thus, the steady-state proportion of families headed by a woman can be predicted from a knowledge of divorce and remarriage rates. For example, if the divorce rate is .02 (20 per 1,000) and the remarriage rate is .20 (200 per 1,000), then the proportion female-headed is .09. Clearly, this proportion varies directly with the divorce rate and inversely with the remarriage rate.

We now move the model somewhat closer to reality by classifying the population of adult women into four mutually exclusive and exhaustive categories as follows:

M = married women with no children under 18.
MC = married women with children under 18.
F = unmarried women (single and formerly married) with no children under 18.
FC = unmarried women (single and formerly married) with children under 18.

This gives us a four-equation model.

$$M = P_{mm}M + P_{mcm}MC + P_{fm}F + P_{fcm}FC$$
$$MC = P_{mmc}M + P_{mcmc}MC + P_{fmc}F + P_{fcmc}FC$$
$$F = P_{mf}M + P_{mcf}MC + P_{ff}F + P_{fcf}FC$$
$$FC = P_{mfc}M + P_{mcfc}MC + P_{ffc}F + P_{fcfc}FC$$

There are a total of 16 transition probabilities. Four of them (P_{fmc}, P_{fcm}, P_{mfc}, P_{mcf}) are equal to zero since, in principle, it is impossible to change marital status and the presence of children simultaneously. (Given a short enough period of time, these must be separate events.) Two of the above probabilities (P_{mmc} and P_{ffc}) represent legitimate and illegitimate first birth rates respectively. Two others (P_{mcm} and P_{fcf}) are the probability that the last child will grow up (become age 18). Four (P_{fm}, P_{fcmc}, P_{mf}, P_{mcfc}) represent changes in marital status (formal or informal) due to first marriage, remarriage, reconciliation, death, divorce, and separation for women with and without children respectively. Since these probabilities summarize a variety of different types of marital changes, further disaggregation would be appropriate. The values of the remaining four (P_{mm}, P_{mcmc}, P_{ff}, P_{fcfc}) are determined as a residual, remembering that all of the transition probabilities from a given state sum to unity.

Given a knowledge of the above demographic flows, we can solve this system of equations for FC (the proportion of unmarried women with children under 18). The usefulness of the model is twofold. First, it allows one to predict the impact of changes in the relevant flows on FC and enables one to sort out the contribution of various demographic factors to changes in female-headedness over time or between groups. Moreover, with sufficient disaggregation of the population by age, race, location, etc., it is possible to sort out the relative contributions of changes in behavior within groups and shifts in the composition of the population. Secondly, once the social and economic determinants of a particular kind of demographic behavior have been estimated (say, the effect of welfare income on divorce rates), then the above model can be used to trace through the effects of these social and economic factors on the stock of female-headed families.

Although the above system of equations represents a major step toward modeling the real world more accurately than the simple two-equation system first presented, it still represents an obvious abstraction from some of the complexities of family life. Of greatest importance is the fact that it ignores the living arrangements of both adults and children. An unmarried woman with a child may live with relatives or may head a household. Her children may live with her or with other relatives (including the father), with friends, or in an institution, or, as in the case of an illegitimate birth, the child may be put up for adoption. Thus, there is no one-to-one correspondence between FC and the number of female-headed families with children. However, with some additional work it may be possible to incorporate "living arrangement" parameters into the system—perhaps by applying living arrangement probabilities to the basic demographic flows. For example, one might want to multiply P_{ffc} (the illegitimate first birth rate) by the probability that the mother will keep the child rather than resort to adoption.

On-going work of The Urban Institute is directed toward collecting and refining the basic data on the transition probabilities, and toward estimating the behavioral determinants of these demographic flows.

APPENDIX 4

Components Analysis

Table 4-A

**COMPONENTS OF GROWTH IN THE NUMBER OF FEMALE-HEADED
FAMILIES WITH CHILDREN LESS THAN 18, 1960-1970**
(Numbers in thousands)

Number of Female-Headed Families with children less than 18	White	Nonwhite
1960	1,191	448
1970	1,891	840
Total growth, 1960-1970	700	392

Components of Change	White No.	White Percent	Nonwhite No.	Nonwhite Percent
Total	700	100	392	100
Living Arrangements (EFHFC/DC + NFHFC/NC)	70	10	31	8
Presence of Children (DC/D)	138	20	92	24
Marital Dissolution (D/E)	161	23	59	15
Population Growth (E + N)	174	25	61	16
Illegitimacy (NC/N)	63	9	82	21
Interaction	94	13	67	17

Technical Note: Based on substituting 1970 values for each individual component into 1960 equation where

$$\text{FHFC} = \frac{\text{EFHFC}}{\text{DC}} \cdot \frac{\text{DC}}{\text{D}} \cdot \frac{\text{D}}{\text{E}} \cdot \text{E} + \frac{\text{NFHFC}}{\text{NC}} \cdot \frac{\text{N}}{\text{NC}} \cdot \text{N}$$

See table 4-C for definitions and raw data from which these calculations were made.

Source: 1960 and 1970 Census (see table 4-B).

Table 4-B

CHANGING PERCENTAGES OF ADULT WOMEN IN VARIOUS STATUSES, 1960-1970

	1960			1970		
	White	Nonwhite	Total	White	Nonwhite	Total
Percentage of Single and Formerly Married Mothers Heading Own Households	82.1	79.7	81.5	86.0	81.5	84.6
Percentage of Ever-Married Women Who Are Divorced, Separated, or Widowed	19.6	33.1	21.0	22.3	38.2	23.9
Percentage of Ever-Married Women Who Are Divorced	3.4	4.6	3.5	4.8	7.1	5.0
Percentage of Ever-Married Women Who Are Separated	1.6	10.7	2.5	1.9	12.5	2.9
Percentage of Ever-Married Women Who Are Widowed	14.6	17.8	15.0	15.7	18.6	16.0
Percentage of Women in Disrupted Marital Status Who Have Children <18	15.3	27.5	17.3	17.1	34.0	19.7
Percentage of Never-Married Women Who Have Own Children <18	.3	4.8	.9	1.0	11.9	2.4
Total Number of Adult Women (Ever Married plus Never Married) (000)	58,040	6,873	64,913	68,873	8,122	76,995

Sources: 1960 and 1970 Census (see sources of table 4-C).

Table 4C

DEFINITIONS AND DATA USED IN COMPONENTS OF CHANGE ANALYSIS
(Numbers in thousands)

	1970 Nonwhite	1970 White	1960 Nonwhite	1960 White
EFHFC = Ever-married female-headed families with own children <18* (excludes subfamilies)	672	1,803	391	1,165
**DC = Women in disrupted marriages with own children <18 = VC + WC + SC (includes subfamilies)	754	2,055	489	1,418
**VC = Divorced women with own children <18	179	952	86	554
**WC = Widowed women with own children <18	168	603	133	530
**SC = Separated women with own children <18	407	500	270	334
V = Divorced women	414	2,559	249	1,609
W = Widowed women	1,078	8,463	954	6,908
S = Separated women	726	996	576	741
E = Ever-married women	5,795	53,825	5,362	47,225
NFHFC = Never-married female-headed families with own children <18 (excludes subfamilies)	168	88	57	26
**NC = Never-married women with own children <18 (includes subfamilies)	277	144	73	32
N = Never-married women	2,327	15,048	1,511	10,815
D = Disrupted marriages = V + W + S	2,218	12,018	1,779	9,258
Total FHFC = EFHFC + NFHFC	840	1,891	448	1,191

*Excludes female-headed families where a woman was married and her husband was absent for reasons other than separation.
**Derived by adding female-headed families with children <18 and female-headed subfamilies in the appropriate marital status category.

Sources: 1970 Census of Population, Subject Reports, "Family Composition," PC(2)-4A, tables 20 and 25, and "Marital Status," PC(2)-4C, table 1.
1960 Census of Population, Subject Reports, "Families," PC(2)-4A, tables 6 and 21, and "Marital Status," PC(2)-4E, table 1.

APPENDIX 5

Components of Growth of the AFDC Caseload 1967-1971

Let N_t = female-headed family welfare caseload in year t

F_t = number of female-headed families with children in year t

E_t = proportion of female-headed families with children who are eligible for welfare in year t

P_t = welfare participation rate of eligible female-headed families with children in year t

then $N_t = P_t \cdot E_t \cdot F_t$

Table 24 provides the following values:

	1967: t = 1	1971: t = 2
N_t (Col. 8)	1385	2837
F_t (Col. 9)	3187	4078
E_t (Col. 7/Col. 9)	.685	.738
P_t (Col. 10)	.634	.942

We wish to observe what proportion of the total caseload increase is attributable to each of the factors independently. Taking 1967 as the base year, we substitute the 1971 value of each individual factor, one at a time, into the 1967 equation.

Total caseload increase	$N_2 - N_1$	1452	100%
Increase due to F only	$P_1 \cdot E_1 \cdot F_2 - N_1$	386	27%
Increase due to E only	$P_1 \cdot E_2 \cdot F_1 - N_1$	106	7%
Increase due to P only	$P_2 \cdot E_1 \cdot F_1 - N_1$	671	46%
Increase due to interaction (residual)		289	20%

210

APPENDIX 6

Regression Analysis—1970 Census Employment Survey

Data on populations in low-income areas of 41 U.S. cities from the 1970 Census Employment Survey are used with operating statistics from the AFDC and food stamp programs to test for effects of welfare programs on family structure. A list of the 41 cities included in the analysis appears at the end of this Appendix.

The general hypothesis about the relationship between welfare and family structure can be expressed as follows:

(1) $$\frac{FHC}{F} = B_0 + B_1 A + B_2 W + B_3 M + B_4 C + e$$

where FHC = number of women in each city who head families with children under eighteen

F = total number of women aged 16 to 54 in each city

A = welfare system variables

W = variables measuring women's own-income opportunities

M = variables measuring income available to women through men and families

C = noneconomic control variables

We wish to observe whether the welfare variables exert an independent influence on the proportion of adult women who head families with children. Our hypothesis is that, other things equal, greater income opportunities for women outside of traditional family support arrangements are associated with higher proportions of women heading families, and that higher incomes available to women within those arrangements are associated with lower proportions. Thus both own earnings and welfare benefits would be positively associated with the proportion of women heading families, and higher male income negatively associated.

There are, of course, many different variables which might appear in vectors A, W, M, and C. From among those which could be constructed from the data base, a number of alternative specifications were explored, resulting in the following equation:

(2) $$\frac{FHC}{F} = a_0 + a_1 WL + a_2 RRE + a_3 UP + a_4 ERN + a_5 MFI + a_6 MWU + a_7 PCP + a_8 WLE + a_9 REG + V$$

The welfare vector consists of:

WL the average AFDC benefit level in the state in which the city is located, plus the average food stamp bonus value in the county in which the city is located, for July 1970, divided by the median full-time earnings of men in the low-income area. This measures the relative generosity of transfer income support available to female-headed families with children and is expected to be positively associated with FHC/F.

211

RRE the welfare recipiency rate among eligible female-headed families with children, calculated as the percent of female-headed families with children with annual income below the state welfare entry level (state AFDC full cost standard) who received some welfare in the previous twelve months. This measures several things —information about welfare available in the community, tastes for welfare and acceptability of welfare among community residents, and administrative ease of obtaining benefits. It is expected to be positively associated with FHC/F.

UP presence in the state of an unemployed parent segment of AFDC, coded 1 if present, 0 if absent. This indicates whether families must be split in order to receive welfare benefits, and its presence is expected to be negatively associated with FHC/F.

The women's own-income opportunities vector consists of:

ERN the ratio of women's full-time median earnings to men's full-time median earnings, expressed as a percent. A higher ratio is expected to be associated with higher FHC/F.

Other variables measuring women's unemployment experience and female family heads' other unearned income receipts did not add significantly to the equation's explanatory value.

The male family income vector consists of:

MFI the median annual income of husband-wife families in thousands of dollars. This reflects the opportunity cost of becoming a female head and is expected to be negatively associated with FHC/F.

MWU median weeks unemployed in the past twelve months for adult males. This measures the stability of the most important income component of MFI, men's earnings. It is expected to be positively associated with FHC/F.

Again, other measures of income, earnings, and the stability of earnings were explored but not adopted.

Finally, the control vector consists of:

PCP the percent of the total population in the survey area which consists of children under eighteen. Since women must have children living with them to be counted in FHC, this variable is expected to be positively associated with FHC/F.

WLE the percent of adult women who have lived in the survey city for five years or less. This is to allow for mobility as a factor in family instability and to control for the possible movement of female-headed families with children to metropolitan areas for other than welfare or earnings reasons. It is expected to be positively associated with FHC/F.

REG   region of the country, coded 1 for the South and 0 for
        elsewhere. This variable controls for regional differ-
        ences in family stability based primarily on cultural
        factors. It is expected to be negatively associated with
        FHC/F.

V   unexplained variable.

Other control variables tried but not retained in the final specification include measures of city size, age distribution of women, and
the proportion of the white population which is Spanish-speaking.

The decision to express WL and ERN in relative form was made
after exploring several alternative specifications in which welfare
benefits and women's earnings appeared directly. These alternative
specifications featured various measures of welfare benefits,
women's earnings, and men's earnings independently in the equation. They were significantly less successful in explaining variation
in the dependent variable than was the equation using the values of
welfare and women's earnings divided by men's earnings. This result
is consistent with the relative income hypothesis developed in chapter 3.

The different measures of earnings and welfare benefits alluded
to above were an effort to specify as correctly as possible the magnitude to which families were expected to be reacting. The major
question here, other than that of absolute versus relative values,
was how to treat the food stamp program. Inclusion of some estimate of the subsidy value of food stamps was necessary not only
because those values were so significant and so widely applicable,
but also because they were unevenly distributed in a way which
tended to offset variations in AFDC benefit levels. For example, food
stamp bonuses added only 10 percent to high AFDC benefits in New
Jersey, but 88 percent to low AFDC benefits in Alabama. However,
food stamps are available to husband-wife families and to female-
headed families who are not on welfare, so there was an issue of
whether food stamp bonus values should be added on top of median
husband-wife family income and median men's and women's earnings as well as on top of average AFDC benefit levels. The specification which introduced food stamp bonus values as a supplement to
AFDC benefits only was most successful in explaining variation in
the dependent variable, and seemed superior on a priori grounds,
given that median husband-wife family income and median male
earnings far exceeded income ceilings for food stamp eligibility in
all but one city.

Regressions run separately for whites, including the Spanish-
speaking, and nonwhites yielded the results shown in table 6-A.
In addition to the linear equation (2) shown above, a logarithmic specification was tried in order to capture some expected
nonlinearities between the dependent variable and the economic
explanatory variables. For example, as the benefit level of welfare
plus food stamps gets higher and higher relative to men's earnings,
it is expected that the proportion of women heading families would
rise at an accelerating pace, both because of the near normal shape

Table 6-A
REGRESSION RESULTS
1970 CENSUS EMPLOYMENT SURVEY FOR 41 CITIES

Variable	Mean Value White	Mean Value Nonwhite	White Population Linear	White Population Logarithmic	Nonwhite Population Linear	Nonwhite Population Logarithmic
FHC/F	10.84	25.32				
WL	.37	.40	-3.51102 (.76032)	-0.11341 (.86779)	10.59730* (2.01277)	0.20747*** (2.75068)
RRE	.86	1.12	0.66420 (.47074)	-0.02012 (.23839)	1.89301 (1.04204)	0.09479 (1.22270)
UP	.68	.68	-1.14029 (1.10096)	-0.11666 (1.28874)	0.40365 (.25863)	0.00389 (.05983)
ERN	.68	.68	16.66356*** (2.75137)	1.15428*** (3.21202)	6.83721 (.87761)	0.15841 (.77942)
MFI	8602	8250	-0.00069* (1.76987)	-0.67555** (2.24172)	-0.00192*** (2.75224)	-0.71527*** (3.09565)
MWU	12.6	14.5	0.57268*** (2.80273)	0.65032*** (3.08160)	-0.00563 (.03492)	0.01408 (.14713)
PCP	.29	.44	30.08015*** (3.85398)	0.66335*** (3.44920)	24.76147 (1.66907)	0.400572 (1.51294)
WLE	.22	.14	3.33724 (.98603)	0.08734 (1.65190)	8.54598 (1.03514)	0.05649 (1.14960)
REG	.22	.22	-1.47496 (.96935)	-0.21633 (1.56087)	-5.41212*** (3.03130)	-0.24107*** (3.30709)
Intercept			-9.24510	4.19567	19.17069	11.69594
R²			.682	.704	.638	.668
N			41	41	41	41
F			7.4	8.2	6.0	6.9

T values (in parentheses) shown beneath regression coefficients
Significance levels denoted by: *** p <.01, ** p <.05, * p <.10

of the male earnings distribution and because of the type of family structure decision process presented in chapter 3. Were the benefit levels to rise as high or higher than median male earnings, the accelerating growth of female-headed families would be expected to taper off, as most families would already be in that status, but this situation is nowhere near reached in the present sample. Results using both the linear and logarithmic specifications are given in table 6-A, but it is the somewhat more satisfactory logarithmic results which are reported in the body of chapter 5.

All the equations explain a substantial portion of the variance of the dependent variable, and have F statistics which are significant at at least the 5 percent level. The few independent variable coefficients which do not have the expected sign (WL in the white linear equation and WL and RRE in the white logarithmic equation; UP in both nonwhite equations and MWU in the nonwhite linear equation) are insignificant.

Given our particular interest in the coefficient of the welfare variable, it is useful to explore the coefficient's sensitivity to the presence or absence of other variables in the equation. Two other variables are of particular interest in this regard, RRE and WLE. RRE, the recipiency rate variable, could be taking away some of the effect of WL, the welfare benefit variable. This would be true if RRE was itself in part a measure of benefit levels, in the sense that high recipiency rates were prompted by high demand for welfare based on the existence of high benefits. Adding RRE to the equation does reduce the size of the WL coefficient, but by only a modest amount (5 percent for the nonwhite logarithmic equation).

Similarly, the introduction of WLE would be expected to reduce the size of the WL coefficient, on the assumption that one of the ways high benefit levels might increase the proportion of women heading families would be to attract female heads from elsewhere. This effect would be captured in part by the mobility variable, WLE, rather than wholly by the welfare benefit variable, WL. However, this is not borne out in the empirical results. Introducing WLE into the equation raises the size of the WL coefficient (16 percent for the nonwhite logarithmic equation). This says that controlling for the effects of in-migration allows WL to play a larger role in contributing to female-headed families than it otherwise would. It suggests that WL is influencing the living arrangements of longer term residents of the city and that this relationship is obscured somewhat by the behavior of the more recent arrivals. This is in line with some other researchers' findings that it is not urban immigrants themselves but their offspring—the first generation raised in the city—who are particularly prone to family instability.

41 CITIES IN 1970 CENSUS EMPLOYMENT SURVEY ANALYSIS

Akron, Ohio
Baltimore, Maryland
Birmingham, Alabama
Boston, Massachusetts
Bridgeport, Connecticut
Buffalo, New York
Charlotte, North Carolina

Chicago, Illinois
Cincinnati, Ohio
Cleveland, Ohio
Columbus, Ohio
Dallas, Texas
Dayton, Ohio
Detroit, Michigan

Fort Worth, Texas
Houston, Texas
Indianapolis, Indiana
Jersey City, New Jersey
Kansas City, Missouri
Los Angeles, California
Louisville, Kentucky

Miami, Florida
Milwaukee, Wisconsin
Newark, New Jersey
New Orleans, Louisiana
New York City, New York
Norfolk, Virginia
Oakland, California

Oklahoma City, Oklahoma
Omaha, Nebraska
Philadelphia, Pennsylvania
Pittsburgh, Pennsylvania
Rochester, New York
San Diego, California
San Francisco, California

St. Louis, Missouri
Tampa, Florida
Toledo, Ohio
Tulsa, Oklahoma
Wichita, Kansas
Youngstown, Ohio

INDEX